"The ideas in *Reverse Innovation in Health Care* could save American health care billions of dollars. Vijay Govindarajan and Ravi Ramamurti have identified a rich new source of cost-saving medical innovation that deserves our most serious consideration."

—**TOBY COSGROVE**, MD, retired President and CEO, Cleveland Clinic

"*Reverse Innovation in Health Care* delivers an important message for health-care reform: focus on delivery cost. Vijay and Ravi show examples from near and far that bend the cost curve without sacrificing quality. These innovations should be embraced and scaled as essential pieces of a reju-venated US health-care system."

—**JEFF IMMELT**, former Chairman and CEO, General Electric; Chairman, AthenaHealth; Venture Partner, New Enterprise Associates, Inc.

"*Reverse Innovation in Health Care* is a book that should be part of any con-sideration of how we improve America's health-care system to benefit our people. Understanding how other nations approach health care is essential when looking at ways to reach a stronger and better system here. This book gives us a great deal to think about and learn from."

—**JUDD A. GREGG**, former US Senator; former Chairman, Senate Budget Committee; and former Chairman, Senate Committee on Health, Education, Labor, and Pensions

"A provocative volume of ideas that could facilitate a needed transforma-tion of our health-care delivery system."

—**KENNETH L. DAVIS**, MD, President and CEO, Mount Sinai Health System, New York City

"*Reverse Innovation in Health Care* is a great and well-rounded approach to tackling many of the current health-care issues by learning from nations that have implemented true value-based health care."

—**TAWFIG AL RABIAH**, Minister of Health, Saudi Arabia

"This book offers inspirational and practical insights on how to significantly improve the accessibility of health care in the face of ever-increasing demand. This will be required reading for my leadership team."

—**MARY ACKENHUSEN,** President and CEO, Vancouver Coastal Health, Canada

"Compliments to Vijay and Ravi for having the courage to write on a very emotional and sensitive topic. The ten reverse innovation lessons need to be deliberated upon earnestly so that millions of people who don't have access to quality health care can benefit!"

—**RAJIT MEHTA,** Managing Director and CEO, Max Healthcare, India

"Both powerful and insightful, *Reverse Innovation in Health Care* exposes what is wrong with the American health-care system. Through vivid examples, the authors show us that our nation's biggest challenge and greatest opportunity is transforming the delivery system. To improve medical care, achieve superior outcomes, and lower costs, we must learn from the success of others around the globe. This book is a great place to begin and a must-read for both health-care leaders and policy experts."

—**ROBERT PEARL,** MD, professor, Stanford University School of Medicine and Stanford Graduate School of Business; author, *Washington Post* bestseller, *Mistreated: Why We Think We're Getting Good Health Care—and Why We're Usually Wrong*

"At a time when the US health-care system is bankrupt, Govindarajan and Ramamurti offer concrete and pragmatic suggestions as to how we can improve quality and reduce costs. Their ideas, if adopted, will transform health care in America. A must-read for anyone who wants to make a real difference in this critical industry."

—**JOHN LYNCH,** former President and CEO, Knoll, Inc.; former Governor of New Hampshire

"*Reverse Innovation in Health Care* definitely delivers on its mission to show how to make value-based health care work. The several compelling case studies from India and the United States clearly demonstrate how innovative health-care institutions deliver superior outcomes for patients at lower costs to them and society."

— **ROBERT S. KAPLAN,** Marvin Bower Professor of Leadership Development, Emeritus, Harvard Business School

"If American health-care leaders—clinicians, executives, board members, policy makers, and others—do not take this astounding book seriously, shame on them. Herein lie badly needed, thoroughly disruptive solutions to our health-care mess. Herein are pathways to better care, better health, and costs we can afford—all at once!"

— **DONALD M. BERWICK,** MD, President Emeritus, Institute for Healthcare Improvement; former Administrator, Centers for Medicare & Medicaid Services

"This book offers inspiration on what is possible as well as badly needed guidance on how to achieve radical gains in health-system performance."

— **ELLIOTT S. FISHER,** MD, MPH, John E. Wennberg Distinguished Professor, Geisel School of Medicine at Dartmouth; Director, Dartmouth Institute for Health Policy and Clinical Practice

"This book is timely and very important for American physicians, health-care executives, and legislators to read and understand. Health care is not underfunded in this country, and many of these case studies are very portable."

— **JOHN COCHRAN,** MD, former Executive Director, Kaiser Permanente Federation

"Given today's imperative to implement new and more efficient ways to provide quality health-care services in the United States, we must all open our minds to the initiatives highlighted in this book. Rethinking how we deploy care begins with efforts similar to those outlined here."

—**ELLEN ZANE,** CEO Emeritus and Vice Chair, Board of Trustees, Tufts Medical Center

"A thoughtful book that appropriately pushes and challenges current boundaries and practices."

—**STEVEN KADISH,** former Chief of Staff to Massachusetts Governor Charlie Baker; Senior Research Fellow, Harvard Kennedy School's Taubman Center for State and Local Government

"As we confront the ongoing and ever-growing need to control health-care costs, Govindarajan and Ramamurti raise intriguing concepts and examples in *Reverse Innovation in Health Care* from which we can learn and deliver value-oriented care."

—**RAJ GARG,** MD, JD, President and CEO, Cancer Treatment Centers of America

REVERSE INNOVATION IN HEALTH CARE

REVERSE

HOW TO MAKE

INNOVATION

VALUE-BASED

IN HEALTH

DELIVERY WORK

CARE

VIJAY GOVINDARAJAN

RAVI RAMAMURTI

HARVARD BUSINESS REVIEW PRESS

Library of Congress Cataloging-in-Publication Data

Names: Govindarajan, Vijay, author. | Ramamurti, Ravi, author.
Title: Reverse innovation in health care : how to make value-based delivery work / by Vijay Govindarajan and Ravi Ramamurti.
Description: [Boston, Massachusetts] : Harvard Business Review Press, [2018] | Includes index.
Identifiers: LCCN 2018002101 | ISBN 9781633693661 (hardcover : alk. paper)
Subjects: LCSH: Medical care—India—Quality control. | Medical care—United States—Quality control. | Medical care—India—Cost effectiveness. | Medical care—United States—Cost effectiveness. | Value analysis (Cost control) | Competition. | Health planning.
Classification: LCC RA410.55.I4 G684 2018 | DDC 362.10954—dc23
LC record available at https://lccn.loc.gov/2018002101

ISBN: 9781633693661
eISBN: 9781633693678

To our families

VG: Kirthi, Tarunya, Adam, Pasy, and Michael;
and in fond memory of Rangan
Ravi: Meena, Bharat, Paige, Neely, Merritt, Gita, Aki, and Arjun;
and in fond memory of Bala and Drew

Contents

Part One

Health-Care Solutions from a Distant Shore

Value-Based Competition in India

1.

An Unhealthy Problem Meets an Unlikely Solution

One spring day a few years back, a fifty-something man named George found himself short of breath. His wife drove him to the emergency room at the University of Texas Southwestern Medical Center, where he was diagnosed with pneumonia. When George was released from the hospital four months later, he was presented with a 161-page bill of $474,064 as his share of the costs.

George survived the pneumonia, but he didn't know if he could survive the bill. His room alone cost $73,376, and respiratory services, oxygen, and breathing tests added up to $94,799. "Special drugs," most of which were listed as "Sodium Chloride .9%," otherwise known as IV saline solution, came to $108,663.

George hired a billing advocate, a woman who had worked as a claims processor for Blue Cross Blue Shield until she was sent an astronomical bill for a daughter's emergency-room visit and decided to go over to the other side. She helped a bit, and the hospital, the president of which was paid $1,244,000 a year, agreed to revise the bill downward to "only" $313,000.

Roughly ten thousand miles away, in a small farming village a couple of days' drive from Bangalore, India, an eighteen-month-old boy named Deep was keeping his parents awake with worry. Deep had a heart condition. He was smaller than other children his age, and he didn't have much interest in eating, or in anything else for that matter. But Deep's parents knew there was hope. They had been in these worry shoes before, five years earlier, when they learned that their daughter would need an operation on her heart. So they took their son to the same hospital, Narayana Health in Bangalore, a private for-profit cardiac hospital that specialized in pediatric heart surgeries, performing sixteen a day—half of its total practice.

Narayana was famous throughout India, not only for its excellent surgical outcomes but for its prices. A typical heart surgery at Narayana cost only about $2,100, tens of thousands of dollars less than the same procedure would cost at hospitals in the United States. More important for families like Deep's, 60 percent of the pediatric surgeries were provided free or at a discounted price. And yet, Narayana was a profitable company, and in December 2017 had a market valuation of over $1 billion.

Deep's parents paid just a fraction of the full price for Deep's heart procedure. "Don't worry about the money," the hospital told them. "Just take Deep home and see if his appetite improves." It did, and the boy flourished.

These two stories raise an interesting question: What can all countries, rich and poor, learn from organizations like Narayana Health about how to deliver world-class health care affordably? In the United States, the question is timely, because Americans are at a pivotal—perhaps decisive—moment in health-care policy. But the question is relevant in every country. In the United Kingdom, for instance, the National Health Service (NHS) struggles with issues of costs, quality, and access. Jim Mackey, head of its statutory watchdog group, says bluntly: "The NHS is in a mess."[1] In France, the health-care system is believed to be near bankruptcy.[2] And in poor countries, the problem is worse: America and Europe may have millions of people who need *better* care, but the developing world has billions of people with *no* care.

It is time to consider some unconventional remedies to the problem, and that is what we attempt in this book. It isn't just hospital leaders, doctors, consultants, and policy makers who should be interested in innovative solutions to the health-care conundrum. We hope this book will also interest insurers; CEOs of companies that spend a fortune on employee benefits; suppliers of drugs, devices, and services to the health-care industry; and entrepreneurs looking to disrupt the industry. We hope there will be more experiments of the kind announced in January 2018 by three big employers—Amazon, Berkshire Hathaway and JPMorgan Chase—to form an independent company to disrupt health care for their million-plus employees.[3] We further hope this book will help mobilize grassroots support for deep and lasting reforms of the health-care sectors in all countries.

Let's begin by taking a closer look at the situation in the United States.

An Unhealthy Problem

The story of the American health-care system involves the good, the bad, and the ugly. The United States is home to the world's best hospitals and the world's best doctors, and it has produced more health-care miracles than any other country in the world. Americans and American universities dominate the Nobel Prize in Medicine. US pharmaceutical companies develop new drugs that save countless lives. And US medical-device companies produce a steady stream of innovations. Americans get to choose their doctors and insurers, and they don't have to deal with care rationing or long waiting times for procedures. The care that Deep was lucky to get in India is routinely available to most Americans, if more expensively. That's the good.

Now for the bad and the ugly. In 2016, the United States spent a staggering $3.3 trillion, or almost 17.9 percent of its GDP, on health care—that's $10,348 per person, at least twice as much as any other country in the industrialized world spent. Between 2000 and 2015, US health-care costs rose at twice the rate of the Consumer Price Index.[4] This has caused health-insurance premiums, copayments, and coinsurance payments to soar for people like George. The collateral damage is widespread. Today's health-care costs add an estimated 15 percent to the cost of every American-made automobile. They cannibalize paychecks by diverting company funds to employer-sponsored health plans.[5] And they crowd out discretionary government spending in important areas such as infrastructure, research, and education. By 2030, when 20 percent of the US population will be over sixty-five years old, the upward pressure on health-care costs will be unprecedented, and US national and household budgets will be looking for life support.

Despite this record spending, the quality of American health care is uneven, with frequent medical errors, failures, and a great many inefficiencies. A 2017 Commonwealth Fund report on health in eleven industrialized nations ranked the United States first in spending and last in overall health-care performance.[6] American life expectancy ranked forty-third in the world, medical errors were the third-leading cause of hospital deaths, and three-quarters of health-care spending was on chronic diseases, many of which could be better managed or even prevented. The thirty-day hospital readmission rate for Medicare patients was a discouraging 15 percent to 16 percent, and it was costing taxpayers $17 billion a year. Access to health care was also spotty: Even after the Affordable Care Act helped twenty million Americans obtain health insurance, twenty-eight million remained uninsured. Underinsurance was also widespread, affecting 23 percent of Americans. And persistent racial, ethnic, and income disparities haunted health-care access and outcomes.[7]

Reflecting on the state of US health care, the Institute of Medicine concluded in a now famously scathing report: "Between the health care we have and the care we could have lies not just a gap but a chasm."[8] That was seventeen years ago, and while there has been a lot of talk— seemingly *endless* talk—about health-care reform in the intervening years, not all that much has changed.

How can that possibly be true? For one thing, there are many special interests in play. Insurers, regulators, doctors' groups, the pharmaceutical industry, workers' unions, political parties—all these players have interests to protect, and those interests put a drag on change.

But the real reason the health-care debate hasn't gotten anywhere is that would-be reformers are debating about the wrong things. *It's not about who pays for what.* Skyrocketing health-insurance premiums are just a *symptom* of the underlying problem. The problem with American health care is that *it costs too much, the quality is uneven, and too many people can't get the care they need.*

When we look at the problem primarily in this way, as a crisis of health-care delivery and not as an issue of who pays for what, we can begin to see new solutions from unexpected places.

Reverse Innovation in Health-Care Delivery

Reverse innovation refers to the case in which an innovation flows from a poor country to a rich country rather than the other way around. We have been studying this phenomenon for over a decade, and for the past five years we have wrestled specifically with the question of how it might apply to health-care delivery. (See the sidebar "About Our Research.")

What Is Reverse Innovation?

The locus of innovation in the global economy is changing, and so are patterns of dissemination. Poor countries no longer just borrow innovations from developed countries.[9] They also contribute innovations to the rest of the world, including developed countries. We call this transfer of new ideas and innovations from poor regions to rich "reverse innovation."

Innovations arising in poor countries typically involve practices that maximize *value* (i.e., the ratio of benefits to price), by making products extremely affordable and easy to use, while also keeping quality high. Although these innovations arise from conditions of poverty and scarcity, they can address needs in conditions of wealth and abundance perfectly well.

Reverse innovation can take on many forms. An American multinational corporation could develop a product for its consumers in poor countries and then turn around and sell the product back home, as an entry-level product or to a niche market. For example, General Electric developed an extremely low-cost, portable ultrasound machine in China and later sold it in many countries, including the United States.

Alternatively, an emerging-market firm could develop products tailored to the unique requirements of poor countries and then market such products to rich countries. Reverse innovation can also occur indirectly through knowledge transfer. For instance, an established company or a startup in the United States might be inspired by business models and management innovations adopted in poor countries and could bring those models to the United States, disrupting the industry.

Reverse innovation in health-care delivery is still a nascent phenomenon. It is a "next practice," the importance and significance of which will grow in the next decade as the United States and other rich countries confront the challenge of maximizing value by dramatically lowering costs.

Few American hospitals operate internationally, and none has a subsidiary in India. As such, reverse innovation in health care must occur indirectly through knowledge transfer, which requires that leaders of US health-care organizations cultivate a global mindset. Leadership requirements for developing a global mindset include:

- Curiosity about health-care innovations in poor countries;

- Willingness to acquire knowledge about such innovations through immersion experiences in poor countries;

- Ability to modify and adapt such innovations to suit the unique US context.

Reverse innovation first came to our attention in our work with General Electric, a multinational company that took a product developed in China for the Chinese market—an inexpensive and portable, high-quality ultrasound device—and marketed it successfully in the United States. What began as a defensive move to counter Chinese competitors in China became a big hit for GE not only in other emerging markets but also in the United States, particularly in rural and far-flung areas, where the nearest large clinic or hospital was hours away. The low-cost ultrasound also pioneered new applications for situations in which portability was critical or space was constrained, such as at accident sites and in operating suites. We wrote our findings up as an article for *Harvard Business Review*, with GE's CEO, Jeff Immelt.[10] We challenged other multinationals to see the innovation opportunities in emerging markets in a new light.

Subsequently, we discovered that reverse innovation was already occurring in several companies, including Harman International, PepsiCo, Procter & Gamble, Walmart, Renault, and John Deere. For example, Harman, a German manufacturer of high-end auto infotainment systems, engineered a new system that would work in smaller,

About Our Research

Five years ago, we began a project to understand how some Indian hospitals were able to provide world-class health care at ultra-low prices. We thought these hospitals could offer lessons not only for other poor countries but also for rich countries, because India seemed to have a form of value-based competition.

In the first phase of the research, we screened over forty Indian hospitals that appeared to be pursuing innovative business models and then selected sixteen for in-depth study through field interviews with their founders, administrators, doctors, patients, technical staff, and investors. We examined their prices, medical outcomes, patient volumes, and financial results. Based on the first-round investigations, we identified seven "exemplars" that consistently delivered world-class care at ultra-low prices and offered their services to all (see table 1-1 later in the chapter). We wrote about their breakthrough business models in numerous *Harvard Business Review* blogs, followed by the November 2013 *Harvard Business Review* article "Delivering World-Class Health Care, Affordably." This body of work fed into part one of this book.

cheaper Chinese cars—and in the process created a platform for new systems in cars all over the world. John Deere developed a smaller, cheaper tractor, specifically for the Indian farmer, and that tractor found a global market. Procter & Gamble innovated a low-cost feminine-hygiene brand, Naturella, for Mexico, which it subsequently marketed in thirty countries. French multinational Renault designed a low-cost car, the Logan, for price-sensitive customers in Eastern Europe and subsequently sold it in developed markets by adding safety features, style, and metallic colors. Walmart innovated small-format stores in South America to meet the needs of local consumers and then brought the concept back

In the second phase of research, we explored the potential for reverse innovation of the *value*-based practices from India to the United States. We looked for US organizations that had adopted practices similar to those of the Indian exemplars to improve quality, lower cost, and expand access to health care. We discovered that such examples existed *even under the prevailing fee-for-service regulatory environment*. To assess the opportunities and limitations for reverse innovation, we selected four of these organizations for in-depth study, each of which attacked a core problem of US health care. We then circulated the findings, which are reported in part two of this book, among two dozen health-care reformers and policy makers to get their feedback.

In all, we conducted over 125 interviews in India and the United States with CEOs, hospital administrators, doctors, patients, medical staff, investors, and industry experts.

to the United States. We wrote about these corporate developments in a *New York Times* best seller, *Reverse Innovation: Create Far From Home, Win Everywhere.*[11]

In parallel, we wrote an academic article on reverse innovation that won two best-paper awards and generated a new line of research in international business.[12] More recently, we wrote a McKinsey Award–winning article for *Harvard Business Review* on how to engineer reverse innovations.[13] Today, reverse innovation is part of the business lexicon. Even journals in other fields are taking note of it. For instance, an editorial in *Nature* observed: "Technologies such as [a solar-powered desalination unit in southern India]—engineered to be inexpensive and off-grid as a matter of necessity—may one day end up in rich countries, as fresh water and other resources become increasingly scarce around the world."[14]

Through all this we have learned one important lesson: innovations created for large, low-resource, emerging markets have a powerful potential to transform and even disrupt business models in the United States and other first-world countries. Innovation for poor countries typically involves maximizing value—that is, making products ultra-affordable and easy to use while also maintaining high quality.[15]

Higher quality, lower costs, expanded access to the underserved. This is exactly what is needed in US health-care delivery.

Historically, innovations in medical science and technology have flowed from rich countries to poor ones: pharmaceuticals, clinical procedures, biomedical devices, and medical equipment have all followed this customary path of invention in the United States and other developed countries and then adoption and adaptation in developing countries. But when it comes to health-care *delivery*, the United States has been less innovative. We see a powerful opportunity for innovations in health-care delivery to reverse their traditional direction and flow the other way, from poor countries to rich ones.

Can practices that originate in emerging markets like India actually work in developed countries?

The Indian Exemplars in Health-Care Delivery

To test our hypothesis, five years ago we began studying a small group of extraordinary Indian hospitals. Narayana Health, where Deep got his heart fixed, was part of this sample. By 2012, it had grown into a multispecialty tertiary-care complex with five thousand beds. We also included Aravind Eye Care System, which was famous for performing more cataract surgeries than any other hospital in the world and with great medical outcomes, yet charging only $100 for the procedure from start to finish.[16] After digging deeper and checking out upward of forty hospitals, we discovered several more that were providing world-class health care at ultra-low prices (see table 1-1). Together, these hospitals (seven in all, which we call our "exemplars") cover the gamut of medical services, from maternity care to open-heart surgery, and they charge just 1 percent to 12 percent of US prices (see table 1-2). All the hospitals are privately owned, and all but two are for-profit hospitals.

As shown in table 1-2, Care Hospitals offers knee and hip replacements for a little over $3,000, including imported implants. LifeSpring performs vaginal deliveries for $120 and cesarean deliveries for $300, including pre- and postnatal care. Health Care Global (HCG) Oncology provides a full

TABLE 1-1

Indian exemplars

Provider's name (short form used in book)	Specialty	Year founded	Was founder a medical doctor?	Legal status
Aravind Eye Care System (Aravind)	Eye care	1978	Yes	Private nonprofit
Care Hospitals (Care)	Cardiac care and other tertiary care	1997	Yes	Private for-profit, acquired by Abraaj Group in 2016
Deccan Hospital (Deccan)	Renal care	2007	No	Private for-profit
Health Care Global Oncology (HCG Oncology)	Cancer care	1989	Yes	Private for-profit, IPO in India in 2016
LifeSpring Hospitals (LifeSpring)	Maternity care	2005	No	Private for-profit, funded by Acumen Fund and others
LV Prasad Eye Institute (LV Prasad)	Eye care	1987	Yes	Private nonprofit
Narayana Health (Narayana)	Cardiac care and other tertiary care	2001	Yes	Private for-profit, IPO in India in 2015

TABLE 1-2

Price of medical care, India versus United States[1]

Procedure	India price (US dollars)	US price (US dollars)	India price as percentage of US price
Cataract surgery (including intraocular lens and all charges)			0.3–14%
• Free or subsidized patients			
• Paying patients (depending on type of lens)	11.50–100 (basic lens) 500 (fancy lens) (Aravind)	3,542 (basic lens)	
Coronary bypass surgery			1–3%
• Paying patients	2,100 (Narayana Health)	76,000–342,000 (Texas)	
Angioplasty (without implants)			2–4%
• Subsidized patients	615	28,000–30,000	
• Paying patients	1,154 (Narayana Health)		
Total knee/hip replacement (including imported implants)			7–8%
• Paying patients	3,255 (Care Hospitals)	39,300 (hip), 49,000 (knee)	
Cancer treatment (full set of radiation)			12%
• Three-dimensional conformal radiotherapy	1,500	12,500	
• Radiosurgery (CyberKnife)	3,800 (HCG Oncology)	n/a	
Maternity care			1–3%
• Vaginal delivery (including pre- and postnatal care)	120 (LifeSpring)	8,802 (average for vaginal and cesarean)	
• Cesarean delivery (including pre- and postnatal care)	300 (LifeSpring)		
Kidney dialysis—peritoneal (per year, including diagnosis, medication, and hospitalization)	8,200 (Deccan Hospital)	89,000[2] (hemodialysis)	9%

Source: Authors' estimates based on inputs from Indian hospitals.

Indian rupees (INR) were converted to US dollars (USD) at the rate of 1 USD to 65 INR, the rate prevailing in mid-2017.
1. Price comparisons are difficult, and this table mainly shows the order of magnitude difference in prices at the exemplar hospitals in India and on average in the United States in 2015–2016. Prices in the United States vary widely, however, depending on the hospital, the insurer, the individual patient, etc.
2. Based on the treatment most widely used in the United States, i.e, hemodialysis, rather than peritoneal dialysis.

set of radiation treatments for $1,500 and radiosurgery using CyberKnife for $3,800. Deccan Hospital offers peritoneal dialysis for $8,200 a year. The much higher prices for treating the same condition with hemodialysis in the United States are also shown in table 1-2. Despite ultra-low prices, the Indian hospitals report excellent medical outcomes and, like Narayana, they are all profitable—even though many of their patients are too poor to pay even their very low prices. The most rewarding part of the research was meeting the inspiring founders of these hospitals— mostly doctors who were trained abroad and wanted to bring modern medicine to average Indians. Faced with shortages and constraints at every turn, they improvised and innovated relentlessly. They used every trick in the book to improve quality, lower costs, and expand access to middle-class and poor Indians with annual incomes of a few thousand dollars at best.

What can these hospital systems teach us about effective health-care delivery? We published our initial thoughts in a groundbreaking November 2013 *Harvard Business Review* article, "Delivering World-Class Health Care, Affordably." We noted how these hospitals had to focus on quality to attract the well-to-do, while driving down costs relentlessly to make care affordable to the poor. In this way they became at once extremely high-quality and ultra-low-cost players who extended the same world-class care to both the rich and the poor.

An HBR webinar based on the article garnered an audience of over one thousand from around the world. The article was picked up by several newspapers and magazines. We also wrote fifteen articles on HBR-online about various promising reverse-innovation ideas that we had come across. We wrote op-ed pieces in *The Washington Post*, *The Boston Globe*, *Forbes*, *Wired*, and other publications describing the innovative practices of Indian health-care exemplars. Now, with this book, we bring together all of our research on reverse innovation in health care to show how revolutionary practices in India can help improve health-care delivery everywhere.

We wrote this book because we believe the Indian exemplars are the Fords and Toyotas of health care.

The health-care-delivery innovations that we describe in this book can be applied in every poor country and in every rich country—not just in India or just in the United States. In fact, we've presented our research on reverse innovation in health-care delivery in major forums of medical professionals in countries ranging from the United States, Brazil, and India to Singapore, South Africa, and Thailand, with consistently positive feedback.

To be sure, we've also encountered our share of skepticism about whether the Indian hospitals can really do what we describe—that is, provide world-class care at ultra-low prices—and whether their practices can be applied in other countries, especially rich countries such as the United States. In appendix A, we catalogue all the particular doubts we've encountered, with our response to each: For instance, can quality of care really be that good when prices are so low? Are prices so low in India because labor is cheap, or because the Indian hospitals don't have to invest in education and research like leading hospitals in developed countries do? Or is it because regulation is lax in India and there are no malpractice suits? If you have such questions, take a look at the sidebar "India? Really? Countering Skepticism about Transferring Practices from India to Developed Countries," or better yet, take a detour through appendix A.

Bottom line: these are all good questions, but they are not grounds for dismissing the Indian innovations as irrelevant to developed countries. This would be similar to discarding Toyota's manufacturing innovations in an earlier era as irrelevant to developed countries.[17] Reverse innovation in health care is not optional. It is oxygen.

How are the Indian exemplar hospitals able to deliver high-quality care to everyone—rich, poor, and virtually penniless—and *make money doing it*? The short answer: they perform this seeming miracle by creating cultures, organizations, and practices that foster value-based health care.

India? Really? Countering Skepticism about Transferring Practices from India to Developed Countries

Was the care in India really of high quality, despite ultra-low prices?

The Indian exemplars are exemplary for a reason. All of the physician founders of these hospitals were trained at very high standards, four of them in the United States and the United Kingdom, and quality health care was their mission. Several of the hospitals are accredited by Joint Commission International (JCI) or its Indian equivalent, the National Accreditation Board for Hospitals & Healthcare Providers (NABH). The data also suggests that medical outcomes at these hospitals for open-heart or eye surgery, for breast-cancer treatment, for maternity care, or for end-stage renal disease are as good as or better than those in the West (see table A-3 in appendix A for details).

What about labor costs? Don't they account for most of the lower prices in India?

Surprisingly, no. The salaries of nurses, paramedical staff, and administrators in India are indeed dramatically lower—only 2 percent to 5 percent of what a US hospital would pay—but medical specialists, who account for half the salary bill at Indian hospitals, are another story. Cardiothoracic surgeons, nephrologists, ophthalmologists, and oncologists cost anywhere from 20 percent to 74 percent of US levels. In fact, we found that even if all the doctors and staff at Narayana Health were paid at US levels, its costs for open-heart surgery would still be only 3 percent to 12 percent of those in a comparable US hospital (see appendix A for details).

The labor-cost differential just isn't as important as you'd think. Moreover, costs of other inputs—such as imported supplies (e.g., stents, valves, and orthopedic implants) and high-end devices (e.g., PET-CT scanners, MRI machines, and cyclotrons), as well as land and capital—can be significantly higher in India than in the United States.

Aren't Indian hospitals spared the costs of running educational and research programs?

Not really. Five of the seven Indian hospitals we profile also engage in applied research and function as teaching hospitals that graduate more medical professionals than most hospitals in India. They have also produced clinical innovations such as the "beating-heart" technique for open-heart surgery, novel methods of corneal slicing and approaches to corneal transplants, innovations in cataract surgery (e.g., manual small-incision cataract surgery), and innovations in treating patients with breast, neck, and throat cancers.

Without a system-level change, can US hospitals really benefit from Indian-style innovations?
Can bottom-up change really work?

Absolutely. It's true that Indian health care is less regulated than US health care. It's also true that US hospitals face many systemic constraints, such as fee-for-service reimbursement, malpractice lawsuits, entrenched unions, and insurance interests. But systems do change. Over time, US regulations can and will change so that innovations to lower cost, expand coverage, and improve quality will become easier to adopt. Both the market and the public good demand it. Not all Indian innovations will reverse easily. Some likely cannot be reversed at all. But many can be transferred directly, or with adaptations, and some will show such promise that their adoption will disrupt the burdensome US system. We have seen it, and we describe several Indian-style innovations already under way in the United States in part two of the book.

Value-Based Health Care

The value-based health care that has proven so elusive in America is alive and well in this handful of exemplary hospitals in India.

For more than a decade, leading thinkers in health-care policy have argued passionately for patient-centered, value-based health care as the solution to America's health-care crisis.[18] Led by Michael Porter, Clay Christensen, Regina Herzlinger, Donald Berwick, Paul Farmer, and Jim Kim, these thinkers imagine a health-care system in which the goal is not profit, or volume, or growth, or even treatment interventions, but *value*. Porter, for example, defines value as "health outcomes achieved per dollar spent," and he describes value-based competition as a system in which all players—providers, insurers, employers, suppliers, and customers—focus on creating value for patients.[19] Choice and competition are regarded as "powerful forces to encourage continuous improvement in value and the restructuring of care."[20]

Proponents would like to see value-based health care replace America's prevailing fee-for-service system, in which players focus on volumes of patients and procedures rather than on value or outcomes. They point out that the prevailing system has led to zero-sum competition in which everyone tries to shift costs to someone else, rather than positive-sum competition in which all participants win.[21] Value-based care would compel providers to lower costs and improve patient outcomes.

Michael Porter and Elizabeth Teisberg spell out several principles of value-based competition, including the following:

1. Players should focus on creating value for patients, not just lowering costs.

2. Competition should center on medical conditions over the full cycle of care.

3. High-quality care should be less costly.

4. Value should be driven by provider experience, scale, and learning at the medical-condition level.

5. Innovations that increase value should be strongly rewarded.[22]

More recently, Porter has spelt out the principles of value-based care, and he also strongly advocates for integrated practice units that provide patients seamless care as they are served by different specialists, as well as the bundling of prices for major procedures instead of the fee-for-service system.[23]

The United States falls short on the defining characteristics of value-based care, notwithstanding many efforts at reform, including those launched in the last few years by the Centers for Medicare & Medicaid Services. Value-based care is a breathtaking prescription for change that Porter and Lee have described as "a fundamentally new strategy," the adoption of which will be "neither linear nor swift."[24]

Indeed, top-down reforms aimed at creating value-based competition have been slow to gain traction in the United States. We've seen a long list of experiments and incremental fixes, such as safety protocols, fraud chasing, health maintenance organizations, hospital consolidation, electronic medical records, and so on. They have moved the system in the right direction, but never quite gathered momentum, and in 2018 the jury was still out on the experiments included in the Affordable Care

Act of 2010 and the Medicare Access and CHIP Reauthorization Act of 2015. Meanwhile, the usual complaints about US health care continue, with good reason.

Value-based competition in the health-care sector has become an urgent necessity, and the way to achieve it is through a combination of bottom-up and top-down reform. In the bottom-up approach, which this book focuses on, individual health-care players, new entrants, and startups could disrupt the industry by applying business models founded upon principles of value-based competition. Bottom-up change doesn't require a grand plan out of Washington, DC, agreement among our divisive political parties, or coordination among all players in the health-care system. It just needs entrepreneurs and intrapreneurs with innovative models for delivering value to patients. We've all seen it work in other industries. In fact, it's another thing that America does best.

But what kinds of bottom-up, radical innovations are likely to be consistent with value-based competition, and where should one look for answers? Proponents of value-based competition see a future in which care will be organized by medical condition and delivered by integrated practice units. They see careful cost accounting and bundled payment systems. They see a concentration of high-cost resources in centers of excellence supported by a network of providers with wide geographical reach. They see purpose-built IT platforms and a renewed emphasis on prevention over treatment.

But we see India.

And what we see is value-based health care: high-quality, low-cost care that offers universal access to consumers and delivers profits to the bottom line.

You've seen the Indian prices. And as we note in the sidebar "India? Really?" and in appendix A, several of the hospitals are accredited by Joint Commission International (JCI), the global arm of the Joint

Commission, an independent, nonprofit organization that accredits more than 21,000 health-care organizations in the United States, or by its Indian equivalent, the NABH. Some of the exemplar hospitals also benchmarked themselves against international standards for medical care. Aravind Eye Care System's overall incidence of complications was as good as or better than those of the United Kingdom's National Health Service. For coronary-bypass procedures, Narayana Health's thirty-day mortality rate, at 1.4 percent, was lower than the US rate of 1.9 percent.[25]

All seven hospitals aspire to make health care a human right. They share a strong commitment to providing quality health care to the poor and middle class, most of whom are uninsured. Universal access is the goal of the physician founders, and free care is often the only way to get there. Our exemplars succeeded not by charging exorbitant prices but by cutting costs to the bone. For example, since its founding, Aravind has provided free or highly subsidized eye surgery to anywhere from 2.5 to 3.0 million people—or 50 percent to 60 percent of its surgical patients. Similarly, free or subsidized care has accounted for 50 percent of the cases at LV Prasad Eye Institute since inception and, in 2016, accounted for 51 percent at Narayana Health and 20 percent at HCG Oncology.[26]

Despite providing high-quality care at ultra-low prices, and despite their willingness to provide free and discounted care, the Indian hospitals are all profitable, and five have raised capital in private markets to fund their growth. The December 2015 IPO of Narayana Health in India was oversubscribed 8.6 times.[27] The company raised $100 million in India, and its market capitalization in 2017 was over $1 billion. Similarly, in 2015, Care Hospitals was purchased by a private-equity firm at a valuation of about $300 million, and in 2016 HCG Oncology went public with a market valuation of $276 million.[28] Over the years, Aravind has garnered a net surplus equal to between 35 percent and 50 percent of revenues. Remarkably, since its inception in 1976, it has covered the cost of all its free medical care and capital expansion out of operating surpluses.[29]

We see the management innovations of Indian exemplars as a powerful answer to many problems in US health care today. We found that the value-based competition in Indian hospitals has five core principles, which will be further illuminated in the next two chapters and which are briefly introduced in the sidebar "The Five Core Principles of Value-Based Health Care as Practiced in India." They can help bring about bottom-up transformation of the health-care sector, because they are not contingent on fundamental changes in the regulatory environment. Moreover, organizations are welcome to adopt parts of the business model even if they can't adopt the model in whole. Some is better than none, but firing on all five cylinders will allow health-care organizations to really push the limits of performance.

We think the five principles can be applied in *all* countries, including developed countries, and not just in India. Lord Nigel Crisp, who ran the United Kingdom's National Health Service, also believes poor countries can teach rich countries useful lessons. In fact, he wrote a book explaining why: *Turning the World Upside Down*.[30] Recently, *NEJM Catalyst*, an affiliate of the *New England Journal of Medicine*, featured an article on what US hospitals can learn from India's private heart hospitals.[31] And the British journal *The Lancet* carried a comment titled "Can Reverse Innovation Catalyse Better Value Health Care?" It concluded that "Western health systems can learn a lot from health-care providers in LMICs [low-income and middle-income countries], who have progressed with far fewer resources and in far more challenging conditions."[32]

We believe it is time for US health-care reformers to get out of their hospitals, lecture halls, and caucus rooms and take a good look at what is going on in poor countries such as India and in hospitals such as Aravind Eye Care, HCG Oncology, LV Prasad Eye Institute, and Narayana Health.

The Five Core Principles of Value-Based Health Care as Practiced in India

How do Indian hospitals practice value-based health care? Simply put, they have cracked the code for delivering high-quality health care affordably. Our Indian exemplars are a heterogeneous lot. They perform simple procedures, such as cataract surgery, and also complex ones, such as open-heart surgery. Some deal with chronic conditions, such as kidney disease and cancer, while others deal with one-time events such as maternity care. What the exemplars all have in common is a breakthrough business model—their "secret sauce"—and it is characterized by five principles:

- **A driving purpose—health care for all.** The purpose driving every exemplar is a determination to provide high-quality, ultra-affordable health care to all, regardless of patients' ability to pay. This purpose leads to a remarkable strategy: exemplars target the rich to drive up quality and margins, and target the poor to drive up volume and motivate cost reductions. As a result, they become extremely high-quality, ultra-low-cost providers that extend the same world-class care to both the rich and the poor.

- **A hub-and-spoke configuration.** The exemplars distribute assets in a hub-and-spoke design, with the scarcest expertise and equipment concentrated in a hub, which serves as a "focused factory" for advanced procedures, while spokes, which are connected to the hub by telecommunication links, serve as gateways and as service points for simpler procedures. In this way, the exemplars simultaneously drive up the quality of care while driving down costs.

- **An enthusiastic use of technology.** These are relatively young Indian companies, and they love their technology. The exemplars use technology to build telehealth networks, conduct remote diagnosis and treatment, create electronic-medical-record and information-technology systems, track and analyze costs, provide home-based care (especially for the chronically ill), and develop low-cost alternatives for expensive, imported devices and supplies. Technology improves patient engagement and satisfaction and quality of care.

- **Task-shifting and continuous process improvements.** The exemplars involve everyone in continuous process improvements. They create protocols for procedures and use task-shifting to optimize the roles of surgeons, doctors, nurses, and other medical professionals. Where they see gaps, they create entirely new job categories and encourage self-service by patients and their families.

- **A culture of ultra-cost-consciousness.** Finally, the exemplars push frugality throughout their organizations. They avoid needless waste and unnecessary procedures, offer bundled pricing, aggressively control fixed and variable costs, are frugal in capital expenditures, and train doctors to think about the financial consequences of every decision. They invest in medically important areas—but no more than necessary—and conserve spending in nonmedical areas.

Each principle of this business model contributes to the goal of providing high-quality care at ultra-low prices to all, but each has its greatest impact when applied with all the others—like the synergy of five cylinders firing at once.

Indian Practices in the West

To assess the likelihood that reverse innovation can seriously influence US health care, we undertook the second phase of our research project, looking for US health-care organizations that were already using Indian-style innovations. And we found quite a few. After interviewing industry experts and checking many leads, we selected four organizations to research in depth (see table 1-3). Each of these organizations used one or more principles of the Indian exemplars to cut health-care costs, improve quality, or expand access—sometimes all three. We see these organizations as role models for changing US health care from the bottom up, and in the second half of the book we will closely explore their accomplishments. Many other US organizations are also experimenting with similar innovations

TABLE 1-3

American innovators

Provider's name (short form in book) and *specialty*	Main US health-care problem tackled	Year founded	Innovation leader	Legal status
Health City Cayman Islands (HCCI) *Cardiac care and other procedures*	Soaring costs	2014	Dr. Devi Shetty, Chairman and CEO, Narayana Health	Private for-profit
University of Mississippi Medical Center, Jackson, MS (UMMC) *Multispecialty tertiary care*	Access—rural areas	1955	Dr. Kristi Henderson, (former) Chief Tele-health and Innovation Officer, UMMC	State-owned nonprofit
Ascension, St. Louis, MO (Ascension) *Multispecialty tertiary care*	Access—uninsured and underinsured	1999	Dr. Anthony R. Tersigni, President and CEO, and John Doyle, Executive Vice President, Ascension	Private nonprofit
Iora Health, Boston, MA (Iora) *Primary care and chronic conditions*	Quality and over-hospitalization	2011	Dr. Rushika Fernandopulle, Founder and CEO	Private for-profit start-up

(see the sidebar "Examples of Value-Based Care" later in the chapter), but the following four examples will be treated in depth in the second half of the book. Let's take a quick look at our featured US innovators.

Health City Cayman Islands (HCCI): Attacking High Costs

The most direct route for reverse innovation may be that taken by exemplar Narayana Health, which in 2014 opened Health City Cayman Islands (HCCI), a 104-bed hospital just a one-hour flight from Miami. HCCI is close enough to the United States to attract Americans, but is free of many of America's cumbersome regulations. Using frugal practices honed in India, it offers world-class surgery, to Caribbean populations as well as Americans, at 25 percent to 40 percent of US prices. By late 2017, it had an impressive record of medical outcomes—zero mortalities over five hundred surgeries—and received accreditation from Joint Commission International. At the same time, it was in advanced discussions with American insurers and self-insured employers, hoping to persuade them to use the hospital for tertiary care. If the discussions bear fruit, US patients could be offered care with zero copayments and zero deductibles, plus free transportation and lodging for the patient and (if necessary) a chaperone, for one to two weeks. For US insurers, the cost savings from using HCCI could be even greater. A team of American doctors that visited HCCI came away very impressed and warned: "The Cayman Health City might be one of the disruptors that finally pushes our overly expensive US system to innovate."[33]

University of Mississippi Medical Center (UMMC): Improving Access for Rural Communities

One reason that innovations flow from poor countries to rich countries is because rich countries have regions or market segments with the same problems as poor countries. We found that situation in Mississippi, the state with the fewest doctors per capita in the United States and one where the average person has to drive forty minutes to reach a community hospital and several hours to reach UMMC, the state's only academic medical center—problems similar to those often seen in rural India. So it's not just coincidence that Mississippi was the first state to implement a comprehensive hub-and-spoke 24/7 telehealth network that connected health workers at understaffed community hospitals with specialists at UMMC in Jackson. It started in 2003, when Dr. Kristi Henderson, in the UMMC trauma unit, first used basic videoconferencing technology to link the medical center with rural hospitals, and it has expanded since then to link thirty-five specialties at UMMC with counterparts in two hundred rural hospitals across the state. As in India, the hub-and-spoke network has improved access to health care for poor rural communities, while lowering costs and improving quality and patient experience. It has even revived community hospitals that were losing patients and money, and it has relieved the pressure on UMMC's resources, allowing the experts there to focus on the patients who need their care the most. Of chief importance, it has saved thousands of lives.

Sixty million Americans (one-fifth of the country's population) live in rural areas that could benefit from a hub-and-spoke arrangement of the kind Kristi Henderson implemented in Mississippi. There is no need to reinvent the wheel.

Ascension: Improving Access for the Uninsured and Underinsured

Ascension, the nation's largest nonprofit health system and the world's largest Catholic health system, has a worthy mission: to serve "all persons, especially those living in poverty and who are struggling the most, and to deliver compassionate, personalized care, and lead health-care transformation in the United States."[34] In recent years, that has meant finding a way to provide high-quality care to uninsured and underinsured Americans.

Ascension has done that well, using strategies similar to those used by Indian exemplars. Like the exemplars, it uses an inspiring purpose to devise breakthrough innovations that have lowered cost and improved quality in ways that other US hospitals may not have considered pursuing. Like the Indian hospitals, it uses a sliding scale to charge for services, and treats the uninsured poor with margins earned by serving the insured rich. To drive down costs, improve quality, and achieve a national scale, Ascension merged several independent Catholic hospitals and implemented programs to reduce variability in care, standardize supplies across the system, leverage volume discounts, and streamline the supply chain. By 2016, Ascension was saving $1 billion a year, or 5 percent of total revenues, in supply-chain costs alone.[35] And to encourage reverse innovation, Ascension has sent dozens of key employees to India to study Narayana Health's practices, and it became a coinvestor in the Health City Cayman Islands venture to get a firsthand feel for how to implement Narayana's breakthrough innovations in health-care delivery.

Iora Health: Improving Quality

One of the biggest problems with the fee-for-service system and with an overbuilt health-care system is overutilization of medical and physical resources. Some experts believe that from 25 percent to 40 percent of US medical care isn't needed.[36] This indicates not only wasted money but also the possibility of worsened health, owing to the increased risk of medical complications and infection. Iora Health's founder, Dr. Rushika Fernandopulle, felt he was more likely to find answers for America's health-care problems in poor countries. Inspired by what he had seen in countries like Haiti, India, and Malaysia, he concluded that the key to keeping people healthy is focusing on primary care. So, at Iora he employs a task-shifting

Examples of Value-Based Care

W e selected four US innovators to profile in part two of the book, because they made particularly promising use of one or more of our Indian principles. However, many other progressive companies and start-ups have been innovating in a similar fashion, spurred on by think tanks and policy researchers, as briefly described below. We also include in the following a few examples from outside the United States.

Progressive incumbents

Among the many progressive companies is Virginia Mason Medical Center, in Seattle, a leading value-based innovator that pioneered quality control and "lean" practices in the early 2000s under the leadership of Dr. Gary Kaplan, who found his inspiration in Japan, in the Toyota Production System.[37]

Children's Hospital of Philadelphia (CHOP) built a hub-and-spoke net-work that links more than forty community hospitals, primary care cen-ters, and specialty care centers to the main hospital. The configuration was born out of desperation in the 1990s, when escalating malpractice costs shut obstetrics and pediatric units in community hospitals across the state. CHOP specialists took over the threatened services, offering clinical consults, arranging helicopter transport to its main campus, and renting beds when they needed them.[38] A similar arrangement connects Cleveland Clinic's Heart & Vascular Institute and its world-class specialists with eleven hospitals ranging from Ridgewood, New Jersey, to Plano, Texas.[39]

Mayo Clinic set up a "focused factory" model for the adult cardiac sur-gical practice within its full-service "solution shop," where it applied ideas similar to what we observed in India, such as mapping the care process, segmenting the patient population, and empowering nonphysicians at the bedside. The result was reduced resource use, length of stay, variability in outcomes, and cost.[40] Surgery Center of Oklahoma operates focused factories for many elective procedures and displays its highly competitive bundled prices transparently on its website.

Many US hospitals are using telecommunication links to improve operations in intensive care units. UMass Memorial Medical Center has, since 2007, linked its adult ICUs to a central group of remote intensivists (doctors and nurses) who use advanced technology and tools to monitor patients and flag cases requiring attention. Such e-ICU systems have been shown to shorten ICU stays, speed recovery, and lower mortality rates by 27 percent.[41] Boston-based Steward Health Care has also established a tele-ICU system across its hospitals. Avera Health of Sioux Falls, South Dakota, has built a regional telehealth network comprising three hundred locations spread across several states (South Dakota, North Dakota, Iowa, Nebraska, and Minnesota). The network covers a population of one million and provides such services as 24/7 e-ICU and remote emergency care to partner hospitals, using a team of intensivists and emergency physicians based in Sioux Falls. Mercy Health System's Virtual Care Center, outside St. Louis, Missouri, provides telehealth support to a growing consortium of partners nationwide. The system targets both early diagnosis and long-term patient monitoring.[42]

California-based CareMore Health uses a new category of workers called extensivists, who, like Iora's health coaches, stay in touch with elderly patients with chronic conditions. Task-shifting is working well for dental-health-aide therapists in Minnesota dental clinics and in underserved tribal communities in Alaska,[43] and also in a Stanford Medical School effort that employs vocational nurses to treat hepatitis C patients in underserved areas far from the university medical center, an effort that involves telemedicine as well.[44]

In Canada, Shouldice Hernia Hospital has leveraged its unique technique for hernia repair and turned a Toronto-based hospital into an Aravind-style "focused factory," where highly productive surgeons perform more than seven hundred hernia operations a year, compared with twenty-five to fifty for most general surgeons.[45] In Finland, Anssi Mikola, a consultant, discovered that if he applied Aravind Eye Care's ultra-efficient system for cataract surgery in one of the country's private practices, it could double or triple productivity. He then helped apply the Aravind style of care delivery in a private dental practice, which was able both to lower its prices by 40 percent and expand its business.[46]

Startups

Numerous startups, too, are applying Indian-style innovations. TripleCare, a New York–based physicians group, uses telemedicine to connect long-term care facilities with doctors and specialists in major hospitals. The system spares many patients expensive and stressful visits to emergency rooms and hospitals.[47] Many technology entrepreneurs are getting into med-tech startups. Among them is John Sculley, former CEO of Apple, who is reinventing himself in health care because he believes it is ripe for innovation, just as computing was when Apple got started.[48] Many providers are using online and mobile apps for mental-health therapy, some offered by weekly subscription.[49]

Several immediate care startups are adding "spokes" to serve the routine needs of families, as an alternative to costly visits to hospitals or ERs. These include a variety of urgent-care centers and MinuteClinics (the walk-in clinic within CVS drug stores), which offer quick, easy consultations with doctors in facilities located in residential neighborhoods. Others, such as Zocdoc, make it easy for people to find and schedule doctor appointments online.

In the United Kingdom, the Netcare Group, a leading South African private hospital, helped to clear the National Health Service's backlog of patients requiring cataract surgery, using Aravind-style "assembly-line" procedures in mobile operating suites. The productivity and cost savings were very Indian-like. According to Netcare's CEO, Dr. Richard Friedland, Netcare "did twenty-two surgeries a day with one theater and one surgeon, while the NHS was doing twelve a day in two theaters with two surgeons."[50]

Promoters of reverse innovation

Several institutions are promoting reverse innovation, even if they don't use that term. In 2014, the Ivey International Centre for Health Innovation, at Ivey Business School, Toronto, Canada, organized a conference on reverse innovation in health care. The Massachusetts-based Institute for Healthcare Improvement, founded by Don Berwick, has done pioneering work advancing the triple aim of lower cost, higher quality, and improved access, including efforts to bring innovations from poor countries—such as the use of community health workers—to the United States. In March 2017, working with G2L, an organization dedicated to adapting "global health strategies to underserved communities" in the United States, it sponsored a conference on global-to-local health.[51]

Meanwhile, in Britain, Lord Nigel Crisp, former chief executive of the National Health Service and Permanent Secretary of the Department of Health, has been advocating for some years that the United Kingdom and other rich countries could learn useful lessons in health-care delivery from poor countries.[52]

The more we look, the more we see that Indian innovations, which we have been calling "next practices," are becoming "now practices." We think that's very good news.

delivery structure that leans heavily on "health coaches," nonmedical staff who personally guide patients toward healthier living. As with Indian paraprofessionals, these health coaches are not just less expensive than doctors and nurses but are also much better communicators than most doctors. And Fernandopulle backs it up with both a custom-built IT system that enables complete and continual communication between health workers and patients, and a capitation-only payment system that eliminates incentives for unnecessary tests and procedures. Fernandopulle's innovative model has seen a 40 percent drop in hospitalizations and a 30 percent to 40 percent drop in ER visits, leading to a 15 percent to 20 percent drop in total health-care costs.[53] By 2017, just six years after its launch, Iora had thirty-four locations in eleven cities. It employed four hundred people and had raised more than $125 million in venture capital.

Scaling, Replicating, and Transforming Health Care

These examples show that Indian-style innovations are working in the United States, even within the existing regulatory environment. UMMC's telehealth model has already been scaled geographically across Mississippi, across many specialties, and across hospitals, schools, correctional institutions, and homes. Ascension has demonstrated that large, established hospitals and hospital systems can save hundreds of millions of dollars by leveraging scale and improving processes across their national networks, freeing up resources to serve more uninsured and underinsured patients. Iora has taken its business model of doubling down on primary care to eight US states and aims to have one to two million patients within a decade. As the youngest of the four, HCCI is still in the process of scaling up, but it is only a matter of time before a large US employer or insurer signs up to use its services. Together, these cases show how the three core problems of US health care—cost, quality, and access—can be attacked through bottom-up innovation by both established health-care players and new entrants in a scalable, profitable, and sustainable way.

We are optimistic that others will replicate these strategies. Progressive, established health-care providers will do so to prepare for a future of value-based care, and even if that takes longer to materialize than expected, they still have much to gain by replicating the strategies of Ascension and UMMC. New entrants will embrace disruptive business models, such as those of Iora and HCCI, because there are great rewards awaiting anyone who can end the industry's wasteful practices. As already noted in the sidebar, many Western health-care providers are already beginning to transform the industry from the bottom up.

But it's too early to declare victory. The current crop of bottom-up experiments are but "green shoots." To put it another way, we think of them as faint signals coming from the future. Our goal for this book is to amplify those signals to embolden others to launch new experiments.

We expect innovations in one sphere to trigger reactions in others, because the players in the health-care system are interdependent. Regulators or self-insured employers may force hospitals to change, and hospitals may persuade suppliers and insurers to change. Startups like Iora may wake up established providers. Foreign entrants like HCCI may disrupt local players. Over time, these changes will cascade through the system, until things reach a tipping point, when the status quo will become unsustainable and transformation of US health care will become a sudden reality. That's how innovation works—first gradually, then suddenly—and we believe the same dynamic will play out in health care in the coming decade.

The Future Is Far from Home

It's time to move beyond the myth that health care in America and other developed countries is so expensive because it is so good. By many measures, it's no better than the care delivered by some of our Indian exemplars. And while we know that costs in the United States will never fall to the level of costs in India, we believe that innovations we observed in India can help drop US costs by 20 percent to 30 percent, saving as much as $1 trillion a year.

Washington hasn't been helpful. Government policy experts consistently misdiagnose the problem and engage in endless debates about how to pay for health insurance for everyone. Instead, they should be finding new ways to rein in the galloping costs of health care and improve its quality. If productivity and effectiveness can be improved, the United States will have enough money, and more, to treat every American needing care.

Regulators, consumers, hospitals, employers, suppliers, and insurers should all prepare for change. In fact, they should welcome it, and as we explain in the final chapter of this book, each of them has an important role to play.

We know that Indian hospitals, doctors, and administrators have traditionally looked to the West for advances in medical knowledge, and we think it's time the West started looking to countries like India for innovations in health-care delivery.

How the Book Unfolds

Because the challenge of health-care reform is so big and far-reaching, we have written this book for a broad audience. It is meant for clinical and nonclinical executives of health-care organizations around the world; health-insurance companies; *Fortune* 500 companies that develop drugs, medical devices, and new procedures; biotech firms; and companies that provide diagnostic services. It will also interest small- and medium-sized companies as well as startups in Silicon Valley and elsewhere that are looking to disrupt existing practices in the sector. It should also be of considerable interest to health-care policy makers everywhere, as well as to academics and consultants working in health care. The book should capture the attention of the general public, too, not only because the Indian exemplars are intriguing and instructive but also because they will be disruptive. It is our hope that the book helps mobilize grassroots support for deep, lasting, and patient-centered health-care reforms in the United States and elsewhere.

In the next two chapters, we take a deeper dive into the exemplar Indian hospitals and show how these organizations apply the five core principles of value-based delivery to great effect. They have revolutionized health-care delivery by streamlining operations, standardizing procedures, reconfiguring their organizations, leveraging technology, experimenting with new methods, valuing every patient, living their mission, and implementing innovations that work.

The full business model that the Indian exemplars use is presented in chapter 2, and illustrated with an in-depth case study (Narayana Health) in chapter 3. We believe it is a very powerful model of value-based health care, and an engine both for social good and for bottom-line results.

In part 2 of the book, "Reverse Innovation in Health-Care Delivery: Four New Models for the United States," we take an in-depth look at the US health-care organizations introduced above that are already using Indian-style innovations. We illustrate how each one uses one or more principles of the Indian exemplars to cut health-care costs, improve quality, or expand access—sometimes all three. We see these organizations as role models for bottom-up innovation to deliver value-based care in the United States.

In appendix A, as noted before, we address skepticism about whether India can really offer lessons for health-care reform in the United States. In appendix B we provide an innovation-diagnostics tool kit to help health-care organizations apply the Indian innovations and transform their organizations.

It's important to repeat that while this book explores innovations that we hope will transform the health-care systems in the United States and other rich countries, the same breakthrough models can—and should—be implemented in developing countries, beginning of course in India, where there is a track record of success. In fact, many Indian innovations are already being applied elsewhere in the developing world. Narayana Health has entered into a partnership to build a multispecialty hospital in Nairobi, Kenya, for instance.[54] And another exemplar, Aravind, has conducted community ophthalmology training in thirty countries, many in Latin America and Africa.[55] New global players are also emerging. In 2016, the profit-minded, Dubai-based Abraaj Group bought India's fifth-largest private hospital group, Care Hospitals, which performs open-heart surgeries for $3,000. Abraaj plans to transplant Care Hospitals' business model to countries in Africa.[56] We hope this book can help accelerate that kind of dissemination.

While we have focused on solutions from Indian health-care providers, we know there are many other solutions in countries around the world. We hope this book will encourage readers to take a hard look at what's working in other countries and to imagine what it would take to make those solutions work elsewhere. Reverse innovation is an equal-opportunity strategy.

Let's begin with a deeper look into the core principles of value-based health care practiced by the Indian exemplars.

2.

Breakthrough Business Model of Indian Exemplars

How Value-Based Competition Works

The business model of the Indian exemplars is founded on a common set of principles that work in a "virtuous cycle" to produce value-based health care that is high quality, low cost, patient-centric, and available to those who seek it (see figure 2-1). The central element—and in our minds the most important element—is each organization's purpose, which is to provide high-quality, ultra-affordable health care to all, regardless of patients' ability to pay (principle 1). The hospitals organize their assets and key people in a hub-and-spoke configuration that sends high volumes of patients to the hub for complex procedures and high volumes of patients to the spokes for simpler procedures. That, thanks to economies

FIGURE 2-1

Breakthrough business model

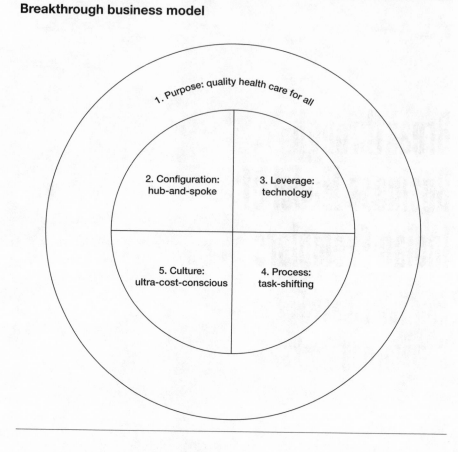

1. Purpose: quality health care for all

2. Configuration: hub-and-spoke

3. Leverage: technology

5. Culture: ultra-cost-conscious

4. Process: task-shifting

of scale, keeps costs down and gives those patients who use the spokes more-convenient and -timely care (principle 2). The hospitals also leverage technology wherever possible (principle 3) and use task-shifting and process innovations (principle 4) to simultaneously lower cost and improve quality. Finally, their ultra-cost-consciousness shatters the cost floor (principle 5), which frees up the resources necessary to support the organization's purpose of serving the underserved.

Before we describe the breakthrough business model, we will highlight why value-based health care took root in India.

How India Got to Value-Based Health Care

At first glance, India seems an unlikely place to look for breakthrough innovations in health-care delivery. After all, India's performance on many health metrics has been abysmal. Per capita spending on health in 2014 was just $75 (see table A-1 in appendix A). Physician density is less than one-third that of the United States and nurse density is roughly one-sixth. The infant mortality rate is almost seven times that of the United States and more than four times that of China. An estimated 63 million Indians live with diabetes and 2.5 million with cancer, but most of them will never be diagnosed with those illnesses, much less treated. Similarly, less than 5 percent of the annual 2.5 million Indians who need heart surgery will actually get it.[1]

But certain conditions unique to India have bred a form of value-based competition in which a handful of organizations have found the key to delivering high-quality, ultra-low-cost health care for all who seek it. *Value-based competition thrives in India because highly motivated companies have found opportunities in three daunting realities of the Indian socioeconomic context.*

Reality #1: The Indian population is huge, poor, rural, largely uninsured, and price conscious. India has a population of 1.2 billion people, and 90 percent of them are poor and uninsured. Uninsured Indians can get care in a government hospital free of charge, but, barring a few exceptions, government hospitals are famous for being crowded and understaffed, for providing poor care, and for being fraught with corruption. The alternative, private hospital care, is too expensive for almost everyone in a country where the average per capita income is $2,000 and where people pay 70 percent of health-care costs out of pocket. *Daunting? Yes. But seen through the eyes of opportunity, India has a vast, untapped market of price-conscious health-care consumers. It is the kind of place where visionary enterprises can find ways to offer high-quality, ultra-low-cost care.*

Reality #2: India has to make do with a severe shortage of doctors and facilities. In per capita terms, India has far fewer doctors and medical facilities than the United States or even China. For example, India has nine hospital beds per 10,000 people, while the United States has thirty. India's practitioner density is less than half that of China (see table A-1 in appendix A). And neurosurgery patients often wait a year for a bed in a public hospital.[2] *But seen through the eyes of opportunity, India is ripe for innovations that make the most-efficient use of the country's limited resources, thereby driving up the productivity of medical experts and facilities and increasing access for people who need care.*

Reality #3: Indian health care is a wide-open industry. In the United States, there are many barriers to innovations in health care, including government regulations, the fee-for-service reimbursement model, powerful insurance and pharmaceutical lobbies, workers unions, an often protectionist doctor culture, certificate-of-need laws that prevent new entrants from competing against established providers, and the constant threat of medical-malpractice lawsuits. The Indian health-care industry is relatively unfettered by regulation. It operates like any other market: consumers pay for what they consume, seeking value for money, while suppliers compete for business with rival offerings. *Seen through the eyes of opportunity, India offers a health-care environment in which value-based competition can flourish.*

Poverty is a great motivator. It produces an intense pressure to create value. The Indian hospitals we write about in this book pursue innovations in every facet of their operations, with a determination that is hard to imagine in rich countries, where medical resources are plentiful and third-party reimbursement is the norm. In fact, it is India's aching poverty that motivated many of the founders of our Indian exemplars to embark on their bold experiments in the first place. Readers will notice that these founders were typically medical doctors raised in India but trained in advanced countries, who wanted to bring modern medicine to the Indian masses. We call them *doctorpreneurs,* because

India's Doctorpreneurs

Dr. Devi Shetty is a remarkable man, and his high moral purpose propelled Narayana Health to the forefront of value-based health care. He is profiled in depth in the next chapter.

Dr. Govindappa Venkataswamy, known as Dr. V, was fifty-eight years old and already retired from an illustrious career in ophthalmology when he founded the nonprofit Aravind Eye Hospital in 1976. A passionate follower of the great Indian philosopher and poet Sri Aurobindo, Dr. V dedicated himself to the poor and uneducated, who suffered four million cases of cataract-related blindness each year. He wondered why cataract surgery could not be performed with the same cost, speed, and consistency with which McDonald's makes hamburgers. If it could, he reasoned, needless blindness could be eradicated from this world. Dr. V started Aravind with eleven beds in his home, and it grew to become the world's largest eye hospital—one that performed more than 1,000 surgeries per day, over half of them on patients who paid little or nothing.[3] In 2013, Aravind's average cost per cataract surgery was $50, yet on metrics of quality it outperformed the United Kingdom's National Health Service (see table A-2 in appendix A). Compared with other Indian hospitals, Aravind was so efficient that it could make enough money on one paying patient to provide free or subsidized care to two nonpaying patients. Aravind has inspired dozens of eye hospitals around the developing world. In FY 2016–17, Aravind had five tertiary care hospitals, six secondary care hospitals, and sixty-two primary care centers. That same fiscal year it served 4.1 million outpatients and performed 463,000 sight-saving surgeries.[4]

Dr. Gullapalli N. Rao followed a very similar path. In fact, his family lived in the same neighborhood of Chennai as Dr. V, and as a child Gullapalli would see the great man come and go. After twelve years of training and clinical experience in the United States, at Tufts University and the

University of Rochester, he and his wife returned to India (Hyderabad), and in 1987 established the nonprofit LV Prasad Eye Institute. Their mission was to deliver excellent eye care to all. The Institute is organized in a five-level, pyramid design. At the bottom are trained "vision guardians," who literally go door to door, each serving a population of 5,000 people. At the top are four specialty-care hospitals that treat complex eye diseases. Throughout the system, half of all patients are treated for free. In recognition of his contributions to improving eye care, Dr. Rao, in 2017, was inducted into the Ophthalmology Hall of Fame instituted by the American Society of Cataract and Refractive Surgery.

Dr. B. S. Ajaikumar, an oncologist, found his purpose in the bleak corridors of India's public cancer hospitals. After completing medical studies at St. John's Medical College, Bangalore, he did his residency training in oncology at the University of Virginia Hospital and his fellowship in radiation and medical oncology at the renowned University of Texas MD Anderson Cancer Center. While he was still practicing in the United States, he founded a nonprofit cancer hospital in Mysore and, with a group of oncologists, started the Bangalore Institute of Oncology (BIO). These early experiences taught Ajaikumar that demand was enormous but that the needs of the day were accessibility, affordability, and high-quality treatment. That's when he started a for-profit enterprise, HCG Oncology, to provide value-based, advanced cancer care, accessible to all. By 2017, HCG had become Asia's largest cancer-treatment network, with twenty comprehensive cancer-care centers and three multispecialty hospitals across India. It is noted for leveraging technology for personalized care and for making cancer treatment affordable to those of low income, who make up more than 20 percent of its patients. In 2016, HCG was successfully listed on the Indian stock market.

Dr. B. Soma Raju was one of the most outspoken critics among a group of cardiologists who declared India's bureaucratic medical system a failure in 1997.[5] He went on to found a private for-profit hospital system, Care Hospitals, naming it for the deep commitment he felt to making modern medicine affordable and accessible to all. As the system grew to fourteen hospitals in six cities, Care became one of the leading centers in India for cardiac care. Dr. Soma Raju also pioneered the development of low-cost stents and other devices that cost 10 percent of imported equivalents. Like the other Indian exemplars, Care has developed detailed protocols for every elective procedure, constantly updating them with experience. As a result, its outcomes on angioplasties, for instance, are substantially better than US averages. Like Narayana and Aravind, Care is imbued with its founder's sense of purpose and commitment to making health care accessible to all. In 2016, 25 percent of Care patients paid the break-even price—or less—for their care. That same year, Care was bought by the Abraaj Group, which hoped to spread the Care model across other poor countries, especially in Africa.[6]

they are part physicians, part entrepreneurs, and part philanthropists. (See the sidebar "India's Doctorpreneurs" for brief profiles of those covered in our research.) Their goal was not to make money through health care but to put health care within reach of the greatest number of people. Profit made it possible to do that, but it was not the end objective.

Now let's take a closer look at the five principles of the breakthrough business model of health-care delivery practiced by the Indian exemplars.

Principle 1: Pursue an Inspiring Purpose: Quality Health Care for All

The most striking commonality across the Indian exemplars is an inspiring purpose—a conviction that high-quality health care should be available to all, rich and poor, regardless of ability to pay. In most cases, this has meant giving free health care to people who couldn't afford even the ultra-low prices charged by the exemplars.

Aravind Eye Care System's stated purpose is to "eradicate needless blindness." At LV Prasad Eye Institute, it is "to create excellent and equitable eye care systems that reached all those in need." At LifeSpring, a maternity hospital for the urban poor, it is to make "dignified maternity care accessible." HCG Oncology aims to be a "leader in oncology care in South Asia, making high quality cancer care accessible by adopting global innovations." All of the hospitals have similar missions that stress the triple aim of quality, affordability, and access.

That commitment appears to put them in the same class as many well-meaning NGOs, but the exemplars have another commitment that sets them apart: they are determined to be financially self-supporting. This means that after providing high-quality care to all and free care to many, they have to balance their books. The exemplars know that charity is not scalable. They know that to sustain their operations they have to be more efficient and more productive than other hospitals, so that the margins from paying patients can be used to subsidize the care of others. And for that, the exemplars have to drive down costs while improving quality. In short, they have to innovate like no one has innovated before. We think they have achieved breakthrough innovations because everyone in these organizations, including the rank and file, is inspired by the respective organizations' purpose. Everyone understands that a penny saved is a penny that can be used to help another poor patient. The founders of these hospitals each have the proverbial social heart and business brain—the key qualification for *doctorpreneurs*.

To translate their purpose into action, our hospitals have to do three things. First, they have to convert the *need* for health care into actual *demand* for health care. Second, they have to target everyone—not just the rich, and not just the poor, but both—and then realize synergies from serving these dissimilar segments to make a profit. Finally, they have to turn that profit back into their pursuit of purpose. Let's look at each of these three imperatives in turn.

Turn need into demand. This is harder than it might seem. Many of the needy patients the hospitals hope to serve live in the remote reaches of India, so the exemplars first have to find them, then educate them about their medical conditions, and then let them know that many health solutions are within their reach. The hospitals know that nonmedical expenses like lost wages and transportation often keep poor patients from seeking even "free" medical care in the cities, so they reach out to the villages and support patients when they need treatment elsewhere. Aravind, for example, runs two thousand rural "eye camps" each year, and also offers poor patients free transportation to the specialty clinics and hospitals, as well as free surgery, room and board, medications, and follow-up visits.

Outreach is geared toward prevention as well as early detection. HCG Oncology, founded in 1989 as India's first private, for-profit cancer hospital, was by 2017 South Asia's largest cancer-care network. Because smoking is the leading cause of cancer, HCG Oncology designs programs, based on principles from psychotherapy and nutrition, to motivate people to quit.

As demand for medical treatment has grown, the hospitals have had to expand supply, which means dealing with a perennial shortage of doctors, nurses, equipment, space, and operating capital. The exemplars have responded with various strategies: they invest heavily in training doctors, nurses, and paramedical staff and even in manufacturing their own critical supplies, such as medical devices, lenses, instruments, or medicines.

Target everyone, rich and poor alike. To make their business models work, the exemplar hospitals need rich patients, those who are willing to pay market prices—and more, for premium amenities such as private rooms, air-conditioning, and television. Those patients expect truly excellent care, and they get it, for a price that subsidizes care for the poor.

This rich-poor dynamic may sound like a modern-day version of Robin Hood, but it is far from it. Like Narayana Health, these hospitals charge their paying patients 20 percent to 40 percent less than other private Indian hospitals do, partly to compensate for the fact that the facilities are not exclusively for the well-to-do.

The arrangement works to the benefit of all, because the same high-quality care that is demanded by rich patients is available to everyone. At the same time, the exemplars' mission to serve the poor forces them to lower their own costs dramatically. The poor increase volume, which improves the quality of outcomes for all, including the rich. It is a perfect match up: rich and poor create value for each other, and the hospitals become high-quality, ultra-low-cost players.

View profit as a means to an end. It might seem that the twin goals of serving the poor and making money are incompatible. After all, the more poor patients a hospital treats, the more money a hospital would be expected to lose. But Indian exemplars manage both to serve the poor and make money, for the following three reasons.

First, free or subsidized care actually contributes to profitability. When a hospital commits to serving all, rich and poor, it has to dramatically reduce its costs, because there is no other way to serve the poor and be financially viable. In other words, serving the poor drives cost innovation to levels that would be unimaginable otherwise. In fact, the exemplars achieve unit costs much lower than those in so-called profit-maximizing hospitals. Second, the high patient volume, which wouldn't exist without poor patients, enables the hospitals to achieve full utilization of resources such as equipment capacity and salaried-surgeons' time. That optimization drives the *fixed cost per unit* to levels far below that of other providers. Finally, poor patients also put inordinate pressure on the hospitals to reduce *variable costs*. Let's say a hospital manages to serve poor patients with little or no increase in fixed costs—for example, by getting machines and doctors to work more efficiently, so that two patients can be processed in the time that other hospitals take to process one paying patient. Such a hospital would still incur the full variable cost for each poor patient, so our exemplars doggedly innovate to reduce variable costs to levels that hospitals serving only the well-to-do could never match.

In short, the exemplars' purpose to serve the underserved motivates them to innovate to achieve the ultra-low-cost position that in turn boosts profit margins on the paying patients and allows the hospitals to serve more poor people. Purpose drives these enterprises, and profit enables them to achieve their purpose. Profit also means that the hospitals don't have to depend on fickle sources of funding—such as government subsidies, charitable contributions, or bank loans—to balance their books.

Of course, it takes more than a noble purpose to produce results. It takes disciplined execution and constant experimentation. This is exactly where the Indian exemplars excel, as the next four principles demonstrate.

Principle 2: Configure Assets in a Hub-and-Spoke Design

Over time, each of the hospitals we studied has evolved into a system of hubs and spokes. That structure helps the hospitals reach India's underserved patient populations, most of which live in villages and towns far from major urban centers, and also helps them to direct all patients to the appropriate level of care. In most cases, the hub hospitals were built first, in dense urban centers, where the exemplars assemble the scarcest talent and house the most expensive and sophisticated equipment. One by one, spokes were added in outlying villages and towns. The spokes, staffed by more widely available talent and outfitted with less-expensive equipment, treat patients with less-serious or -urgent conditions, and send those requiring higher-level diagnosis and treatment to the hub. Unlike suburban outposts of urban hospitals in the United States, the spokes are not miniature hubs, attempting to treat all things for all patients. Rather, they are gateways, focusing mainly on diagnosis, routine treatment, and follow-up care.

HCG Oncology has three hub hospitals in major cities, including a center of excellence in Bangalore, and it has twenty spoke hospitals oriented around those hubs. The hubs provide radiation, medical, and surgical oncology, while most spokes provide only radiation and chemotherapy treatments but no surgeries. Similarly, LV Prasad Eye Institute has a five-tiered "pyramid" model extending up from the village level through small towns and major urban areas and ultimately to its lead hospital in Hyderabad. (See the sidebar "LV Prasad Eye Institute's Five-Tiered Pyramid.")

There is a good reason that the hub-and-spoke configuration has been adopted by every exemplar: it works. It allows them to capture a high volume of patients and to put that volume to work to lower costs and improve quality. Let's see how they do it.

The Hub-and-Spoke Configuration and Costs

The hub-and-spoke configuration drives down costs in three ways.

- *It concentrates the use of expensive equipment.* The exemplar hospitals concentrate their expensive equipment in the hubs, avoiding costly duplication in the spokes. For example, HCG Oncology's three hubs have high-level imaging equipment—PET-CT scanners, cyclotrons, CT scanners, and top-of-the-line MRI machines—while its spoke hospitals make do with linear accelerators, ultrasound equipment, x-ray machines, and more-basic MRI machines

LV Prasad Eye Institute's Five-Tiered Pyramid

The LV Prasad Eye Institute (LVPEI), founded on an awareness that 75 percent of blindness is avoidable and that 90 percent of blind people live in developing countries, uses a unique five-tiered pyramid of differently skilled staff serving differently sized populations that require distinct levels of care. The LV Prasad system deploys its tiers in a configuration that serves 3,600 towns and villages across India. In January 2018, its 168 "primary" eye-care centers, near the base tier of the pyramid, diagnose problems, treat simple conditions, and send more urgent cases up the pyramid to higher tiers, in this case 26 secondary care centers, three tertiary centers, and ultimately the center of excellence in Hyderabad.[7] Here's how it works.

The bottom-most level of LVPEI's pyramid is staffed by local workers who either volunteer their time or are paid a small salary. Called vision guardians (VHGs), they receive a mere two weeks of training, primarily in eye care but also in general health screening, before going to work, where they are responsible for raising community awareness and conducting screenings for various eye conditions, as well as for diabetes and hypertension. Based out of the institute's primary centers, each cadre of VHGs serves a population of 5,000.[8]

Each of LV Prasad's second tier of 168 vision centers is managed by a vision technician (VT), often a local high school graduate with a full year of training in optometry. Vision technicians serve a population of 50,000 and are charged with executing "three *R*s": refraction, recognition, and referral.

The third tier consists of twenty-seven secondary care units, including nine centers run by partner organizations, each of which is linked to a network of ten vision centers. Secondary care units, each staffed by two dozen technicians and medical professionals, accept cases from lower tiers and, when necessary, send needier patients up to higher tiers. Secondary care teams, which serve a population of 500,000, diagnose almost all eye conditions and perform surgeries for cataracts, primary glaucoma, corneal tears, and some other, nonblinding eye conditions.

At the top of the LV Prasad pyramid sit two tiers that handle only the most demanding cases. One comprises three LVPEI tertiary centers, each located in an urban area and each serving a population of approximately five million. The other, at the very top of the pyramid, is LVPEI's center of excellence, located in Hyderabad and said to serve a population of fifty million. These tiers provide tertiary level care and training for virtually all eye conditions. They also offer eye-banking services, conduct research, and advocate for eye-care policy.

Like all of our exemplars, LV Prasad is driven foremost by a strong sense of purpose, and it is empowered by its tiered-pyramid model, which functions like the hub-and-spoke models of the other exemplars. From its founding, in 1987, by Dr. G. N. Rao, and until early 2018, the nonprofit has served more than twenty-four million people, with more than 50 percent of its services provided free of cost.[9]

(or none). As the center of excellence, HCG's Bangalore hospital houses equipment that HCG couldn't afford to duplicate even in other hubs, such as an $8 million CyberKnife (a hyperprecise, noninvasive, robotic radiosurgery system). Similarly, LV Prasad's rural centers have just one simple ophthalmic instrument, but its second-level centers are equipped to perform simple cataract surgeries, and its top tiers have state-of-the-art equipment for advanced procedures, such as corneal transplants.

- *It centralizes scarce expertise.* Medical expertise is allocated the same way, with the hubs housing most of HCG's cancer specialists, while the spokes are staffed by more-general physicians. Specialists whose expertise is expensive or in short supply in India—e.g., oncologists, oncopathologists, and medical physicists—are concentrated in the center of excellence in Bangalore. Once a patient's treatment plan is finalized in consultation with doctors in the hub, chemotherapy or radiation treatment is generally provided by lower-level staff in the spokes, minimizing cost and inconvenience for patients. And because diagnosis and treatment of cancer often saddles patients with severe psychological stress, spokes develop cancer wellness programs designed to help patients reduce stress and better cope during chemotherapy and radiation. The programs integrate the latest concepts in stress management with yoga, including yoga postures and breathing and meditation techniques. Yoga not only provides mental relaxation while building confidence in an individual coping with cancer, it also improves lung capacity through breathing techniques.

- *It turns hubs and spokes into focused factories.* During fiscal year 2016–2017, Aravind served 4.6 million outpatients at its farthest spokes, the mobile "eye camps," and performed 463,000 eye surgeries at its hubs—making it the world's largest eye-care system.[10] Such high patient volumes allow the hubs to function as focused factories for complex procedures and the spokes to function as focused factories for simple procedures, enabling economies of scale and lowering unit costs.[11] As volume rises, costs fall, because doctors, equipment, and facilities are used more intensively and more efficiently. For example, the average Aravind hub doctor performs between 1,000 and 1,400 eye surgeries per year, compared with a US average of about 400. At Aravind, the morning is usually reserved for routine cataract surgeries, which account for 70 percent of all surgeries. Surgeons begin at 8:00 a.m. and usually perform from twenty to twenty-five surgeries by 1:00 p.m.[12] Equipment has a similarly rigorous routine. While leading US hospitals might use operating suites for one shift on weekdays and only for emergencies on weekends, the Indian hospitals use them for two shifts seven days a week. Likewise, US hospitals may use a PET-CT scanner for up to five patients a day, whereas HCG's scanners are used between fifteen and twenty times a day. As HCG's founder, Dr. B.S. Ajaikumar, says, "You have to make the equipment sweat!"[13] He runs his MRI machines day and night, charging lower nighttime prices as an inducement for patients to come in when machines would otherwise be idle. Higher volumes allow these hospitals to more quickly amortize the cost of machines, supplies, and medical equipment.

The Hub-and-Spoke Configuration and Quality

The hub-and-spoke configuration helps improve quality in three important ways.

- *It accelerates learning and skill development.* Research has shown that specialization and volume markedly improve a surgeon's performance.[14] Practice really does make perfect, or at least close to perfect, as specialization reduces errors. For example, despite doing cataract surgeries at an extremely fast rate in the hub hospitals, Aravind has fewer medical complications than hospitals in the United Kingdom's National Health Service. The high volume and the variety of cases attract talent. Doctors know they can build their capabilities faster in such environments. All the academic hospitals we studied recruit many of their doctors from among their own students. The caliber of the recruits, in turn, contributes to better outcomes for patients at these hospitals.

- *It facilitates the development of system-wide protocols.* High volume and centralized medical decision making encourage the hub hospitals to develop standard treatment protocols, and to continuously update them with evidence-based feedback, which reduces errors. Care Hospitals provides a case in point. Its CEO, Dr. Krishna Reddy, believes that any medical procedure that can be scheduled in advance, including complicated surgeries like coronary-bypass operations, can be guided by standardized procedures and protocols. The hospital assigns all its angioplasty patients, for instance, to one of three risk categories based on a set of criteria that includes age, weight, medical history, and lifestyle. It then treats each patient according to the protocol developed for that risk category. The results are impressive. While studies suggest that one in every two hundred angioplasty patients worldwide will require emergency surgery after treatment and half of those will likely die on the operating table, at Care Hospitals only one in every twenty thousand angioplasty patients has required emergency surgery and only one has died on the table.[15]

- *It encourages ultraspecialization.* As volume increases, doctors at the hubs treat many uncommon and even rare conditions often enough that they became world-class practitioners in those areas. Narayana Health, for example, has developed a center of excellence in pediatric open-heart surgery, attracting poor patients from across India, Bangladesh, other parts of Asia, and Africa. In 2016, its eighty-bed pediatric open-heart ICU was the largest in the world. Similarly, HCG has built deep capabilities in the treatment of breast, neck, and throat cancer, and LV Prasad is world-class in corneal transplants.

As the Indian exemplars have evolved into efficient hub-and-spoke systems, the US health-care system finds itself propping up too many hubs.

Hospitals in the United States invest in duplicate equipment and offer a full range of services even in their suburban facilities, when the investments are hard to justify. Even in specialty areas where the United States has higher volumes of care than India, such as cardiac care, kidney care, and cancer care, treatment is often spread inefficiently across many hospitals. For instance, over 500,000 Americans underwent open-heart surgery in the United States according to a study published in the *Journal of the American Medical Association*, compared with only 100,000 in India, but the US volume was spread across many hospitals.[16] Thus, Cleveland Clinic and Mayo Clinic—two premier cardiac hospitals—did far fewer open-heart surgeries per year than Narayana Health, which performed 14,700 cardiac surgeries in 2016. Similarly, in fiscal year 2016–2017, Aravind served 4.6 million outpatients and performed close to half a million surgeries, which was vastly more than any US eye hospital. When US hospitals consolidate, the motive often is not to rationalize operations and lower costs but to gain brand recognition with the public and bargaining leverage with insurance companies.

Principle 3: Leverage Technology

Our Indian exemplars see technology as a means to extend their reach, lower cost, and improve quality of care. Generally unencumbered by legacy investments or practices, they leverage technology to offer telehealth services across their hub-and-spoke networks, facilitate home care for the chronically ill, reduce the cost of critical supplies and equipment, and build information systems and electronic medical records across their organizations. In doing so, they take advantage of India's considerable capabilities in frugal innovation and software development. Let's see exactly what they do.

Promote telehealth services. HCG Oncology has built a telemedicine network across its hub-and-spoke system that allows doctors in the hubs to efficiently and economically serve patients seeking care at the spokes.

Hub specialists can read medical images and design radiation treatment plans remotely. Unless expensive equipment, complex tests, or in-person consultations with superspecialists are required, patients can get care closer to their homes. This lowers their nonmedical out-of-pocket expenses (lost wages during time away from work, the cost of travel, and room and board), the kind of expenses that often deter poor patients from seeking even "free" care. Indian hospitals are highly sensitive to the *total cost to the patient*, factoring in not just medical expenses but also collateral nonmedical costs. Telemedicine dramatically lowers the cost of treating patients.

Support home care for chronic conditions. Some Indian hospitals encourage patients with chronic conditions to get treatment at home rather than in costlier outpatient facilities. One interesting example is Deccan Hospital's practice of encouraging home-based peritoneal dialysis instead of the hospital- or clinic-based hemodialysis that is more common in the United States (see the sidebar "Deccan Hospital's Home-Based Renal Care"). In 2017, the annual cost of Deccan's home-based treatment was about $8,200, roughly 9 percent of the cost of outpatient hemodialysis in the United States ($89,000), yet the five-year survival rate for Deccan was better than that of the US average for hemodialysis: 50 percent versus 41 percent.[17]

Engineer cheaper, locally manufactured supplies. Several of the Indian hospitals have developed cheap local substitutes for expensive imported supplies and devices. In the 1980s, when the intraocular lens (IOL) used in cataract surgery was introduced in the West, lenses cost $200 apiece—a price that was unaffordable for all but a very few affluent patients in India. Aravind signed a technology-transfer agreement with an obscure Florida firm and created its own manufacturing operation called Aurolab, which made IOLs for $5 apiece.[18] By early 2013, the price had dropped to $2, and the lab had expanded its product line to include rigid

Deccan Hospital's Home-Based Renal Care

Deccan Hospital, led by chief nephrologist Dr. K. S. Nayak, has developed a system for home-based dialysis called peritoneal dialysis (PD), a treatment option for patients with severe and chronic kidney disease, so-called end-stage renal disease (ESRD). The alternative, which is commonly used in the United States, is a clinic- or hospital-based treatment plan called hemodialysis (HD).

With PD, fluid is introduced through a permanent tube in the abdomen and then flushed out either every night while the patient sleeps or via regular exchanges throughout the day. Unlike HD, PD does not require visits to a hospital and is consequently cheaper and more convenient for the patient. The primary disadvantage is a risk of infection, because PD involves permanently attaching a tube to the abdomen.

Initially, the highest barrier for PD in developed countries was concern that patients might lack access to a doctor. As a result, less than 10 percent of ESRD patients in the United States are treated with PD. The end result? The United States treats ESRD patients with HD for about $89,000 a year, compared with $8,200 for Nayak's PD patients, who also have better survival rates than US patients.

Deccan Hospital uses technology to deal with the distance barrier. The hospital uses mobile-phone short messaging service (SMS), inexpensive digital cameras, and the internet to address patient accessibility issues. Those technologies, coupled with a dedicated PD team of medical and paramedical professionals, have enabled the hospital to develop a unique PD remote-monitoring system. Patients who use the system are in constant touch with kidney specialists. To monitor complications from infection, patients and their caregivers are trained during their initial PD period to use their own mobile-phone cameras to take photographs of the PD effluent bag.

Health complaints from patients receive immediate responses, and remote monitoring is backed up by a home-visit protocol involving a well-trained clinical coordinator (CC), who follows a checklist for a step-by-step assessment of patient well-being. That information, along with a summary of the patient's most recent laboratory results, is sent to a nephrologist by SMS from the patient's home. The CC waits until the nephrologist responds (usually within fifteen minutes), and advises the patient accordingly. CCs also assess and advise patients on nutrition, anxiety disorders, mental depression, psychological well-being, and physical fitness.

HD, on the other hand, requires patients to visit the hospital three times a week, which is burdensome and more expensive and which hampers the patient's lifestyle. Nayak says: "Our success can easily be replicated in the United States. Conservatively, even if 15 percent of ESRD patients chose PD over HD, it would save Medicare and Medicaid many millions of dollars a year."[19]

and foldable IOLs as well as low-cost sutures, blades, other ophthalmic consumables, and equipment for eye surgery. In 2017, Aurolab's low-cost supplies were being exported to 120 countries.[20]

Similarly, Care Hospitals' founder helped develop stents priced between $240 and $360 whose performance was comparable with that of imported stents costing between $2,000 and $3,000. Care Hospitals subsequently created a subsidiary to manufacture stents, catheters, and other devices for sale in India and abroad.

Embrace value-added technological innovation. The Indian hospitals take advantage of India's flourishing ecosystem for frugal innovation to source ultra-low-cost equipment and tests. Oncologist Dr. Vishal Rao at HCG

Oncology, for instance, invented a $1 voice prosthesis device that helps patients with stage 4 cancer whose voice box has been removed to speak properly. Similar devices in the United States cost as much as $700. Another example is the 3nethra, an inexpensive portable ophthalmic instrument developed in India that can take refractive index measurements and screen patients for four eye conditions (cataracts, diabetic retina, glaucoma, and cornea issues) without requiring a skilled operator. In the United States, the same tests require three expensive instruments and trained operators. 3nethra uses an image-processing algorithm to generate a report within five minutes of screening and can be integrated into a telemedicine network for remote diagnosis. LV Prasad partnered with the Massachusetts Institute of Technology to develop the next generation of optometric technologies. An Indian entrepreneur developed an easy-to-use, Android-based health tablet (Swasthya Slate) that can conduct thirty-three diagnostic tests and if produced in volume could cost only $150 per unit.[21] Another entrepreneur, Myshkin Ingawale, developed a noninvasive (needleless) test for anemia that features a portable, easy-to-use device that costs between $200 and $300 to buy and less than ten cents per test. The standard Western procedure costs several times more and requires equipment priced up to $10,000.[22]

Create EMR and IT systems. Well before health care in the United States made meaningful use of electronic medical records, our Indian exemplars were knee-deep in bits and bytes. HCG Oncology created electronic medical records (EMRs) for its cancer patients from the outset as a way to lower recordkeeping costs and avoid errors when patients were treated across the hub-and-spoke system. Narayana Health developed and installed a software program called iKare on iPads connected to all ICU beds. The software automatically updates patient records as changes are generated and directs staff on next steps of care, helping to reduce hospital errors. Narayana has also built an information system across its entire twenty-three-hospital network, with data stored in the cloud and easily accessible at all levels. There is a cultural norm for data sharing that allows the hospitals to compare performance measures for such things as surgeon productivity and operating-suite utilization, which encourages the diffusion of best practices across the chain.

Instead of leveraging telehealth opportunities or offering inexpensive home-based care, as the Indian exemplars do, health-care providers in the United States tend to keep their patients in expensive hospital settings, even those patients with chronic conditions or in end-of-life situations who prefer to be at home.

Principle 4: Adopt Task-Shifting

By shifting tasks from highly specialized workers (primarily doctors) to nurses and paramedical staff, the best Indian hospitals match the skill level of their people with the requirements of the tasks (see figure 2-2). In India, where highly skilled workers are scarce, this kind of task-shifting is often necessary to optimize specialists' time and energy. The practice saves money, of course, but it also improves quality, because doctors and paramedics perform tasks that best fit their expertise. The exemplars have redesigned their staffing and delivery of health care in three ways.

Create new job categories. The Indian exemplars have taken task-shifting to the next level by creating new categories of low-cost health-care workers at one end of the spectrum and highly focused specialists at the other. When Dr. Venkataswamy founded Aravind, he had plenty of patients but too few ophthalmologists and optometrists to screen them. His solution was to hire village women with high-school diplomas and train them for two years to work in a new position called "midlevel ophthalmic paramedic." Over time, these village-based paramedics have made up 64 percent of Aravind's workforce and perform tasks such as admitting patients, maintaining medical records, and assisting doctors. Similarly, unable to lure

FIGURE 2-2

Task-shifting

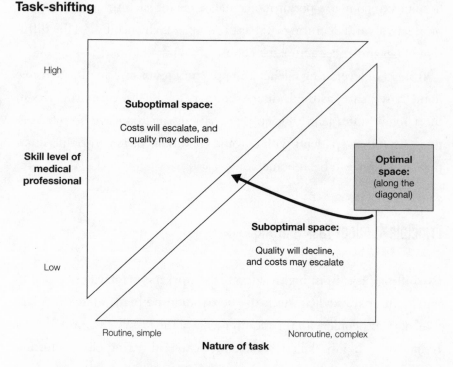

Source: Albert G. Mulley Jr., MD, MPP, Managing Director, Global Health Care Delivery Science, The Dartmouth Institute for Health Policy and Clinical Practice.

trained personnel to rural villages, LV Prasad, as mentioned already, has developed a cadre of vision guardians and vision technicians to carry out basic vision tests at the village level. In addition to being inexpensive, the paramedics bring previously unseen skills such as cultural competency, loyalty to the organization, strong work ethic, and the ability to connect more deeply with patients and families whose socioeconomic background is similar to their own. This last contribution is especially helpful in dealings with rural patients, who are unfamiliar with the health-care system and may even fear physicians.

At the high-skills end of the spectrum, HCG has developed a new category of "onconurses" to assist doctors in chemotherapy and radiation treatments, and Narayana Health trains nurses to advance to the higher-skilled position of "nurse intensivist," akin to a nurse practitioner in the United States. Narayana Health also encourages general physicians to become specialists, and specialists to become superspecialists. Similarly, LV Prasad's vision technicians have the option of enrolling at its optometry school to become optometrists. This practice has opened up new career possibilities for rural Indians: for instance, one vision technician at LV Prasad rose to become an optometrist and later obtained a PhD in ophthalmology.

In these ways, the hospitals have expanded their organizations' skill base, enlarged their patient reach, and created new labor pools that make up for deficiencies in India's public education system.

Pursue process innovations. The exemplar hospitals maximize their efficiency by *over*investing in the staff supporting their most skilled surgeons and specialists, radically extending their reach. Each Aravind surgeon, for example, has help from six paramedics in the clinical domain and four assistants for administrative and support services. Paramedics go to villages, screen patients, transport them back to the hub hospital, measure their vitals, have tests performed, prepare the patients for surgery, deliver postsurgical care in the ward, transport them back to the village, and provide follow-up care. The surgeon performs only the actual procedure, which is a small but vital fragment of time to which all other tasks contribute.

Like Southwest Airlines, the best Indian hospitals focus on reducing the turnaround or downtime of their most costly resources. They increase surgeons' productivity by decreasing the amount of time it takes to move one patient out of the operating suite and to bring in the next one. Turnaround time is the key factor limiting efficiency and a key driver of costs, according to a global study of performance benchmarks in knee-replacement surgeries. Dr. Eric Wadsworth, a cofounder of Dartmouth's Master of Health Care Delivery Science program, concurs. "Instead of looking at 'wheels in to wheels out,'" he said, "we must reframe the question to look at 'wheels out to wheels in.' Of course, efficiency is possible during surgery itself, the time when patients are wheeled in to and out of surgery. But the bigger cost savings are during the interval between when one patient is wheeled out and the next is wheeled in."[23]

Aravind tackles the challenge in cataract surgery by setting up two surgical stations side by side, with the surgeon positioned between them, assisted by a swiveling microscope and two pairs of nurses. For each patient, one nurse assists the doctor by administering local anesthesia, providing sterile instruments and the right implants, focusing the microscope, and bandaging the patient. The other—actually a paramedic called a "running nurse"—replaces used surgical instruments with fresh surgical tools from a sterilization area about thirty yards away and moves patients in to and out of the operating suite. Switching smoothly from one patient to another, Aravind's doctors perform surgeries briskly in ten-to-twelve-minute intervals. This is how Aravind's doctors are able to perform five or six surgeries per hour, compared with one or two per hour in a conventional operating suite with a single assisting nurse.

Aravind's doctors are *not* overworked. They are more productive because of rational task-shifting and clever process design.

Encourage self-service. An extreme form of task-shifting is self-service, in which patients or their family members take over tasks traditionally performed by hospital staff. For example, LifeSpring Hospitals, a maternity center, provides an extra bed next to the new mother so that a family member can stay and help care for her. Another hospital encourages family members to use a shared kitchen to prepare meals for their patients. Similarly, Narayana Health encourages family members to provide post-ICU care for patients after undergoing a four-hour audio-and-video curriculum developed with Stanford University. This kind of self-service care backed by training reduces staffing costs and allows for more-personalized care for the patient, while also ensuring continuity and uniformity of care when the patient goes home, thereby reducing postsurgical complications and readmissions. More broadly, self-service encourages patient ownership of health and disease management.

While the Indian exemplars have developed protocols for all scheduled procedures, such as knee and hip replacements, angioplasties, and open-heart surgery, not all US hospitals have done so, as Atul Gawande, an American surgeon and writer, famously pointed out in his *The Checklist Manifesto*.[24] Similarly, when US hospitals go after costs, they seldom embrace the kinds of task-shifting strategies we saw in India. Instead, cost reduction typically starts with cuts in low-cost staff jobs, forcing doctors to spend more time on simple, routine tasks such as transcription, logistics, and billing. At Mayo Clinic, for example, doctors reportedly spend more than half their time on nonmedical matters. This is exactly the wrong kind of task-shifting, and it has led to physician dissatisfaction and burnout.

Principle 5: Create a Culture of Ultra-Cost-Consciousness

In the best Indian hospitals, the goal is to maximize the number of patients treated rather than the number of procedures conducted. To achieve that goal, those hospitals embrace a mindset of old-fashioned frugality. In medical matters, of course, frugality must not come at the expense of quality. But absent a compelling medical reason not to cut costs in each particular case, the hospitals are relentless. Cost cutting is an ongoing priority, even among doctors. Had the hospitals served only rich patients, as many private providers in India did, cost wouldn't have mattered so much, but when the goal is to serve as many poor patients as possible, every penny of cost matters.

Here are six cost-cutting measures widely used by our exemplars.

Avoid needless waste. Some hospitals selectively reuse medical devices that are sold by their foreign manufacturers for single-use applications. One such device is a $160 single-use steel clamp used during beating-heart surgeries that Care Hospitals and Narayana Health routinely sterilize and reuse from fifty to eighty times before throwing away. "If no hospital in the world throws away its needle holders, forceps, and scissors, which are drenched in blood after every operation, why throw out the clamps?" asks Devi Shetty, Narayana's founder and chairman.

Other hospitals have asked their suppliers to shorten the length of sutures—and to lower the price accordingly—after finding that their doctors were routinely discarding one-third of each suture after tying it off.

Avoid unnecessary procedures. The exemplars strive not just to control costs and prices but also to be *cost-effective*. That means avoiding unnecessary procedures and tests. At Care Hospitals, for example, new recruits are specifically taught that the hospital exists *solely* to provide quality health care at affordable prices, not to generate income from unnecessary tests. Care's doctors' compensation is team-based, a structure that creates peer pressure to avoid unnecessary tests. Unlike many private clinics and hospitals in India that engage doctors mainly as consultants who use its facilities, Aravind, LifeSpring, LV Prasad, and Care pay their doctors a fixed salary and engage them directly on the hospital's payroll, offering no bonuses or other incentives for internal referrals for tests or procedures.

Offer bundled pricing. Indian exemplars offer fixed-price packages, or bundled pricing, for common medical procedures rather than à la carte pricing. At LifeSpring, prices for delivery (vaginal and cesarean) are displayed prominently all over the hospital. Bundled pricing motivates the hospital to accurately measure the costs incurred in each step of the treatment process, to eliminate waste and unnecessary steps and tests, and to reduce inefficiencies. To ensure quality outcomes, hospitals have established protocols that make sure necessary procedures are not skipped.

Control variable costs. The zeal of our exemplars to lower costs through frugal innovation has no end—otherwise Aravind would have been content with a $5 intraocular lens and would not have pushed the cost threshold lower. Aravind knows, down to a fraction of a penny, its variable costs for every type of cataract surgery and patient. It watches material consumption very closely, looking to shave pennies here and there. If it were serving only rich patients with high willingness to pay, as many private providers do, there would be no pressure to track costs with such precision. But when the price is often zero (for free patients), even a few cents can seem like a lot.

Be frugal in capital expenditures. The hospitals we studied think carefully about fixed costs as well. For instance, they match the sophistication of equipment to the task. LifeSpring, for instance, orders smaller and simpler beds for its maternity wards, but the company does not skimp on the delivery tables for operating rooms in its twelve hospitals in Hyderabad. It also uses low-resolution black-and-white ultrasound machines unless a complicated case requires more-advanced equipment. Rigorous maintenance and repair of equipment are also high priorities among the exemplars so as to prolong the working life of expensive technology. For example, Narayana Health contracts with an American maintenance company, TriMedx, to double the life of the hospital's expensive diagnostic equipment.

Leasing arrangements are also common, even for land and buildings, which are both very expensive in India. Some hospitals negotiate pay-per-use deals with equipment suppliers instead of buying expensive diagnostic equipment outright. Many hospitals economize on furnishings for their lobbies, wards, patient rooms, hallways, and offices. LifeSpring has a no-frills, simple physical space. The non-air-conditioned rooms feature basic furniture, and the hospital has no food services. Senior managers at Aravind and Care often share small offices, freeing up space for more mission-critical needs such as operating suites.

The capital-investment savings add up. In 2013, Narayana Health spent just $7 million on a 300-bed superspecialty hospital in Mysore, which it built as a prototype for expansion into smaller cities. The Mysore hospital's capital expenditure per bed ($23,300) is a little more than 1 percent that of comparable hospitals in the United States.[25]

Focus doctors' attention on consequences of their decisions. One particularly interesting way of building cost consciousness across the organization is Narayana's practice of sending daily updates to doctors by cell phone that include data on occupancy, emergencies, and numbers and types of surgical procedures. The practice encourages doctors to be prudent: they can see how their decisions about which medicines to prescribe, supplies to use, or tests to order affect the cost of treating patients. Taking its cue from the Toyota Production System, Narayana also encourages frontline medical practitioners to continually suggest ideas for cost savings and improvement.

While Indian health care focuses on frugality, for the last fifteen to twenty years US hospitals have splurged on excess capacity and costly, high-tech equipment, which has led to even more pressure to utilize hospital facilities. Despite all this spending, cost accounting in US health care is rudimentary at best. When it comes to the cost of procedures, for example, few US doctors—or even hospital CFOs—can provide accurate or fine-grained estimates. Eric Wadsworth of Dartmouth put it this way:

> *Very few doctors and nurses can tell you how much they charge for a clinical procedure. The clinical folks don't know, the administration doesn't know, and the dirty secret is the finance department doesn't know really, either, because they've never had to measure cost. All they had to do was add up all their revenue on one side, all their expenses on the other, and make sure there was some sort of a positive margin or, if not, find some way to fill in the gap with philanthropy.*

Conclusion

The five principles, unsurprisingly, work best when used in conjunction to reinforce one another. Aravind, LV Prasad, and Narayana probably apply all five principles to the fullest, and they see greater success in serving a larger proportion of free or subsidized patients while still remaining profitable. Purpose, which really stems from the desire to bring modern medicine to the greatest number of people, energizes innovation on all fronts, and leads to fuller use of the remaining four principles. But the principles can also be applied individually. Structuring a hospital network as a hub-and-spoke system can stretch resources without compromising on quality, but when done in conjunction with technology (such as telemedicine) it is even more effective. Task-shifting by itself is a useful principle, but when combined with continuous process improvements and technology, it pushes even farther the boundaries of what the hospitals can do. Similarly, frugality in operating and capital expenditures lowers costs without lowering quality, but purpose influences the fervor with which frugal practices are discovered, adopted, and diffused.

The five principles are also consistent with bottom-up innovation. Pursuing an inspiring purpose, configuring the assets of a health-care system in a hub-and-spoke design, deploying technology effectively, or being frugal in operating and capital expenditures does not require the consent of anyone in Washington, DC, or the government. Task-shifting may be constrained by regulations on who can do what, and telehealth consultations may not be reimbursable in some policy contexts, but organizations that are determined can still pursue one or more of our five principles to improve the quality of care while lowering costs.

In conclusion, the key lesson for other hospitals in India and elsewhere is this: Consider adopting parts of the business model described in this chapter even if you can't adopt all of it. Some is better than none, but firing on all five cylinders will allow health-care organizations to really push the frontiers of high quality, low cost, and maximum access. And each of the principles can be applied to some extent by any established player or new entrant, regardless of the prevailing policy environment. That's what makes them particularly powerful as a means for bottom-up transformation of health care.

In the next chapter, we will take you on a close-up tour of one of our exemplars, Narayana Health.

3.

Value-Based Competition in Action
Narayana Health

The young cardiac surgeon was making the rounds in a pediatric ward in the B.M. Birla Hospital in Kolkata, India, walking with an older woman he had recently treated for a heart condition, when the woman suddenly turned and looked him in the eye.

"I know why you are here," she said.

"Really?" Dr. Devi Shetty responded. "Tell me, please. Why am I here?"

"Because when God created these children with heart problems, he was preoccupied," the woman answered. "He sent you here to treat them."

It's easy to see why, many years later, Shetty would say that the older woman, who was known throughout India as Mother Teresa, was an inspiring force behind Narayana Health, the Bangalore-based hospital system that Shetty founded in 2001 with a vision of treating all patients regardless of their ability to pay.

Shetty did fix many children's hearts, and he often did it for free. This was a major medical accomplishment and the work of a great humanitarian. But Shetty's greatest accomplishment was the creation of a value-based health-care system, and that is the achievement we will investigate in this chapter. It is Shetty's lifework and it began with a simple observation:

"If a solution is not affordable," Shetty says, "it's not a solution."[1]

Creating Value from Nothing

Shetty was determined to find a way to repair hearts in circumstances of extreme poverty. He engineered a business model for cardiac care in which wealthier patients paid more than poor patients, some of whom couldn't pay at all, and he ended up with a health-care system that treated close to 2.1 million people a year. Along the way, he accomplished many things. He made universal access to excellent health care his first priority; he built hospitals across India; he tied in with satellite clinics in the countryside; he cut hospital costs to the bone; he offered a bundled price for cardiac operations; he redefined health workers' roles; and he leveraged emerging technologies to improve both hospital finances and patient care. (See table 3-1 for basic facts on Narayana Health.)

By 2017, Shetty had achieved his affordable solution, with results that were impressive to Western observers. For example, Narayana hospitals charge little more than $2,100 for open-heart surgery that would cost between $100,000 and $150,000 in the United States. The *cost* of the surgery is even lower: approximately $1,100 to $1,200 per surgery. Shetty has thereby fulfilled his high-minded purpose and also built a profitable company.

He doesn't do it by soaking the rich. From the beginning, even the most expensive surgical stays at Narayana hospitals have been priced 20 percent to 40 percent less than the same offerings at other private Indian hospitals.[2] He doesn't do it by cutting corners on quality, either.

TABLE 3-1

Narayana Health, key facts, 2017

Prices

Cardiac surgery, subsidized patients	$1,307
Cardiac surgery, paying patients	$2,100
Angioplasty without implant, subsidized patients	$615
Angioplasty without implant, paying patients	$1,154

Volume (FY 2016–2017)

Number of outpatients, all ailments (annual)	1,907,677
Number of cardiac surgeries (annual)	14,700[1]

Subsidized patients, cardiac care

Share of subsidized patients among all outpatients	11.8%
Share of subsidized patients among all cardiac surgeries	54%

Productivity[2]

Cardiac surgeries per senior surgeon per year	600 to 700
Cardiac surgeries per surgeon (junior and senior) per year	480 to 500

Quality

Mortality rate within 30 days of heart surgery	1.4%[3]

Financial information (FY 2016–2017)

Total revenues	$288.9 million
Salaries as % of total revenues	40.5%
Supplies and consumables as % of total revenues	24.1%
Total annual compensation for doctors (3,011 doctors as of May 1, 2017)	$39.6 million (13.7% of total revenues)
Total annual compensation for nurses (14,330 full-time nurses as of May 1, 2017)	$20.5 million (7.1% of total revenues)
EBITDA margin (% of total revenues)	13.1%
Net profit margin (% of total revenues)	4.4%

Indian rupees (INR) converted to US dollars (USD) at a rate of 1 USD to 65 INR, the rate prevailing in mid-2017.
1. Mayo Clinic performed less than one-third the number of cardiac surgeries performed by Narayana in FY 2016–2017, see https://www.mayoclinic.org/departments-centers/cardiovascular-surgery/home/orc-20123417.
2. On average, Narayana's cardiac surgeons performed two to three times as many open-heart surgeries per year as their US counterparts.
3. Based on Faheem Ahmed et al., "Can Reverse Innovation Catalyse Better Value Health Care?" *The Lancet* 5, no. 10 (2017); and Lord Carter of Coles' 2015 "Review of Operational Productivity in NHS Providers: https://www. gov.uk/government/uploads/system/uploads/attachment_data/file/434202/carter-interim-report.pdf). See also Tarun Khanna, Kasturi Rangan, and Merlina Manocaran, "Narayana Hrudayalaya Heart Hospital: Cardiac Care for the Poor (A)," Case 505-078 (Boston: Harvard Business School, 2005, revised 2011). Khanna, Rangan, and Manocaran reported the thirty-day CABG mortality rate as 1.27%. Narayana Health's patients were probably of higher risk than US patients for four reasons: 1. As the largest cardiac hospital in India (and the world), Narayana accepted patients with complications who may have been turned down by other hospitals 2. Indians tend to be prone to more serious heart problems than people in many other countries 3. Indians generally go for heart surgery in advanced stages of disease and 4. Poor hygienic conditions and higher pollution outside the hospitals may increase postoperative complications and mortality.

All Narayana patients, no matter what they pay, receive identical, first-rate medical care, and the hospitals report outcomes on metrics—such as the hospital-acquired infection rate (2.8 per 1,000 ICU days)—that rival those of the best hospitals in the world.[3]

He does it by being an innovator, by stepping over traditional boundaries and painting outside the lines. When, for example, a multinational supplier of hospital gowns refused to budge on a prohibitively high quote, Shetty partnered with a local manufacturer to make gowns of the same quality for a fraction of the price. And when dairy farmers in the state of Karnataka couldn't afford medical care, Shetty helped them set up an affordable insurance scheme that became the largest of its kind in the world. Shetty also launched a data-mining project to help predict disease outbreaks and steer public health policy. In these ways, Shetty has created value not only for patients and providers but also for society as a whole, turning Narayana Health into a catalyst for progress.

It is also a profitable enterprise. Driven by the twin goals of high quality and low cost—objectives that are seemingly incompatible and that have not been pursued by most health-care organizations in the United States—Narayana has enjoyed steadily rising results. In FY 2016–2017, the company's operating profit margin (EBITDA margin) was about 13.1 percent, compared with 6.3 percent for Mayo Clinic and 10.3 percent for Cleveland Clinic.[4]

Those profits have driven Narayana's growth and expansion beyond cardiac care. In 2017, Narayana's flagship facility in Bangalore was operating as a full-fledged "health city," with a heart hospital, a cancer center, an orthopedics and trauma hospital, an eye hospital, an organ-transplant institute, and departments of neurosurgery, neurology, pediatrics, nephrology, urology, gynecology, and gastroenterology. Altogether, Narayana has twenty-four hospitals across India as well as a hospital in the Cayman Islands (keep your eye on that one). That year, Narayana performed more than 343 surgeries and procedures every day, including 39 heart surgeries.[5] Its hospitals receive patients from more than seventy-seven countries, and it has the largest telemedicine network and the largest pediatric cardiac ICU in the world.

Narayana's results have impressed both health-care experts and investors. In 2008, AIG and J.P. Morgan paid $100 million for 25 percent of the company. In 2015, when the company went public, its IPO was oversubscribed nearly nine times and raised around $100 million. In 2017, Narayana's market cap was around $1 billion.

How did Narayana Health do it all? By respecting the poor and understanding the value of nothing.

"We started with the idea that the problem we face is not the heart operation per se," says Dr. Ashutosh Raghuvanshi, Shetty's right-hand man and the vice chairman, managing director, and group CEO of Narayana. Raghuvanshi, a pediatric cardiac surgeon, paints a picture of the heartbreaking scene he saw every day: a mother, with a baby on her lap, struggling to take in the news that the child needed a heart operation. Devastated, the mother could frame only one question: *How much will it cost?*

"Early on," Raghuvanshi says, "we realized that the health-care problem in this country was not a science problem. It was an economic problem. Our objective was not only to do the heart operation but to close the gap between a patient's financial abilities and the cost of the operation. Every single thing we did started from the assumption that *There is no money.* Then we started planning how to deliver what we needed to deliver."[6]

A Purpose-Built Hospital System

Devi Shetty was born in 1953 in the southwestern state of Karnataka, the eighth of nine children. His boyhood hero was South African surgeon Christiaan Barnard, who performed the first successful human heart transplant when Shetty was a wide-eyed eighth-grader. Shetty earned a medical degree at Kasturba Medical College in Mangalore in 1982 and then honed his skills at Guy's Hospital, one of the premier teaching hospitals of Great Britain. He returned to India in 1989, at the request of some wealthy Indian patients, and quickly became known as one of the top heart surgeons in the country.

He also became known for his compassion. In Kolkata, where he met Mother Teresa, he cofounded the Asia Heart Foundation (AHF), which supported medical education and cardiac care for the poor. He also signed on as director of the B.M. Birla Heart Research Institute, where in 1992 he performed the first neonatal open-heart surgery in India. It was there that Shetty first refused to take money for heart surgeries on children whose parents couldn't afford to pay.

"Health care is a human right," Shetty often says, with the serene insistence he is known for. "Everyone, rich or poor, should receive the same quality medical treatment. We must disassociate health care from affluence."

Fortunately, Shetty's commitment to the poor and his talents in the operating suite are matched by his gift for raising money, because money for health care is in very short supply. In India, the government spends only about 1 percent of its GDP on health care. Participation in health insurance is low, and monthly per capita income is around $100. Not surprisingly, under these circumstances, the vast majority of cardiac conditions go untreated, this despite the fact that Indians are especially prone to coronary artery disease, which is the nation's leading cause of death. About 2.5 million people in the country need heart surgery every year, but even in 2010 fewer than 100,000 people received it.

Shetty set out to change that, first by building more cardiac hospitals and attracting like-minded surgeons. Using private funds raised through the Asia Heart Foundation, Shetty helped launch the Manipal Heart Hospital in Bangalore in 1997 and, three years later in Kolkata, the Rabindranath Tagore Institute of Cardiac Sciences, a 150-bed hospital that quickly became the largest heart hospital in east India.

Shetty downplays the achievement. His years in the nonprofit space have taught him some lessons. "It's not difficult to arrange for funds when your cause is noble," he told *New Scientist* magazine in 2002, and while he appreciated the power of charity, he had also come to appreciate its crippling limitation.[7] He put it this way in an Al Jazeera documentary on Indian hospitals: "Charity is not scalable. Irrespective of how wealthy you are, if you want to give away things free of cost, there is a definite amount you can give away. After that, you will become broke!"[8]

What *did* scale, he knew, was a business that earned a profit, and he was convinced he could find a market-based solution to delivering the much needed cardiac care. Shetty envisioned what he has called "the Walmartization of health care," whereby high volume and relentless cost cutting would help lower prices and in turn drive growth, scaling up to reach "millions and millions of people."

In 2001, Shetty got the chance to test his theory. His father-in-law, who owned a thriving construction company, fronted $20 million for the construction of a new, for-profit cardiac-care hospital on twenty-five acres of land adjoining Bangalore's famous Electronic City. The family also agreed to provide any kind of support Shetty needed for equipment and medical supplies. Shetty penned a mission statement aligned with his vision of universal health care.

"We have a dream," he wrote. "A dream of making sophisticated health care available to the masses, especially in a developing country like our own."[9]

The mission statement didn't mention Shetty's determination to drive profits and growth by cutting the cost of heart surgery in half, but that intention was there from the beginning, too. Shetty, as the saying goes, has both a social heart and a business brain. Shetty's ability to turn inspiration into profit paid off. In its first year, the two-story, 225-bed hospital posted a profit of 7.7 percent after taxes, ahead of the average 6.9 percent after-tax profit for hospitals in North America. Within four years, the hospital had grown to six stories, ten operating suites, and 500 beds.

Key to the positive performance is Shetty's pricing model. Rich patients, who typically elect to stay in private rooms, pay more than poor patients, who recover in the public wards. The profit on the amenities helps subsidize care for the poor. Everyone is happy because the total base price for open-heart surgery is so much lower than at other private Indian hospitals. In 2017, the bundled price for patients paying full price was $2,100, including all tests and care, no matter how complicated the case, and about half of the patients paid less than that—some paid nothing at all (see table 3-1).

To accommodate the growing patient loads in the early 2000s, Shetty recruited ninety cardiac surgeons and cardiologists, many of whom had trained at Mayo Clinic, Harvard Medical School, and other world-class teaching institutions, and all of whom shared Shetty's sense of purpose. At Narayana's flagship hospital in Bangalore, most are paid a fixed salary, commensurate with the pay at other Indian hospitals. There are no bonuses, incentives, or fees for services. Dr. Shetty inspires a culture of hard work, excellence, compassion, and service to others.

The surgeons came to Narayana, and almost all of them stayed, Shetty says, for the same reason he did: They believed in Narayana's commitment to quality health care for all. "Purpose is even more powerful now than it was ten or twenty years ago," Shetty told us. "That's because today health care can do amazing things. People who we would have declared dead fifteen years ago we can operate on today and can almost guarantee that they'll go home and have a normal life."

Process Innovation through Task-Shifting

When patients are being wheeled into a Narayana operating room, they probably don't know that the lifesaving procedure they are about to undergo was modeled, in part, on the assembly line at Toyota— something Devi Shetty sees as a point of pride.

"Japanese companies reinvented the process of making cars. That's what we're doing in health care," he told *The Wall Street Journal*. "What health care needs is process innovation, not product innovation."[10]

The process innovations that Shetty implemented in his operating rooms allow Narayana surgeons to do three operations in the time it takes surgeons at other hospitals to do one. That is not because the surgeons are especially speedy. It is because every motion in the operating suite is choreographed to reduce turnaround time and optimize pay grades.

For example, in Narayana hospitals, all equipment is cleaned and sterilized outside the operating suite. Clean sets of equipment are kept at the ready in dedicated equipment rooms. As soon as one procedure is finished, the contaminated instruments and drapes are wheeled out of the operating room and a fresh set is wheeled in. According to Raghuvanshi, this change alone has freed up from forty-five to ninety minutes of operating time per suite per day.

Other changes involve who does what. In general, higher-paid senior surgeons do little or nothing that can be done by less-skilled staff. For example, in routine heart surgeries, a junior surgeon opens the chest and harvests a vein from another part of the body for grafting, and then moves on to the next patient to perform the same tasks.[11] A senior surgeon then performs the high-skill, critical procedures on the first patient and moves on to the next, while a different junior surgeon comes forward to close the chest. The entire procedure is supervised by junior surgeons and nurse intensivists, highly trained nurses who earn more than ward and surgical nurses but less than junior surgeons. Outside the operating suite, paramedical staff perform almost all pre- and postop tests. This kind of strategic task-shifting helps Narayana get the most out of its scarcest resource: highly skilled surgeons. As a result, at Narayana total employee costs, including doctors' salaries, make up barely 40.5 percent of revenue, compared with 60 percent in Western hospitals.[12]

At Narayana's multispecialty hospital in Mysore, task-shifting is taken even further. There, post-ICU care is provided by an intensely devoted support team that is paid nothing at all: family members.

In India, the entire family comes to the hospital with the patient. The family members typically spend three days at the hospital while the patient recovers. Anxious about their loved one, they were previously underfoot but powerless to help.

Narayana decided to put those family members to work tracking vital signs, changing dressings, feeding the patient, cheering on physiotherapy, and watching for signs that the prescribed anticoagulant drugs were working properly. Families get their training from a four-hour video curriculum, some of it delivered in the form of a sappy but irresistible soap opera that holds the families spellbound. The practice of training families for in-hospital postoperative care not only frees up the nursing staff for other work but also eases the transition to reliable, high-quality home care, reducing readmissions by 30 percent.[13]

Task-shifting at Narayana saves time and money, promotes teamwork, and increases productivity. Raghuvanshi and Shetty believe it also improves the quality of care. Take surgery, for example. "When we talk about assembly line," Raghuvanshi told us, "we mean that the main part of the surgery is done by the senior surgeon and the noncritical part is done by somebody else. But there is no compromise on quality. In fact, quality *improves*, because the senior surgeon may not be interested in putting stitches on the skin, whereas technicians whose job is only to put the stitches on the skin will do a really fine job. The outcome actually improves."

Shetty highlights another advantage. "Surgery happens in three phases," he has observed. "First, in a surgeon's mind prior to the operation. Then, on the operating table, and then again in the mind, postsurgery, when the doctor evaluates how performance could be further improved. For other surgeons, the next opportunity for improvement is after a few days or weeks, but in our case, because of the numbers involved, it is the next day."[14]

In other words, the deconstruction of tasks allows Narayana's surgeons to evaluate critical skills constantly and put new insights to work immediately. Outcomes improve, even as the cost for the procedure goes down. As noted earlier, Narayana's cardiac outcomes are excellent, even by US standards.

"We strive to provide the best quality at the lowest cost," Raghuvanshi says. "That is what we mean by value. We call ourselves a value provider."

A Culture of Frugality

Like Aravind Eye Care System, with its legendary frugality, Narayana looks at every cost component to see how it can be reduced dramatically.[15] In the early days of the enterprise, Shetty operated on a shoestring, ever mindful that, as Raghuvanshi stressed, *There is no money.* At his flagship hospital in Bangalore, where the average daily high temperature is eighty-five degrees, he limited air-conditioning to the surgical suites. He negotiated pay-per-use contracts for expensive equipment like MRI machines. He ordered surgical gloves from Malaysia by the container load, and he developed a digital x-ray plate on an expiring patent, at less than 1 percent of the original cost.

As the enterprise has expanded, Narayana has been able to reap economies of scale. By 2012, Narayana had strengthened its negotiating position with suppliers by combining the sourcing for its hospitals in Bangalore and Kolkata as well as two smaller units. Together, these operations accounted for 10 percent of cardiac diagnostics and treatments in India—a market share sufficient to wrest a 35 percent discount on supplies. By May 2017, when Narayana controlled twenty-four hospitals and was contemplating still more, it had leverage even with multinational vendors whose equipment was both expensive and subject to high transportation costs.

"If you are a large-volume purchaser, you can get fantastic deals from the vendors both in terms of supplies as well as in your capital equipment," Raghuvanshi says. "We work closely with the large vendors like Philips as well as GE. Because we buy, say, ten catheterization labs in a year, we get a very good deal."

Narayana also began leveraging economies of scope. By 2012, Shetty was operating several multispecialty hospitals, including the Health

City complex in Bangalore and the Multispecialty Hospital in Mysore. In these hospitals, several different medical services—e.g., cardiology, neurology, orthopedics, and oncology—were located in a single hospital or campus, where they shared key resources such as diagnostic departments, labs, blood banks, administration, and IT services. Intensive cross-utilization of these resources minimized unit costs.

"You run one service, you run twenty services—it costs the same," Raghuvanshi points out. "Blood bank is one example. Laboratory is another. The more the utilization, the better it is, especially with automation in labs. If you put one hundred samples in or one thousand samples, the cost of the test is almost the same."

A Thousand Small Things

In these ways, Shetty takes advantage of the opportunities he was looking for when he founded his first for-profit hospital. As his experience in health-care operations has grown, Shetty has realized something else. "In health care," he says, "you cannot do one big thing to reduce the price. We have to do a thousand small things."[16]

It is this culture of frugality that has become the defining spirit of the Narayana enterprise, and it is evident in some very effective practices and innovations. Some, as Raghuvanshi says, were "very basic and simple." For example, Narayana hospitals use generic drugs whenever possible, at 20 percent the cost of brand-name pharmaceuticals. It uses digital imaging instead of x-rays for chest scans, to save the high cost of film. It reuses surgical supplies, like the $160 octopus clamp used in some heart procedures. In the United States those clamps are routinely thrown away after a single surgery, but in Narayana hospitals they are carefully sterilized and reused as many as eighty times. (This practice is in fact allowed by the American accreditation organization, Joint Commission International.)

Narayana also standardizes the list of equipment and supplies it makes available to physicians and staff, reducing the number of SKUs in its inventory from 12,000 to 4,000. That decision not only streamlines purchasing, it also has a big impact on the bottom line.

"In a Western environment, the cost of medicines and supplies is about 15 percent to 17 percent of total costs," Raghuvanshi says, "but in an Indian scenario, about 24 percent to 27 percent of the cost is in material itself, so that's the biggest lever you've got. If you are doing a large volume, and you have just one or two brands of a particular product on your shelf, you have better negotiating ability with the vendors."

Other cost-saving practices are more strategic. For example, Shetty avoids long-term contracts whenever he can, hoping to take advantage of price fluctuations, which are common in India. He sometimes renegotiates his supply contracts weekly. And when it came time to seek hospital accreditation, Narayana put forward only two of its hospitals to the esteemed Joint Commission International. Why? Because accreditations are expensive: $200,000 apiece. "We didn't do it for bragging rights," Raghuvanshi told us. "What we needed was to establish a culture of quality in the enterprise."

Shetty is also stingy with capital investments. He negotiates pay-per-use contracts for PET-CT scanners, MRI machines, and other expensive equipment. Where Narayana owns the equipment, it contracts with TriMedx, an equipment-management company, to extend the life of the machines through aggressive maintenance and repairs. "We fly a jumbo jet for thirty years," Shetty says mockingly, "but we junk an MRI machine in only six years. It makes no sense!"

The cost consciousness was effective. By 2017, Narayana had driven down the cost of coronary bypass surgery to the range of $1,100 to $1,200.

How Small Things Become Big Things

We mentioned earlier Shetty's willingness to step outside hospital boundaries and into the manufacturing space. This happened when Narayana took a hard look at the cost of its surgical gowns and drapes. For many years, the hospitals used linen for these purposes, as was traditional in India. The linen could be laundered for reuse, but heart surgery was a bloody business and the cleanup was expensive, so Shetty approached the two leading multinational suppliers of disposable gowns and drapes for price quotes. He met a stone wall.

"They wanted us to pay five thousand rupees for each heart operation," Shetty remembers. "We wanted them to sell it to us for two thousand rupees. They refused to come down, so we had them stitched locally using the same material used by the multinationals. In less than a year we reduced the cost of gowns and drapes to nine hundred rupees, and the local company customized the gowns and drapes for each medical procedure." Within four years, this firm became the largest manufacturer of disposable surgical gowns in India, and was looking to export its product to the United States. The multinational suppliers, unable to compete on price, left the market.

At Narayana, frugality also applied to hospital construction. While all urban construction projects in India have to swallow the high cost of land in the cities, Narayana has found ways to build hospitals for 50 percent less than its competitors.[17] There is a strict no-frills policy: no marble foyers, no chandeliers, just ordinary tile and discount furniture. An abundance of natural light saves on electric bills, as does the very frugal use of air-conditioning. The hospitals are not luxurious, but they are extremely cost-effective.

Narayana's Multispecialty Hospital in Mysore, for example, is a defiantly plain, one-story building, and much of it was fabricated off-site. It isn't fancy, but it optimizes the use of space and took only ten months to build, at a capital cost of only $23,000 per bed. In the United States, the cost would be closer to $2 million a bed.

Frugality also contributes to surgical practices, including Narayana's adoption of "beating-heart surgery," especially for coronary artery bypass graft (CABG) operations, in which the heart is operated on "live,"—that is, while doing its work of circulating blood. The technique saves the hospital the cost of expensive heart-lung bypass machines, which are standard in US heart surgeries. It also leads to fewer complications, requires shorter hospital stays, and results in a lower incidence of hospital infections. The beating-heart procedure requires great surgical skill and a sizeable investment in staff training, but high patient volumes and quality drivers at Narayana Health have helped an entire generation of Indian surgeons master the technique.

It is a good example of the kind of high-quality, low-cost solutions that Narayana is always striving for. It is also proof that quality and cost can operate in ways quite different from what is expected in Western healthcare models, which are often based on the assumption that high quality has to engender high costs. In the Narayana universe, high quality always drives low costs and vice versa.

"For us, quality is a kind of journey or a process that can help us reduce our costs," says Raghuvanshi. "We believe that if you have quality, your systems and processes are going to be better, and that in turn reduces cost. You reduce your morbidity, you reduce your mortality, you reduce the cost of your antibiotics, your ICU stays, et cetera. We feel that these are not two separate things. They go hand in hand."

Reaching Out with a Hub-and-Spoke Model

Shetty's dream of making "sophisticated health care available to the masses" faced another big challenge: geography. While India's cities certainly have many needy heart patients, the patients Shetty especially hoped to serve live in villages scattered all over the countryside. Unfortunately, open-heart surgery is not the kind of procedure you can perform in the countryside under a banyan tree. And impoverished villagers with broken hearts were not going to just appear on Narayana's doorsteps. Unless Shetty found ways to reach out to them, they were going to die before they got any kind of care.

"Market creation," economists call it. "Saving lives," Shetty says.

In its early years, Narayana conducted mobile outreach camps. The camps were funded by the Asia Heart Foundation and organized by local groups like Lions Clubs and Rotary Clubs. Every weekend Narayana would outfit two buses, each carrying three physicians, EKG machines, and emergency medical equipment, and dispatch them as far as eight hundred miles into the countryside. The buses went from village to village, and the doctors performed cardiac screenings on anyone who showed up. Minor issues were treated on the spot, usually at no cost, while serious conditions were referred to the hospitals in Bangalore and Kolkata.

Over time, the outreach camps evolved into cardiac-care units (CCUs), more permanent regional clinics that served as satellites and gateways for the urban hospitals, where greater expertise and expensive medical equipment were always available. The arrangement served both patients and providers. It distributed care to the doctor-starved villages, and it allowed Narayana to centralize its investment in talent and technology.

But the villagers they screened often didn't make the trip to the city, because they could not afford the treatment when they got there. Narayana wasn't making enough money yet to subsidize all their care, so Shetty had to think up a new plan. In 2002, when a milk cooperative in his home state of Karnataka approached him for a product endorsement, Shetty saw a very different opportunity.

On the one hand, Shetty knew that most of the 1.7 million members of Karnataka's farming cooperatives could not afford medical care. On the other hand, he knew that (largely for this reason) many hospitals in the region had very low occupancy rates, about 35 percent. Insurance could solve the problem, and the cooperative was big enough to spread the risks involved. Shetty took his numbers to the co-ops' administrators and persuaded them to set up a microinsurance scheme called Yeshasvini, which was launched in 2003.

For only five rupees, or about eleven cents, a month, members of Yeshasvini could get free treatment at 150 hospitals for any procedure whose cost did not exceed $2,200. Yeshasvini turned out to be good for everyone: It improved the health of the co-op members, it filled local hospital beds, and it generated business not only for Narayana but for other specialty hospitals across southern India. In the first twenty months of coverage, 85,000 farmers received medical treatment of some kind. About 22,000 had surgery, of those 1,400 had heart surgery. For each heart surgery, which then cost about $1,500, the heart hospital received $1,200 from the insurance fund. By 2017, Yeshasvini had four million members and eight hundred network hospitals across the state, and the plan had subsidized more than 100,000 heart operations. And while the premium had climbed to twenty-two cents a month, the obvious success of the plan had persuaded half of the Indian states to launch similar programs.

What is noteworthy here is not only Shetty's ability to think outside the operating suite and not only his understanding of the power of networks, but that his vision of health care is entirely patient-centered and that the value he creates flows from his calling to service.

Digital Medicine: Technology Takes the Lead

For a man with an old-fashioned devotion to service, Shetty has a very modern enthusiasm for cutting-edge technologies. In fact, the Narayana operation has been tech-driven from the outset. In 2001, for example, Shetty persuaded the Indian Space Research Organization to share its communications satellites so Narayana could connect its hub hospitals in Kolkata and Bangalore to nine rural-based critical-care units housed in government hospitals. Ten years later, he replaced that network with a better and cheaper technology: Skype.

In 2017, Narayana's vendor list reads like a who's who of high-tech firms. Oracle supplied its cloud-based enterprise-resource-planning (ERP) system. Hewlett-Packard designed its cloud-based mobile health units. Cisco supported its virtual diagnostics system. Its portable ECG machines were made by Schiller, the German diagnostics giant, and its patient data system was delivered on Apple iPads.

"The thing that addresses the problem of poverty in this world is going to be technology," Shetty told us. "Technology gives rich people what they have always had, just in a better format. But it will give poor people what they could never even dream of. It will make this industry very, very efficient. I believe it will reduce mortality and morbidity by at least fifty percent."

Take those portable ECG machines from Schiller, for example. They are hand-held devices that can help detect coronary heart disease, irregular heart rhythms, and heart failure in the field. They aren't sophisticated, but they are effective and very inexpensive—so inexpensive that in 2017 Narayana could afford to deploy them in nearly two thousand villages. There, minimally trained technicians could turn on a machine, administer the test, and transmit the readouts electronically to a hospital hub for analysis.

"They can do the ECG on anyone who complains of chest pain, and the ECG would come to our center in Bangalore, and in about ten minutes our cardiologist would send back a report," Shetty says. "We get eight hundred of these ECGs every day, and they diagnose a significant number of heart-attack patients." The system is not intended to recruit patients, Shetty says, but rather to reduce medical costs, because the earlier a condition is detected the easier it is to treat through monitoring, lifestyle changes, medication, or minor surgical intervention.

The use of technology in the hub hospitals is equally impressive. Narayana's ERP system, which took more than a year to design and another year to implement, connects all of Narayana's hospitals and provides them with 24/7 access to financial metrics, imaging, lab results, and other critical information. New hospitals could be added seamlessly and at little cost. In 2010, when many US hospitals were struggling with the very idea of keeping electronic medical records, Narayana's system was already humming along, centralizing all patient data. Any physician seeking a second opinion could consult with specialists anywhere in the network, anytime, night or day.

That year, Narayana teamed up with Stanford Hospital and Accenture on a proprietary technology project that came to be called iKare. The goal was to reduce the number of physician consults at patients' bedsides by developing "decision support software" that automatically considered treatment plans in the hospital room. Designed to run on iPads, the software updated patient records as soon as new data was entered, then analyzed the data and recommended any actions that could be undertaken by nonphysician staff. The software also issued medical alerts to appropriate staff when the information spelled trouble.

"The moment the parameters are haywire, the system generates a list of possible scenarios, along with possible solutions," Raghuvanshi explains. "It saves thinking time and reduces medical errors."

In 2017, iKare was running on iPads connected to all of Narayana's ICU beds. When the system detected that a patient's condition required a physician's opinion and no specialist was available in the hospital, care providers turned to another high-tech support—the virtual diagnostics system Narayana developed with Cisco in 2016. That system enabled live video, voice, and data streaming from the ICUs directly to a physician's home, a good solution for night coverage.

"The biggest problem we have scaling up critical-care services is the lack of intensivists to work around patients twenty-four hours a day," Shetty says. "Cisco has an excellent videoconferencing system, and we use it all the time to do ICU rounds. Doctors can directly see the data on patients' charts. It's a game changer."

Changing the Game

Here's another game changer: Make doctors unnecessary.

Like many progressive health-care providers worldwide, Narayana has increasingly turned its attention from treating disease to preventing disease. It is certainly a more affordable solution. But Shetty wants to go a step further: to *predicting* disease. In 2014, Narayana began working with Hewlett-Packard to design twenty cloud-enabled, rapidly deployable eHealth centers: quasi-mobile, self-contained medical units that can be housed in shipping containers or installed in vacant buildings in the countryside. Each eHealth center is outfitted with diagnostic equipment and videoconferencing capabilities. Their main purpose is to deliver primary care in remote areas. But the diagnostic units can also be used to collect community health data in sufficient quantities for health workers to spot disease outbreaks early on, or identify risk factors that are elevated in local communities.

"A big idea is that you don't need doctors," says Raghuvanshi. "Health-care workers can assist patients and consult doctors from base units, but they can also use those units to understand disease demographics in particular geographies."

Shetty says such efforts are just the beginning. As technology presents new possibilities, Narayana will pursue those possibilities as well. For example, in 2017 the company deployed self-help diagnostic kiosks in rural gas stations, aimed at truck drivers. It also developed an electronic-medical-records app for mobile phones. The idea was that whenever patients felt ill, wherever they were—at home, in their truck, at work, visiting family—they could send their records to their doctor, who could call back with advice on treatment. According to Shetty, from 70 percent to 80 percent of medical complaints could be resolved in this manner.

"Today, telemedicine is used by very few people," Shetty observes, "but I can almost bet that within the next five to seven years almost all of these doctor clinics are going to disappear. Most patients will consult their doctor online using their mobile phone and videoconferencing."

This kind of thinking has made Narayana a leader in telemedicine, not only in India but throughout the world. "We've been doing these things for fifteen years," says Shetty. "Eventually, it will become the mainstream of medicine. We are making the building blocks for that transition, which will happen first in India. Then it will move to the Western hemisphere."

Once again, Devi Shetty is thinking big. But he's not just daydreaming. In fact, Mother Teresa's man in Kolkata has already sent his medical mission abroad. In 2015, Narayana Health opened its own multispecialty hospital in the Western hemisphere—in the Cayman Islands, just 450 miles from Miami, a story we turn to in the next chapter.

The Promise of Reverse Innovation

The Indian hospital exemplars that we have profiled in these three chapters show us that even under extremely constrained circumstances, it is possible to deliver world-class health care at ultra-low prices. Their business model is based on five principles that are mutually reinforcing, and it applies equally to complex and simple medical conditions. It is also financially sustainable over time.

But is reverse innovation of these practices to other parts of the world possible? In developing countries that wrestle with doctor and equipment shortages, poverty, and self-paying patients, the answer is clearly yes. In fact, Aravind has already shared its innovative practices with more than 335 hospitals in India and twenty-seven other poor countries across Asia, Africa, and Latin America. Dr. Aravind Srinivasan, administrator of Aravind Eye Care, estimates that its best-practice evangelism group had helped such hospitals increase their annual treatment volume to more than 800,000 surgeries per year—twice Aravind's own volume. LV Prasad has similarly helped dozens of centers and hospitals in India and abroad.

Several of the Indian hospitals also treat patients from other poor countries, especially in South Asia and Africa, a practice that led some of them to set up hospitals in those regions as well. The new owners of the Hyderabad-based Care group are looking to take its model to Kenya and Ethiopia. Narayana Health plans to open a 130-bed cardiac hospital in Nairobi and offer its services for 20 percent the price of those offered by local competitors. Similarly, HCG Oncology is setting up comprehensive cancer centers in East Africa, modeled after its Indian practice.

But what about developed nations, and specifically the United States, which is the focus of part 2 of this book?

For many years, while Indian patients shopped around for value, American patients were indifferent to price, because of third-party payment. While Indian exemplars developed hub-and-spoke networks, too many US hospitals became hubs with excess capacity and little specialization. For instance, in 2016, almost half a million people underwent open-heart surgery in the United States, versus only 100,000 in India, but the US volume was spread across so many hospitals that none (including Cleveland Clinic and Mayo Clinic) came close to matching Narayana's volume of 14,700 cardiac surgeries that year. And even when US hospitals consolidate, they do so to gain bargaining power over insurance companies rather than to lower costs. Similarly, US hospitals do the wrong kind of task-shifting, by cutting low-cost staff jobs, which forces highly paid doctors to waste time on medical transcription, logistics, and billing. And frugality is the last thing on hospital administrators' minds, as they build hospitals with the ambience of seven-star hotels.

Yet this cannot go on forever. US health care has crossed the point of financial unsustainability. In the coming decade, change is inevitable. In 2017, Medicare was already demanding that providers sign risk-sharing agreements involving capitation and bundled pricing—steps consistent with value-based competition. And as Medicare goes, so too will go private insurers, eventually. Therefore, the things that the Indian exemplars are good at—high quality, low cost, and access—will become much more important in the United States.

We turn next to the innovators who are already putting the Indian principles into practice in the United States.

Part Two

Reverse Innovation in Health-Care Delivery

Four New Models for the United States

In chapters 4 through 7, we profile four US and offshore innovators that have employed one or more Indian principles to address a core problem facing US health care: cost, quality, or access. Each innovator solved its core problem and did so without compromising performance in other areas (see figure P2-1 and table P2-1). We see these organizations as role models for radically transforming US health care. Here is a preview.

FIGURE P2-1

Core US health-care problems addressed by four innovators

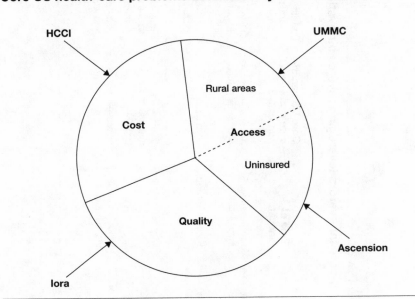

TABLE P2-1

US health-care innovators leveraging reverse innovation

Case	Type of innovator	Core US health-care problem addressed	Main Indian health-care-delivery principle(s) adopted	Inspired by poor countries?	Founder/change maker
Ascension Health	Progressive US incumbent	Access—uninsured and underinsured	Using an inspiring purpose to drive cost and quality innovations	Yes. Inspired by Narayana Health and others	CEO Anthony Tersigni, John Doyle, and others
Health City Cayman Islands	Foreign startup	High cost	Ultra-cost-consciousness (frugality)	Yes. Brought Indian business model to near US shores	Doctorpreneur Devi Shetty
Iora Health	Domestic startup	Quality—patients' overuse of specialist services	Task-shifting (from doctors to "health coaches" and from specialists to primary care)	Yes. Inspired by health-care practices in poor countries	Doctorpreneur Rushika Fernandopulle
University of Mississippi Medical Center	Progressive US incumbent	Access—rural areas	Hub-and-spoke configuration and leveraging technology	No, but independently arrived at same solution as Indian exemplars for same problem	Dr. Kristi Henderson

Chapter 4: Health City Cayman Islands (HCCI). This new entrant, founded by Narayana Health, attacked the problem of bloated costs in the United States by offering world-class care for 25 percent to 40 percent of US prices, using frugal practices honed in India. Narayana deliberately located its hospital in the Cayman Islands, close enough to the United States for a one-hour hop from Miami but far enough to escape the perverse pressures of US regulation. It targeted Caribbean patients as well as Americans. It received accreditation from Joint Commission International and had signed up a few major cruise lines and US medical-tourism outfits, but was waiting to sign up a large self-insured employer like Walmart or a major US health insurer like Aetna or Cigna. By September 2017, that had not happened, although Cigna had signed up HCCI to provide emergency treatment for customers visiting the Cayman Islands.

Chapter 5: University of Mississippi Medical Center (UMMC). Like much of India, the state of Mississippi has a severe shortage of doctors and medical facilities, especially in rural areas, and the state has only one academic medical facility: the University of Mississippi Medical Center (UMMC), in Jackson, Mississippi. And as in India, the problem was tackled by creating a hub-and-spoke telehealth network that connected UMMC's specialists with two hundred rural hospitals across the state. An entrepreneurial trauma nurse at UMMC, Kristi Henderson, helped create the system, which offered rural citizens better, cheaper, and more convenient care. Most important to Henderson, the telehealth system saved many lives.

Chapter 6: Ascension Health. Driven by its Catholic mission to care for the "poor and vulnerable," Ascension, like the Indian exemplars, worked on a strategy of driving down costs through innovation, so that margins from serving the insured and well-to-do could be used to subsidize care for greater numbers of uninsured and underinsured patients. Ascension used its inspiring purpose to increase productivity and efficiency in health-care delivery, and to generate resources to serve its purpose. This chapter also looks at a US nonprofit, Pacific Vision Foundation, which had the goal of applying Aravind's model for ophthalmic care to serve the uninsured poor in the San Francisco Bay Area.

Chapter 7: Iora Health. Frustrated by the quality of primary care in the United States and inspired by health-care-delivery models he'd seen in poor countries, Dr. Rushika Fernandopulle created Boston-based Iora Health to address the problem of overuse of hospitals and specialist care. Iora pioneered a remarkable task-shifted delivery structure that leaned heavily on "health coaches," who are nonmedical staff akin to Aravind's midlevel ophthalmic paramedics or LV Prasad's vision technicians. As in India, these nonmedical staff were not just cheaper than doctors and nurses but also better at connecting with patients and helping them to stay healthy and avoid unnecessary medications, hospital admissions, or treatments. Iora's approach saved 15 percent to 20 percent in total health-care costs.

Loose Bricks for Innovation

In the following pages, you will see how these innovators dealt with some of the many obstacles that discourage the adoption of Indian-style innovations. The Mississippi telehealth team, for example, found ways to fund its operations while working to change state regulations that prohibited insurance payments for telehealth consults. And Iora got its primary care experiment off the ground by going it alone and working with self-insured employers desperate to lower their costs.

Our research tells us that success in health-care reform depends greatly on the creativity and determination of the innovators, and that change requires sustained effort by the same leader over a decade or more. It's not always true that "where there's a will, there's a way," but it is true that sufficient will can usually find some loose bricks to provide openings for reform. And it is those loose bricks that will provide the footholds for reverse innovations.

In well-known examples of reverse innovation, companies like General Electric and Harman International moved innovations from emerging markets to other parts of the world, including the United States, through their own global organizational networks. It is a fairly straightforward, top-down, intraorganizational process. But few American hospital chains operate internationally, and hardly any have operations in emerging markets such as India. (Among the exceptions is Cleveland Clinic, which opened its first major hospital abroad in Abu Dhabi in 2015.) For this reason, reverse innovation in American health care will have to occur through other pathways, following the footholds presented by the loose bricks.

We can't tell you what the loose bricks may be for you—you see them every day as you struggle with your broken health-care system. We can only present examples to inspire you. But we can tell you that the Indian principles of health-care delivery can work just as well in the United States, *even in the prevailing regulatory environment*. The innovations we studied in the United States, like those in India, were all introduced from the bottom up, by private organizations led by "doctorpreneurs" or "nursepreneurs" with a passion for fixing some aspect of US health care. There is no need to reinvent the wheel. Solutions that have worked well in India, under value-based competition, are worthy of serious consideration by US organizations looking to reinvent US health care. They can work here, and they can work now.

4.

Disrupting US Costs
Health City Cayman Islands

If there is a hospital on a ship, and it is parked outside US
territorial waters, that's going to be the most profitable hospital
simply because you have different cost structures; you don't have
to deal with US regulations but you have the US price umbrella.

–Dr. Devi Shetty, Cofounder and Chairman, Narayana Health

Wayne Wright was sixty-eight when the pain in his knees reached the breaking point. Too many years of hopping on and off dragline excavators had left the six-foot-four, 250-pound Texas construction worker unable to walk more than thirty feet without stopping for a few seconds for the pain to subside. In March 2015, when it became clear that both knees would have to be replaced, Wright's self-insured employer put him in touch with Companion Global Healthcare, a South Carolina company that evaluates and recommends offshore health-care providers. There was good reason to listen to what Companion Global had to say. If Wright's bilateral knee replacements had been done in Texas, he says, he would have been hit with a $6,700 deductible. If he went with one of the offshore hospitals, his insurer would pay the deductible, the cost of the surgery, plus travel and lodging for both him and his wife. The total cost to Wright would be exactly zero.

The medical travel agency suggested two hospital options. One was in Costa Rica. The other was Health City Cayman Islands (HCCI), a new hospital on Grand Cayman, a sunny island in the western Caribbean south of Cuba, just an hour's flight from Miami. Wright had vacationed on Grand Cayman, so he chose to go there. He was soon surprised to find himself talking by phone to his surgeon at HCCI, Dr. Alwin Almeida, for more than an hour.

"He talked to me for longer than I had spent talking to a doctor in ten years combined," Wright remembers. "He talked me through the entire procedure, from start to finish, and he didn't miss a thing."[1]

One of the things Almeida told Wright was that the Cayman hospital required that he be screened for MRSA, a group of drug-resistant bacteria that can cause a dangerous staph infection during hospital stays. The test turned out to be easy—a quick nasal swab that was taken by Wright's local doctor, who was impressed by HCCI's precaution.

"He told me, 'Wayne, this is one of the things that's wrong with our medical system,'" Wright remembers. "'In twelve years of practice, I've never had a single surgeon require this medical test.'"

Two years after his bilateral knee replacement, Wayne Wright couldn't recall a single bad moment during his three-week stay on Grand Cayman. His room was spacious, the food was delicious, and the service, for both him and his wife, was worthy of a luxury hotel. But his most indelible memory is of checking out.

"They handed me a single sheet of paper with just four lines on it and one number," Wright says. "It was $22,000."

Wright's bill, paid in full by his insurance, covered everything from English muffins to anesthesia, plus the two-week recuperative stay at a beachfront hotel. His research indicated that the same surgery, done in Texas, would have cost between $100,000 and $120,000.

"In this country," Wright says, "we've got a broken medical system any way you shake it."

An Offshore Disruptor

The hospital that replaced Wayne Wright's ailing knees was part of a very different medical system, one that was conceived in Bangalore, India. In fact, Health City Cayman Islands was the first overseas venture of Narayana Health. In chapter 3, we noted several remarkable things about the Narayana hospital system in India: its ultra-low prices, its strong medical outcomes, its high profit margins, and its commitment to treating all patients regardless of their ability to pay. Narayana's Cayman operation is, in fact, a textbook example of reverse innovation in practice. Narayana perfected an innovative business model in India and then brought it to America's shores hoping to disrupt US health care. Three years after the hospital opened its doors, disruption was only just beginning to happen, but Narayana's reasons to be hopeful were starting to multiply.

Dr. Devi Shetty, Narayana's founder, had always dreamed big, and by 2008, with his Indian operation thriving, he was looking to make a global impact on health-care delivery. But to do that, Shetty knew he would have to change health care in the United States.

"For the world to change, America has to change," Shetty told us in 2013. "So it's important that American policy makers and American think tanks can look at a model that costs a fraction of what they pay and see that it has similarly good outcomes. If Americans believe there is a better way to do things, and if they say 'Let's try it out,' then the rest of the world will follow."[2]

Shetty decided to help that process along by setting up a demonstration hospital in the Caribbean that would attract American attention—as well as American patients. At one level, the Cayman hospital would put pressure on the US health-care system to reduce costs, but Shetty had an even deeper strategic disruption in mind. If HCCI helped drive down US health-care costs, it would have a boomerang effect, lowering costs and expanding access to health care not just in India but all around the world.

"When US medical-equipment, -device, and pharma companies drop prices, it could help Narayana expand access to poor Indians," Shetty explained. "When I speak to Americans or Europeans, I ask them how much they pay for their mobile phones today compared to twenty years ago. It's a fraction. How did that happen? Because nine hundred million Indians started buying mobile phones, and that volume benefited everyone. Similarly, Indian hospitals could buy a lot of CT scanners, MRI machines, or anticancer drugs, and the price of all those things could come down—not by just 5 or 10 percent, but by 80 to 90 percent!"

Shetty knew that the policy makers and think tanks were unlikely to seriously consider adopting a business model that had succeeded only in India, so he had to choose his test site carefully. He settled on the Cayman Islands, a British Overseas Territory, because it was close to the United States in some important ways. He saw in Grand Cayman a first-world infrastructure and a western-hemisphere orientation. The location also put him within shouting distance of the legions of stakeholders who claimed to be searching for more sustainable alternatives to American health care. In this case, Shetty's message could be boiled down to two words: "Watch this."

In 2014, HCCI opened the doors of its 104-bed specialty hospital on the south shore of Grand Cayman Island. Focused first on cardiology and orthopedics, it had plans to expand, within ten years, to a facility offering all major medical and surgical specialties, as well as a medical school and an assisted-living facility. By 2017, HCCI surgeons were performing open-heart surgeries at 25 percent to 40 percent of US prices with a mortality rate, after five hundred surgeries, of zero—true value-based care. The hospital has been awarded full accreditation by Joint

Commission International; has added oncology care, bariatric surgeries, endocrinology, pulmonology, pediatrics, and dental services to its list of offerings; has opened a sleep lab; has greatly expanded its ambulatory-care services; and is already breaking even.

The hospital's sole note of discouragement involves the patients that the hospital most wanted to attract: American patients. They aren't coming, at least not in the numbers that Shetty and his team had hoped. American insurance companies were watching, but they weren't signing on. Neither were large self-insured companies. Shetty knew why. Insurers are risk-averse, and they wanted more hard data before signing on to HCCI.

Robert Pearl, CEO of the Permanente Medical Group and a clinical professor of surgery at Stanford University, was nonetheless optimistic. "Most American doctors and hospitals see India as far away," Pearl said in an op-ed in *USA Today* in 2017. "They underestimate the dangers they face from global disruption. They assume that people won't be willing to travel halfway around the world for surgery. And they may be right. But before they become too complacent, they should look to the Grand Cayman Island, with its seven-mile white sand beach and its tourist culture. There Shetty is building a 2,000 bed hospital for a population of more than 50,000 citizens. Maybe it's just a coincidence that by airplane Florida is less than an hour away."[3]

Coming to America, Almost

Devi Shetty took great satisfaction from knowing that India had spawned the innovations behind the remarkable performance of his health-care chain. "We believe that India will become the first country in the world to dissociate health care from affluence," Shetty told us. "India will show the world that the wealth of a nation has nothing to do with the quality of health care its citizens can enjoy." But despite his pride in his heritage,

Shetty knew that for his Caribbean outpost to attract Americans, it would have to be a little less Indian. Every reverse-innovation effort must adapt the business model to the rich-country context.

"Americans can't even pronounce Narayana Hrudayalaya, the original name of the company," says Viren Shetty, Devi Shetty's son and the company's senior vice president of strategy and planning. "When you tell Americans that you are with Narayana Health, they don't know who you are."[4]

Narayana needed a name that Americans felt comfortable with. It also needed a business partner that Americans felt comfortable with. In 2008, Devi Shetty started shopping around for both, and for the ideal location for his medical showcase. Before Grand Cayman, Shetty considered St. Kitts, but it was a three-hour flight from Miami, and it was expensive. He also looked closely at Guadalajara, Mexico, but couldn't come to an agreement with the municipal leadership, and some of Shetty's medical staff worried about personal safety there.

Then, in the summer of 2009, Shetty got a phone call from Harry Chandi, a wealthy Indian jeweler whose father had been Shetty's patient years earlier. Chandi, who was living in George Town, on Grand Cayman, had an idea that could benefit both Narayana and Grand Cayman, which happened to be in need of help.

For decades, the Cayman Islands, which has no corporate tax, had lived comfortably off two industries: tourism and financial services. Newly elected Cayman premier McKeeva Bush believed it was time for the country to diversify its business offerings. He asked the local burghers, including Chandi and developer Gene Thompson, if they had any ideas. Chandi told him he did.

For several years, medical tourism had been a growing industry around the world, thanks largely to cost-conscious Americans who were willing to fly to Central America and the Far East to have their hips replaced or their teeth capped. Just two years earlier, more than 150,000 Americans had traveled overseas for medical treatments. Chandi figured that if those thrifty shoppers could get the care they wanted in the Cayman Islands, they could save on airfare and spend some of that savings at the islands' ailing resorts. A Narayana hospital in the Caymans could help get the islands' economy back on track, not to mention provide excellent and affordable care for the Caymans' own heart patients, who struggled to find quality cardiac care locally. One study reported that in 2008, four hundred Caymanians had gone overseas for treatment of heart conditions. Most went to Florida, after struggling through a cumbersome three-week-long visa process, and most paid full freight for care when they got there.[5]

Shetty told Chandi that Grand Cayman sounded like a possibility. He put his right-hand man, Narayana's vice chairman, Dr. Ashutosh Raghuvanshi, in charge of a special team to explore the opportunity.

It was a big assignment. Initially, Raghuvanshi recalls, some team members weren't sure where the Cayman Islands were.

A Match Made in Heaven

Among the roughly 100,000 companies registered in the Caymans were several insurance entities owned by the St. Louis–based Ascension group. Like Narayana Health, Ascension was driven by a very strong sense of purpose. Its corporate parent was Ascension Health Ministries, a Catholic entity that reported to the Vatican.

By 2013, Ascension was the largest Catholic nonprofit health-care provider in the United States, with eighty hospitals. Including its other for-profit subsidiaries, the parent company had $18 billion in revenues and $32 billion in assets. Inspired by the example of Jesus as healer, Ascension strove not only to deliver universal health care but also to transform health care and create a compassionate and just society. The similarities to Narayana's mission were striking. Here was a match made in heaven, just waiting to happen.

In 2009, Ascension's Cayman-based insurance companies brought Ascension president Anthony Tersigni to the island, where he heard that an Indian hospital system planned a beachhead for its radically innovative model for health-care delivery. When Tersigni returned to St. Louis, he met with John Doyle, then Ascension's general manager for transformational services. It was Doyle's job to search out opportunities for innovation for Ascension anywhere he could find them—the more radical and disruptive the better.

"Tony said, 'John, I've heard about this thing down there,'" recalls Doyle. "'There's a guy named Devi Shetty, and he's going to build a hospital. I'd like you to find out about it. There may be something we can do.'"[6]

At the time, Shetty wasn't looking for an American partner. But he was happy to talk to Doyle, and both men were always happy to talk about their common mission to serve the poor and reinvent health care. That's what they did when Shetty invited Doyle to come to India to see what Narayana had done.

In Bangalore, Shetty showed Doyle around his heart hospital, and Doyle told Shetty about some of the things that Ascension had done in the United States, like creating a venture-capital group to percolate innovation throughout the Ascension group, and creating a medical-equipment-servicing company called TriMedx. That's when Shetty perked up. "Stop, stop right there," Shetty told Doyle. "That's one of my biggest problems. The equipment manufacturers charge me high prices for servicing, and then they tell me they can't fix it." Doyle told Shetty that TriMedx could fix just about anything, and over an extended discussion about lowering the cost of equipment ownership, improving uptime, lowering the unit cost of service, and extending useful life, Shetty agreed to give TriMedx a try.

Two social hearts with business brains had found each other. The men kept in touch, and one day Shetty called Doyle to ask if Ascension was interested in a partnership in Narayana's Grand Cayman venture. Ascension was.

Clearing the Decks

Back on the island, things were moving quickly. Less than a month after Chandi called Shetty, Shetty was in George Town, the Cayman capital, talking with Premier Bush, and less than a month after that, the two men signed a memorandum of understanding. Narayana would develop not just a hospital but an entire "health city" at an estimated cost of $2 billion over ten to fifteen years.[7] But first, Shetty would use the leverage of his promising venture to clear the land of a few obstacles. Shetty drew up a nine-point list of requested concessions and handed it to the Cayman government.

Point 1: The Cayman government would cap the amount of insurance claims related to noneconomic losses in medical-malpractice cases.

Point 2: The Cayman government would recognize medical qualifications from India and approve Indian doctors and nurses to practice in Cayman.

Point 3: The Cayman government would issue work permits for HCCI staff from India so that they could come and work.

Point 4: The Cayman government would support the Health City in Cayman initiative in principle as it would bring large economic opportunity to Cayman.

Point 5: The Cayman government would allow HCCI to set up a large-scale medical school to train nurses and doctors.

Point 6: The Cayman government would permit HCCI to build a large assisted-living community.

Point 7: The Cayman government would help HCCI obtain land at reasonable costs for the project.

Point 8: Cayman Airways would work with HCCI to provide cheap fares and new flights to bring patients to Cayman.

Point 9: The Cayman government would upgrade the airport to accommodate the increase in arrivals.[8]

The Cayman government (which owns Cayman Airways) was largely on board. If there was a deal breaker on Shetty's list, it was point 2: Cayman's recognition of Indian medical degrees. Shetty wasn't interested in training a new medical staff in the ways of Narayana, not when he had his own people ready to parachute in. But the Cayman Islands had its own medical professionals who were recognized and represented by professional boards that were quite entrenched, including the Medical Council, the Nursing Council, the Pharmacy Council, and the Council for Professions Allied with Medicine. Was there some reason the Indian doctors couldn't meet those councils' requirements?

Shetty responded as he always did when people appeared skeptical of Narayana's capabilities: He invited Premier Bush to see what he had accomplished in Bangalore. In December 2009, just four months after Shetty had gone to George Town, a handful of Cayman leaders, including the minister of health, toured the Bangalore heart hospital. Four months after that, in April 2010, all parties signed an agreement to build a multispecialty hospital and to recognize Indian medical credentials. Persistence had paid off.

The Cayman deal stipulated that HCCI would be exempt from taxes for twenty-five years—even if tax laws were to change. HCCI was also granted partial exemption from the typical 22.5 percent customs duty rate: the first $800 million of medical equipment and supplies brought to the island would be duty-free. Noneconomic damages in medical-malpractice cases would top out at $620,000, an amount that lowered the cost of HCCI's own insurance premiums. The government also agreed to create a new medical-tourism visa, which would be available to incoming patients within seventy-two hours of the hospital's request.[9]

The deal was signed, and Shetty told his architects to get busy.

Ultra-Cost-Conscious Mindset

Hospitals built by Narayana Health were not like hospitals built in the United States at that time. In the United States, architects created show-cases for competing hospital brands and submitted projects that typically cost hundreds of millions of dollars. But Narayana believed in frugality. The company preferred functional buildings with shared wards, no central air-conditioning, and few private offices. In fact, while Shetty was designing the Grand Cayman hospital he was also building a 300-bed hospital in Mysore, India, that would cost only $7 million.

The Grand Cayman facility adopted some of the cost-saving features from the Mysore hospital. It had large windows to take advantage of natural light, and it used insulated concrete forms to save on air-conditioning costs. It had a spacious, open-bay, seventeen-bed intensive care unit that could be overseen from a single nursing station, saving floor space and reducing the number of nurses needed. It harvested rainwater for its own use and used ocean water to help cool the place, which cut energy costs by nearly 50 percent. It used treated sewage effluent for landscape irrigation, and its onsite recycling reduced its landfill use by 60 percent. From the standpoint of sustainability, it was a cutting-edge building, but even with the cost savings, it didn't come cheap. The price tag—$70 million—was ten times the cost of the Mysore hospital for a third of the beds. But by American standards, it was a bargain: about $700,000 per bed, versus $2 million per bed on the mainland.

"Our cost of building the hospital was one of the lowest that anybody has seen in that region," Raghuvanshi told us. "And that despite the fact that Cayman is in the hurricane zone."

The building was financed with $30 million in debt. The balance was fronted by Ascension and Narayana in a 70-30 split. Despite the higher-than-customary construction costs, the project was well within budget. In any case, the real savings at HCCI would be found in operational costs, Narayana's celebrated competency, and Shetty went after those like a terrier.

Over the years, the volume of Narayana's operation in India had created some formidable buying power. In the Caymans, Shetty used that buying power to persuade many of its suppliers to abide by price structures in place in India. Sutures were purchased at Indian prices, for example, and medicines—all of them FDA approved—were as little as one-tenth the cost of the same medicines in the United States.[10] A similar deal allowed Shetty to pay $7 million for equipment that would have cost $20 million had it been sourced in the United States.[11] Even greater savings were expected from Narayana's ability to leave many back-office functions in Bangalore.

"Our biggest advantage is that we can outsource many things to India," Viren Shetty told us. "Paperwork, human resources, finance, medical transcription, radiology—all of that can be done from India. If it couldn't be, we wouldn't even bother building HCCI."

The business plan called for most of the work on the island to be done, at least initially, by Indian staff. There were two reasons for this: Indian workers were less expensive than American or Caymanian workers, and Shetty believed Indian staff and administrators would be harder working, more collaborative, more agile—more accustomed to the Narayana way of doing things.

"We were very clear with our American partners," Viren Shetty says. "The place would be managed by us. We were used to pushing the envelope."

This arrangement suited Ascension, which was not looking to manage the enterprise. Instead, Ascension wanted to learn best practices from HCCI that it might subsequently adopt in its US facilities—reverse innovation, once removed.

In July 2013, seven months before HCCI's scheduled opening, Narayana required its nonphysician Indian staff who had signed on to

HCCI to attend training programs in cultural sensitivity, accent neutralization, and interpersonal skills suited for interaction with people from many cultures. It was the kind of careful prep work that Narayana had always done, only this time the vision was global.

"Innovation comes when you present a new model," Viren Shetty says. "We would like to present our Cayman operation as an alternative health-care model, and at some point, if the environment is conducive enough, we would definitely like to be in the US. No Indian company has achieved great scale without having some US operations. We are trying to do low-cost health care. When you look at the world from Africa to the richest countries, you see our lessons are universal. There is no limit to where we could be. In the end it boils down to execution."

While landscaping crews were readying the grounds, and Indian staff were readying their English, marketing staff at HCCI were preparing a sales pitch. For a fixed price that was less than half of what most hospital procedures cost in the United States, HCCI would provide all medical care, plus round-trip transportation for two (the patient and a companion, often a spouse), and put them up in a hotel for as long as required. There would be no tricks, no contingencies, and no extra charges.

Shetty's team took the pitch to several large, self-insured employers in the United States—such as Walmart, Lowe's, and Home Depot—as well as to several smaller employers. They also talked to health administrators in poorer states, such as Kentucky and Louisiana, where medical specialists were in short supply and insurance coverage was spotty. Potential customers listened carefully, and then gave their answers:

Maybe, they said. *Not yet . . . We'll think it over.*

"They didn't know us," Viren Shetty explains. "There was concern about quality standards. There was a bit of hesitation."

No one wanted to go first, and all of them wanted to see outcomes— lots of outcomes. Shetty resolved to deliver them.

Island Life Is Not Always Easy

When HCCI opened for business in February 2014, it was staffed by eighteen doctors, thirty nurses, twenty-six paramedical technicians, and twenty-two administrative staff from India. The doctors, some of Narayana's highest performers in India, were all fixed-salary employees, with no incentive pay or referral fees for additional tests or procedures. They were paid about 70 percent of what they would have been paid in the United States. The doctors signed on for eight months, and they were chosen, as is always the case at Narayana, with efficiency in mind.

"In the United States, a hospital of this size requires one adult cardiac surgeon, one pediatric cardiac surgeon, and one thoracic surgeon," Devi Shetty explains. "We have one surgeon who covers all those specialties and does them all extremely well—much better than a lot of stand-alone surgeons. You can see the cost benefits. We want to demonstrate that things can be done differently."

In fact, HCCI did many things differently, sometimes by design, and sometimes from necessity. Raghuvanshi was tasked with transferring Narayana's innovative practices from India and applying Narayana's spirit of opportunism when problems and barriers arose. And they did, all the time.

For example, Narayana needed to purchase medical oxygen from US sources, as it was not available on Grand Cayman, but the cost of transporting it from Miami turned out to be higher than anticipated. For Raghuvanshi, it was déjà vu. Back in India, when suppliers of hospital gowns refused to drop the price to one that Narayana was willing to pay, Narayana arranged to have gowns made locally—so inexpensively that other hospitals started buying gowns from them. In Grand Cayman, HCCI generated its own oxygen, and before long, other hospitals on the island were buying oxygen from HCCI.

"Energy was another thing," says Raghuvanshi. "We were totally dependent on energy generation on the island, and that was a problem." The hospital began thinking about building its own 1.2-megawatt solar farm, using technology that would join the photovoltaic energy storage with the hospital's HVAC system and, conceivably, reduce energy consumption by 40 percent.[12]

As the months went by, other operational challenges arose. Shipments from India took longer than expected, forcing Narayana to either carry larger inventories than they liked or buy equipment and supplies from high-priced American suppliers. HCCI couldn't reuse materials and supplies in Cayman, as Narayana did in India, which increased consumption. And inter-island air travel, which was part of HCCI's bundled pricing, proved surprisingly complicated, raising the cost of transportation for off-island patients.

"Over and over we saw that the costs of materials and other fixed costs were higher than in India," says Raghuvanshi.

The margins were lower on this side of the globe, and the barriers higher. But the big problem was volume. It wasn't there yet. In India, volume was the driver for several of Narayana's most effective cost-saving practices, such as radical task-shifting and bulk purchasing. But the numbers in Cayman were slow to rise. In 2016, two years after HCCI opened, the hospital was averaging about 1.5 heart surgeries and 3 orthopedic surgeries a day, far fewer than in India, where each surgeon did 2 to 4 surgeries a day.

The limitations became circular. "We didn't have the volume, so it wouldn't have made sense to provide joints and joint prostheses from India," says Raghuvanshi. "Those are expensive products, and we were procuring them from an American supplier, where the cost was much higher."

The low volume, and uncertainty about how soon it would change, also kept Narayana from negotiating the kind of advantageous pay-per-use deals that it had with equipment suppliers in India. "We had to buy equipment outright," says Raghuvanshi. "The pay-per-use would be difficult for vendors to accept because they didn't know what kind of patient flow to expect, so all of the equipment we put there was a capital expenditure."

Another change to Narayana's Indian model evolved around the practice of task-shifting, which in India optimized the assignment of tasks to skill and salary levels so that higher-paid doctors never wasted a moment doing things that a lower-paid staff member could do. HCCI's occupancy rate, stuck in 2016 at 15 percent to 20 percent, rendered the strategy irrelevant. With time on their hands, the senior surgeons performed all their procedures themselves.

It was a shaky start, and the combination of high-cost local purchasing and lost efficiencies pushed the cost of bypass surgeries up to about $15,000—seven times the cost in India. But that was still a fraction of the cost of the same operation in Florida, and Shetty was known for taking the long view. Narayana would work through the growing pains.

If You Build It, They Might Come

When HCCI was in the planning stages, Shetty was hoping to see 17,000 patients from overseas each year, with a sizable share coming from the United States. Why weren't they coming? Raghuvanshi thought there were several reasons. For one thing, they couldn't get there.

Even in India, where relatively few people could afford to buy a car, buses routinely carried patients from rural villages to Narayana's hub hospitals. In the Caribbean, things were more complicated. Established air routes often zigged and zagged from island to island. Travelers from nearby islands were often routed through Miami, where layovers required visas. Other routes took people through Kingston, Jamaica, which had a reputation for being dangerous.

"Marketing has been extremely challenging," Raghuvanshi admitted. "One major factor is air-travel connectivity, which we hadn't considered as carefully as we should have. We are speaking to other airlines now, trying to set up some kind of hub."

Another problem was inertia. People tend to get health care the way they've always gotten it. In the Caribbean, that meant people with money went to the United States for treatment and people without money just went without. Because there was, as Raghuvanshi put it, "a total lack of infrastructure for diagnosis" on most of the smaller Caribbean islands, many people didn't even know that they needed treatment or, say, having received the rude diagnosis of a heart attack, thought nothing could be done about their ailments. But affordability was the main issue. Most Caribbean islanders didn't have health insurance, and many did not have cash incomes adequate to cover even the low-cost care at HCCI out of pocket.

In some cases, Narayana's efforts at marketing actually complicated things. Bundled pricing, which was designed to attract customers with the security of knowing that there would be no unexpected charges, ended up scaring some away. "People had never seen anything like it," Raghuvanshi says. "The insurance companies were extremely hesitant, because they thought there was a catch and they could end up paying more." And HCCI's state-of-the-art billing system, designed to handle the most complex transactions, stumbled over the easy ones. It had a hard time handling self-payers, and at HCCI, there were a lot of them.

Still, HCCI was able to build up a moderate business from the Caymans and neighboring islands. Through April 2017, HCCI had seen almost 30,000 outpatients and over 3,500 inpatients, plus over 300 sleep-study patients. It had performed nearly 2,000 procedures, including 759 cath-lab procedures.[13] Hoping to increase those numbers, hospital doctors engaged in outreach efforts in off-island clinics and camps. More elaborate was the hospital's outreach to Haitian children, whose access to quality care had been disrupted ever since that island's catastrophic 2010 earthquake. With help from the Have a Heart Foundation, the Red Cross, and the Caribbean mobile-phone company Digicel, HCCI performed more than 100 surgeries on children from Haiti, as well as on children from Jamaica, Honduras, and Belize.

It wasn't like there was no American business. By the summer of 2017, HCCI had seen 17,000 Americans on an outpatient basis. Most were vacationers in need of urgent or emergency care. Elective-surgery patients like Wayne Wright, who got his knees done in 2015, were less common, though emergency surgeries on American patients were rising slowly. One of those patients, a vascular surgeon from Massachusetts, was so impressed with the lifesaving treatment he received after a heart attack that he offered a testimonial for HCCI that appears on the hospital website. "I see plenty of patients post cardiac surgery," he says there. "My care and recovery, in my opinion, is as good as or better than what I have seen. The model here is what the US health-care system is striving to get to."

HCCI also secured contracts with three large cruise lines—Carnival, Disney, and Royal Caribbean—to provide care for their crews and vacationers. And medical-tourism consultants were aiming customers like Wayne Wright in the direction of Grand Cayman, where the appeal of inexpensive joint replacements was enhanced by white-sand beaches.

Still, as of 2017, the big fish were not biting. HCCI had been hoping for commitments from insurance companies and from large, self-insured US employers like Walmart, which employed 1.4 million people (1 percent of the American workforce), and Home Depot, which had nearly 400,000 employees. Both companies had heard the sales pitch, and neither was sold yet. Insurance companies also had listened, politely. Raghuvanshi believed that the hospital's approximately 20 percent occupancy rate, while sufficient for HCCI to break even, was too low to impress the insurers. Though patient outcomes were excellent and patient satisfaction was near perfect, insurers wanted to see a busier hospital. Raghuvanshi believed that 50 percent occupancy might be the magic number.

"They find the idea interesting," Raghuvanshi said. "But no big employer has signed on the dotted line. Many people who have come and seen us feel this is a good option. They think this is what they should be doing, but they're hesitant to recommend it because of how it might be perceived by their customers."

That perception, says Raghuvanshi, the fear that cheap medical care on a Caribbean island couldn't possibly equal the quality at a renowned US hospital, remained a problem. But Shetty's conviction that it would pass was shared by forward-thinking analysts.

"Ask most Americans about obtaining their health care outside of the United States, and they respond with disdain and negativity," says Robert Pearl, former Permanente CEO. "In their mind, the quality and medical expertise available elsewhere is second-rate. Of course, that's exactly what Yellow Cab thought about Uber, Kodak thought about digital photography, General Motors thought about Toyota, and Borders thought about Amazon."[14]

Raghuvanshi was more charitable. "There is nothing we are doing that any group in the United States cannot do," he told us. "We believe that we can be a catalyst by doing something like this in their backyard."

Time will tell. The Cayman Islands are closer than you think.

Lessons from HCCI

Why worth replicating?

- Health-care costs in the United States are too high, at least twice as much per capita as those of any other industrialized country, yet the United States trails these countries in outcomes. Only radical solutions, including models like HCCI's, can make a significant dent on costs—*while maintaining or improving quality.*

How to replicate?

- *Established health-care players should self-disrupt:* Established players, including leading hospitals, should consider adding facilities in locations close to the United States but outside the US regulatory system to experiment with novel approaches to health-care delivery that lower cost without lowering quality.

- *Startups should promote near-shore medical tourism:* New entrants should also consider replicating the HCCI model by opening facilities in places like the Cayman Islands or St. Kitts to complement facilities in the United States and disrupt existing high-cost models of delivery.

- *Adopt a frugal mindset:* Frugality cannot come at the expense of quality, but absent a compelling medical reason, hospitals should cut costs in nonmedical areas. All employees, including doctors, must be encouraged to take the cost of health-care delivery into consideration, alongside the benefits of such care.

- *Be frugal in capital expenditures:* Hospitals feel like seven-star hotels, but such luxury is not essential for providing high-quality care. Hospitals must evaluate carefully their capital expenditures on hospital design and construction and the purchase of costly equipment.

- *Be frugal in variable costs:* To keep unit variable costs low, hospitals should use fixed assets, such as operating suites, and scarce expertise, such as specialists, as productively as possible. They must increase throughput rates, reduce the idle time between procedures, minimize waste (especially of expensive supplies), reuse supplies wherever possible, and minimize expenses on medicines.

- *Avoid unnecessary medical procedures:* Providers must offer patients bundled pricing, which both blunts the incentive to conduct unnecessary tests and procedures and strengthens the incentive for all staff and departments to collaborate in care delivery.

- *Leverage offshoring:* Health-care organizations must consider the merits of outsourcing and/or offshoring certain activities (e.g., diagnostics, transcription, and back-office work) to lower-cost vendors and locations, taking advantage of the internet and the growth in digitization.

5.

Expanding Rural Access
University of Mississippi Medical Center

We use technology in all areas of our life. Think about it—in banking, in retail, or with travel. We are a tech-savvy population. Why don't we leverage technology to transform health care?

–Dr. Kristi Henderson, UMMC

Five miles into the frantic race to the hospital, fourteen-year-old T. J. Brewer looked up from his stretcher in the back of the ambulance and told his mother and father that they had been great parents. He told them he loved them, and he told them goodbye. Bleeding profusely from a chest wound, T. J. was convinced that he would die from the shooting accident in the fields behind his house in rural Richton, Mississippi.

There was good reason for his fear: Perry County Hospital, where the ambulance was headed, had neither the expertise nor the equipment to treat a gunshot wound to the chest. It had no surgeons—in fact, it had no board-certified physicians of any kind. But the hospital did have something that could give T. J. a fighting chance. It had a live video connection linking its emergency department to some of the best emergency doctors in the state, who were a two-hour drive away at the University of Mississippi Medical Center (UMMC), in Jackson.

As the ambulance arrived at the hospital in Richton, a UMMC emergency team slid in front of a TV monitor in Jackson and began talking and gesturing, showing a Perry County nurse practitioner exactly how to treat the wound until T. J. could be transported, first by ambulance and then by helicopter, to the critical-care unit that would save his life. During the ordeal, T. J. lost thirty-four units of blood and his heart stopped three times, but the boy survived, because Perry County Hospital, in the little town of Richton, population 1,088, was one of several spokes on a hub-and-spoke telemedical network born of the determination of one emergency-care nurse in Jackson.[1]

The nurse was Dr. Kristi Henderson (her doctorate was in nursing practice), the daughter of a longtime Mississippi family, who saw a life-threatening problem and devised a high-tech solution to fix it.

Henderson led the development of a homegrown hub-and-spoke telemedicine network—a remarkably Indian-like response to a serious problem of American health-care delivery. In Mississippi, the state that consistently scored at the bottom of US health rankings, access to health care was seriously constrained by a shortage of doctors and by poorly distributed resources. As in India, the underlying problem was poverty. As in India, medical resources were scarce. As in India, solutions emerged from the bottom up, in this case led by a "nursepreneur" who would not take no for an answer. And as in India, a hub-and-spoke telehealth network improved access to health care for poor rural communities, while lowering costs and improving quality and patient experience. It was a powerful example of value-based care.

In 2017, UMMC was selected as one of only two Telehealth Centers of Excellence in the United States by the Health Resources and Services Administration (HRSA), an agency of the Department of Health and

Human Services. HRSA, as it detailed in its call for applications, expected each Telehealth Center of Excellence to "serve as a national clearinghouse for telehealth research and resources, including technical assistance. To achieve that goal, the Telehealth Center of Excellence should have substantial experience operating a telehealth program that offers a broad range of clinical services and has experience demonstrating how [its] efforts have improved access to care and enhanced health outcomes for [its] patients."[2]

Hub-and-Spoke Model

T. J. Brewer's life was saved on New Year's Day 2008, when the University of Mississippi Center for Telehealth was just five years old. Since then, the network has expanded far beyond emergency care. In 2017, Mississippi Telehealth connected specialists in thirty-five fields of medicine with medical staff and patients at 225 sites across Mississippi, including not only community hospitals and clinics but also mental-health facilities, schools and colleges, businesses, prisons, mobile health vans, and even some oil rigs in the Gulf of Mexico. It also linked to hundreds of private homes, connecting patients suffering chronic diseases such as diabetes and hypertension with a team of chronic-disease experts. Today, Mississippi Telehealth is widely recognized as a pioneering model for rural telemedicine delivery, ranked in 2015 by the American Telemedicine Association as one of the seven best programs of its kind in the country.[3]

In 1999, Henderson managed the nonphysician staff in the trauma center at UMMC, the only level-1 trauma center in the state. She handled the budget, oversaw operations, and tracked quality and patient satisfaction. She knew trouble when she saw it, and she saw it every day: emergencies that couldn't be handled where they happened; local emergency departments staffed by a family physician or nurse practitioner; community hospitals with no imaging equipment; local hospitals on the brink of bankruptcy; bottlenecks, backlogs, and long waits for patients in Jackson when the beds were full.

The underlying problem was obvious. "We needed to get the existing medical resources and expertise out into the rural areas," Henderson told us. "I thought we could train community-based nurse practitioners and use videoconferencing to comanage the emergency cases. We jumped in with both feet to a 24/7 operation for emergency care, and it just grew from there."[4]

Henderson, driven by a strong sense of purpose, built her hub-and-spoke delivery network with UMMC at the center, and leveraged technology to connect the hub with the spokes—similar to what HCG Oncology and Narayana Health did in India. The best doctors, specialists, and equipment were housed in the hub at UMMC, while the spokes in the small towns were staffed by generalists and supplied with basic equipment. And it worked as well in Mississippi as it did in India. Thirteen years in, the telehealth network that Henderson first imagined in 1999 had recorded more than 500,000 patient contacts.[5] The telecommunications equipment, which started out as TV sets hooked up to T1 lines, grew to include wireless communication with computer tablets in the homes of the chronically ill. Those tablets recorded health data that aided in the local treatment of more than 100,000 rural patients a year, whose health outcomes rivaled those of patients seen at the UMMC hub in Jackson.

The hub-and-spoke telemedicine network was also a great boon to local hospitals. It reduced the need for patient transfers, increased local hospital admissions by 20 percent, and cut physician staffing costs by 25 percent.[6] Several hospitals that had been headed for closure were spared.

Limited Access in the Magnolia State

Mississippi has one of the lowest standards of living in the United States. In the mid-2010s, it had the lowest median household income of any state, and roughly 21 percent of its three million residents lived below the federal poverty line, including 246,000 children. Twenty-one percent of the adult population held a bachelor's degree, and more than half the people lived in rural communities where resources and opportunities were limited.[7]

The states of health and health care were especially disheartening. Mississippi had ranked at or near the bottom of United Health Foundation's state health rankings for twenty-five years. The 2016 rankings reported that Mississippi had the worst infant-mortality and premature-death rates in the nation, the highest rates of diabetes and cardiovascular deaths, the second-highest incidence of cancer deaths, and alarming numbers of people reporting "frequent physical or mental distress."[8]

Health-care delivery was long a big part of the problem. In a 2015 Commonwealth Fund ranking that looked at forty-two health-care metrics, Mississippi came in last. That year the state had fewer primary care doctors per capita than any other state and only one top-tier hospital: UMMC. Twenty-two percent of the adult population under sixty-five had no health insurance, and Mississippi had the largest percentage of adults who went without medical care because they could not afford it. On measures of access, prevention and treatment, avoidable hospital use and costs, healthy lives, and equity, Mississippi consistently scored at the bottom of the charts.[9]

In 1999, when Kristi Henderson began her work, the disparity between medical care at UMMC and care in the rural parts of Mississippi was shocking. Several counties didn't have a single physician. The entire state had just ninety-nine acute-care hospitals, three-quarters of them in rural areas. Many of those facilities were critical-access hospitals—that is, hospitals with fewer than twenty-five beds, located more than thirty-five miles from another hospital. They had no medical specialists on staff, performed no surgeries or deliveries, and could provide inpatient acute care only on a limited basis by law. In 1999, not one of these critical-access hospitals even had a ventilator.[10]

Community hospitals, the next level of rural health-care facilities, were better staffed, often with a cardiologist and pediatrician as well as an internist, but not with the kinds of skills and knowledge needed for emergency situations or specialty care. For many rural hospitals, the expertise gap was filled by *locum tenens*, doctors who would fly in, work for a couple of days, and fly out, often leaving behind as many problems as they solved. It was expensive, inefficient, and it did nothing to build bonds of trust between the hospital and the community. For chronic-disease patients, especially, reliance on *locum tenens* was unsustainable.

"We were seeing people come in from all over the state who had bad outcomes because of inconsistent care and delays in care," Henderson says. "The health-care system isn't easy to navigate and doesn't make it easy for us to be healthy or manage our own health. That's magnified in a state like Mississippi, where sixty-five percent of our patients have to drive over forty minutes to see a specialist."

To us, Mississippi looks a lot like India: the large rural population, the widespread poverty, the shortage of doctors and medical equipment, the prohibitive distances to high-quality hospitals and specialists, the unequal access to care. It's a system of haves and have-nots, a system working poorly, a system ripe for innovation.

Leveraging Technology

As Henderson looked out over the workings of her busy emergency department, she noticed something different. She noticed that every day, the most highly trained specialists in the state were sharing their valuable medical knowledge with the nurse practitioners in the ER, helping the nurses manage their emergency patients.

She wondered: *Why did it have to stop there?*

"I felt this need to share what we were doing," says Henderson. "I thought we could expand it for more people. I had a path and somewhere

I wanted to go. I just made a list of what I needed to check off to get there and just kept doing it."

Henderson also had the vision to see how technology could be used to replicate the live knowledge-sharing she saw every day at UMMC. Instead of sending trauma patients on hours-long trips to Jackson, or sending *locum tenens* on jitney tours of the countryside, the resources of Jackson would be transmitted to local hospitals on T1 lines, both audio and video, in real time, and handled there by specially trained nurse practitioners. Only those patients who needed extra special care would be brought to UMMC. It was a clever idea, one that delivered quality health care through a hub-and-spoke system of telemedicine.

"The whole thing was based on necessity, really," Henderson says.

We looked at the challenge: We have only these resources, so how are we going to provide health care? The only way to do that was to use simple videoconferencing technology to connect the resources and bring them there virtually. At the other end, in the rural hospital, we would use the health-care professionals who were in the community. Instead of trying to convince a high-price medical specialist to live in Belzoni, Mississippi, for example, we'd use the family doctors and nurse practitioners who were already there. We would make the best of what we had.

Henderson worked closely with her boss, Dr. Robert Galli, who encouraged her to draft a proposal for a network that would run a T1 line from the emergency department in Jackson to community hospitals, as a proof of concept. She consulted the American Telemedicine Association, which had come into being six years earlier and from which she gained insight from the pioneers in the field. While the association offered many examples of telemedical services, none of those examples had involved emergency care, as Henderson hoped to provide. Moreover, the equipment used by other members of the association was expensive. The monitors and software cost tens of thousands of dollars apiece. Henderson figured she could put together something cheaper, and she knew that technology would get better and less expensive every year.

Henderson and Dr. Galli, along with Greg Hall, the team's technology wizard, ramped up their knowledge of technology procurement, consulting with medical experts to identify equipment that was reliable, affordable, and easy to use. Henderson then pitched her idea to telecommunications providers AT&T and C Spire, with whom the state had a special rate. Henderson, Galli, and Hall bought television sets off the shelf and connected them to the T1 line. They weren't fancy TVs, either.

"We literally had those old-fashioned box TVs on carts," Henderson remembers. "When I look back at pictures it's pretty comical. I didn't have any model to go by." To make sure the system would provide adequate resolution over long distances, university faculty tried connecting it via satellite phone to the most distant place they could think of: a medical outreach location in Kigali, Rwanda. Success.

Henderson was cheered, but she knew technology would not be her biggest challenge. That would be the health-care system itself, and her concern was justified by the caution with which the hospital and medical establishment approached the project. "This wasn't what they learned how to do," Henderson explained to us. "The business model was one that brought people to the hospital and to the clinic. It didn't push it out into the communities and to the homes."

Skepticism and Pushback

For three years, from 1999 to 2002, Henderson inched her way over that barrier. She met with members of state medical and nursing boards, explaining the potential of telehealth to regulators, many of whom were disinclined to change things despite the obvious deficiencies in the system they oversaw. Some fretted that medical care could never be truly effective without hands-on contact between physician and patient. Others worried about the reliability of the technology, and about the capabilities of nurse practitioners.

At the time, the practice environment for nurse practitioners was limited, and Henderson, herself a nurse practitioner, wasn't surprised that an attempt to expand their purview would meet with resistance, from both physicians and nurses. But Henderson knew that, working with the academic medical center, she could create a training program that would expand the skill sets of rural nurses and take advantage of their invaluable local knowledge and their hard-earned patient trust.

Other doubters, while enthusiastic about the potential of telemedicine, worried about starting the service with emergency care, an area where there was little room for mistakes. But the most widely voiced concern was that UMMC would steal local practitioners' patients.

"That was the exact opposite of what we wanted to do," says Michael Adcock, the administrator who ran the Center for Telehealth at UMMC. "We were trying to keep the patients in the community and keep them close to home. We wanted patients to come to UMMC only if they absolutely had to, and in most cases, they didn't."[11]

"There were just a lot of naysayers," Henderson remembers.

Henderson designed an extensive program to teach medical generalists and nurse practitioners to better recognize and treat emergency patients. She didn't cut any corners. The program had a curriculum and a clinical residency provided by the faculty in the department of emergency medicine. It had written exams and clinical check-offs. It required each practitioner to perform certain listed procedures under supervision, with a final check-off in the trauma center. All ER patients were covered.

In 2002, the boards and Henderson finally came to agreement: Henderson and her team could wire up three hospitals with the medical center, if they agreed to send quarterly reports of patient outcomes to the boards. More good news followed. The TelEmergency program, as Henderson's brainchild was then known, was given a startup grant of $260,000 from the private Bower Foundation. In October 2003, the network went live. Henderson was off and running.

Purpose: Social Heart and Business Brain

Over the next eight years Henderson built a hub-and-spoke telemedicine network on hard work and persuasion. She had no dedicated staff and no hospital budget line, but she had perseverance and a strong sense of purpose. Henderson will say she just did what she had to do, but Adcock says she just refused to take "no" for an answer.

"She is a steamroller," Adcock says. "She believed it was the right thing to do, and she was going to make it work, and that's what she did."

Funding was tough, but once the three-spoke pilot was underway, money started to come in. Not big money from private-equity investors or plum grants from the National Institutes of Health or the National Science Foundation. But money nonetheless. In 2004, the Bower Foundation came through with another $405,000, and in 2006 the United States Department of Agriculture (USDA) made the first of many contributions that over the next several years would add up to $2.4 million. (Why the USDA? Because it is concerned about rural development and gives grants for rural telecommunications.) Henderson also got help from the Federal Communications Commission, through the Rural Health Care Program of the agency's Universal Service Fund.

The money went into training and to building out the spokes of the network. Henderson met regularly with representatives of AT&T and C Spire, not only to arrange for new T1-line connections but also to learn where the companies' newer, high-speed lines were being laid. Henderson traced those lines to the nearest critical-access and community hospitals, and then drove across the state to those hospitals to make her pitch.

That pitch included a hybrid payment system that Henderson devised because insurance companies in Mississippi did not, at the time, reimburse providers for telehealth services. The system worked like this: insurers reimbursed the local receiving hospitals for the services provided locally, such as lab tests, use of the facility, and the nurse practitioners' time, and the local hospitals in turn paid UMMC a monthly "clinic fee," based on hours of remote consultation, to cover the services of the physicians taking the calls in Jackson. It was a clever solution, and proof that a hub-and-spoke model for health-care delivery could work in parallel with a traditional fee-for-service payment system.

Rural hospitals began to sign up, and the network began to generate both cost savings and revenue. More and more patients treated by the TelEmergency network were discharged directly from the receiving hospital (57 percent by 2013). Others were transferred to better-equipped area hospitals (22 percent in 2013).[12] And the rest were admitted to local hospitals, where their stays—instead of costing $10,000 a day, as would have been the case at UMMC—cost $7,500 a day at community hospitals and less than $5,000 at critical-access hospitals.

"It was much cheaper for patients to stay where they were," says Adcock. "At Jackson, we were constantly full. We'd much rather that patients were taken care of somewhere else. It freed up a bed for someone here who really needed it, like a complex trauma victim or a kidney-transplant patient, and it filled beds in the local hospitals, which often had too few patients to sustain the operation. It was a win-win all the way around."

In this way, the network was built out in hops and skips, aided by positive reports from participating hospitals. It was also aided by Henderson's wide-ranging vision of what *value* meant in *value-based* health-care delivery. It wasn't only the *lifesaving* value of medical care for the trauma patient—although that was the original impulse. It wasn't just the *cost-saving* value to the patient, either. It was also the *hospital-saving* value to Mississippi's beleaguered health-care system and rural communities.

"We ended up bringing some of those small critical-access hospitals to a different level," Henderson says. "It became much more than telemedicine consults. It became a relationship where we really supported these hospitals any way we could. It became a system that brought together what typically were competing hospitals to work together to fill each other's gaps." As she told *Telemedicine* magazine in 2015: "When they had to deal with those high-risk but low-frequency patients, the poisoned child or the near-drowning victim or the survivor of a multi-car accident, we were there for them."[13]

Expanding the Network beyond Emergency Care

This hospital-saving value was magnified in 2008, when UMMC began to add specialties other than emergency care to the telehealth network. The TelEmergency network now had a modest infrastructure and a dozen participating hospitals. UMMC also had a separate store-and-forward system in place that allowed rural hospitals to send cardiology images to Jackson to be read by specialists there. Why not use all that capacity to deliver other specialty services to the rural hospitals electronically?

Expanding the service offerings would solve another problem that Henderson had noted. Many rural clinics routinely referred their patients to Jackson for specialist care—cardiology checkups, dermatology consultations, and so on. Henderson identified the clinics with the highest such referrals and paid them a visit. "We'd say, 'Hey, a large number of patients from your town are coming to see our cardiologists,'" she remembers. "'How about we partner and the patients stay there, and we'll bring the cardiologist to your clinic virtually?'"

As the network grew laterally, adding clinics and hospitals in town after town, UMMC also expanded the menu of service offerings, starting with telepsychiatry in 2008. Next in were radiology, pathology, and cardiology and, in a later wave, ophthalmology, obstetrics, neonatology, dialysis, dermatology, and pulmonology. In 2011, UMMC officially launched its Center for Telehealth, which rolled the original TelEmergency program in with all the new telemedicine services.

In expanding the services, Henderson was careful not to cannibalize rural specialists' practices. Before proposing a telelink, she would comb state records and map out where specialists were already practicing. Where there was coverage, she backed off. Where there was a gap, she'd step in.

"We'd find a region of six counties where none of them had a dermatologist," she told us by example. "Then we'd find a couple of clinics to contract with to provide that service. That way we didn't have pushback. We were enhancing, not taking away. I wanted to build a model of collaboration."

As the service offerings diversified, payment arrangements evolved. Mississippi insurers still didn't pay for telehealth consults, so the spoke hospitals continued their monthly payments to UMMC, but that fee was customized to the particular services for which the hospital or clinic contracted. While all spokes paid an "administrative fee" to cover UMMC's technology and support costs, each also paid a "clinic fee" based on the number of specialty services and consult hours it would use, with charges calculated at fair market value. And as the network grew, the administrative share of the cost decreased, and the savings were passed on to local hospitals.

"We worked hard to get the costs and benefits right," Henderson says. "I'm not going to say it was a rose garden. There were plenty of times I thought I would be escorted out of meetings."

But Henderson had pulled off a kind of health-care trifecta: The community hospitals benefitted from the opportunity to perform the lab or diagnostic tests locally. Their patients benefitted because they didn't have to travel so far to see a specialist. And the specialists in Jackson benefitted because they received a monthly take from the clinic fee.

The new telehealth business also bolstered the bottom lines of many smaller hospitals, saving some such hospitals from closing, and it made many rural communities more attractive to new businesses, whose CEOs had been reluctant to move their employees to a health-care wasteland.

Before long, the state was using UMMC'S telehealth network as a selling point when recruiting new business to Mississippi.

"What Kristi did empowered our community hospitals to provide better care to their local population," says Ryan Kelly, executive director of the Mississippi Rural Health Association. "That allows more of those patients to stay close to home and to receive lower-cost care with often better outcomes. It's a win-win for everyone."[14]

The Nursepreneur Plunges Ahead

All our value-based exemplars, both Indian and American, were shepherded to prominence by the most powerful person in the organization: founders, CEOs, physicians and surgeons, usually educated at world-class universities—and, not incidentally, all men. For an innovator, Henderson was an outlier: a nurse, a woman, Alabama born and Mississippi bred.

But Henderson had the great advantage of understanding the cultures at both ends of her network: she knew the UMMC hub like the back of her hand, yet she was sympathetic with the plight of nurses and nurse practitioners in the spokes. She also had an open mind. Not having been anointed in the most hallowed halls of medicine, she was unmoved by the objection she often heard in the corridors of power: "That's not the way we do things here."

Indeed, Henderson's hub-and-spoke solution to health-care delivery was at odds with the model that most big-name US hospitals embraced. That delivery model, the build-and-brand solution, involved building out each hospital's own physical capacity, either by adding beds and clinics at the hub, or by gobbling up community hospitals and duplicating services in those satellite locations. In this way, hospitals hoped to leverage their big-name brand to attract customers and crowd out the competition, maximizing their bargaining power with insurance companies.

The build-and-brand model had its critics, including Ellen Zane, CEO emeritus and vice chair of Tufts Medical Center. "There is a mentality among a lot of old-fashioned hospital CEOs that is very oriented toward 'bigger is better,'" says Zane. "They like lots of bricks and mortar, and they like being able to pound their chests about their hospital being all things to all people. These hospitals need to understand that not everybody should do everything."[15]

Still, UMMC's hub-and-spoke telehealth system had some challenges that build-and-brand expansions didn't have to face. One was data sharing—a mission-critical function that not only raised all kinds of HIPAA concerns but also posed many logistical problems. In the early 2000s, electronic record-keeping was new in the United States, and there was no centralized repository for patient information or even a shared billing system. With the exception of two sister hospitals to UMMC, all the partner hospitals in the Mississippi Telehealth system were separate businesses, some run by counties and others by large health systems, each with its own budget and record-keeping system. Henderson felt she needed to keep things simple, so she elected to share only those records that absolutely had to be shared and then wait for a better solution to arise from federal mandates and market pressures.

Over time, improved technology and bandwidth made data transmission more manageable. It also made computers, monitors, and software more affordable. "Everything has gotten smaller, lighter, faster, and cheaper," says Adcock. "The fifty-five-inch monitor that would have been $10,000 back in the day is now $500 or $600. Resolution is much better, and storage has gone way, way up." Reliability improved, too. By 2013, network downtime due to technical problems fell to 0.00025 percent across the Mississippi Telehealth network. As the network grew, Henderson saw efficiencies of scale, and the costs of each spoke continued to decline, allowing UMMC to further lower the fees for participating hospitals and clinics.

"One of the things we learned was that to get adoption, it has to be easy," Henderson says. "It has to be something that proves to have real value, not only in its clinical impact but also in efficiency, and it has to be financially sustainable. There are such cultural barriers to change, but if you make the new process easier, better, and cheaper, there is little reason not to adopt it."

Adoption was also aided by UMMC's status as a teaching hospital. In the fourteen years since Henderson launched the network, the hospital has graduated ten classes of physicians for whom Mississippi Telehealth was a mainstay of their medical training, a working system with evident benefits. The hospital also had many fellows and residents rotate through the telehealth programs. These physicians had all gone on to spread the word to other hospitals, serving as emissaries, boosters, and implementers of telehealth delivery in hospitals throughout Mississippi. In this sense, teaching hospitals were perfect replicators for health-care innovations, and facilitators for their dissemination.

The chief roadblocks to widespread acceptance of Mississippi Telehealth were insurance companies and state regulators, who were reluctant to pay for telehealth consults, citing concerns about quality control and fee-for-service payment arrangements. State legislators, in particular, didn't pull any punches. "We don't need that," they told Henderson. "We can't afford that. That's not the way we do things here."

So Henderson did what she always did: she made a list. Then she outlined a strategy and headed to the capitol to win those legislators over.

"Every legislator had an area they were focusing their attention on— maybe it was prisons, or schools, or small-business development," Henderson remembers. "So before I met with them, I would pull their key agenda items and do some research. Then I told them exactly how telemedicine could impact prisons, or the educational system, or whatever it was. I couldn't find any area where telehealth did not promise some benefit."

It took two years of persuasion to get the state legislature to mandate the change. In 2012, legislation passed, and the next year Mississippi governor Phil Bryant signed legislation requiring public and private insurers to cover telehealth services at the same rate as in-person services. The telehealth program could now be subsumed under the fee-for-service system.

"After that," says Adcock, "the network really took off."

Ultimately, Kristi Henderson did manage to win over her many critics and doubters. Her most powerful weapon was her perseverance, but her most potent ammunition was data.

The Ultimate Spoke: Home-Based Care

For ten years, the spokes that linked to the UMMC hub were local hospitals, clinics, and health centers in rural Mississippi towns, but after the state passed legislation in 2012 requiring insurers to cover telehealth consults, the doors swung open to a multitude of possibilities. Over the next four years, the spokes multiplied rapidly. The network extended to elementary schools, where it helped school nurses treat student illnesses and injuries; to high-school sidelines, where it helped coaches to recognize concussion injuries in real time; to colleges, where mental-health consultations were made available; and to prisons, where it provided evidence-based care to HIV-positive inmates.

Even as Mississippi Telehealth was reaching out to those institutions, Henderson felt that she and her team were still just scratching the surface of the potential of telemedicine. She was thinking of places like Ruleville.

Ruleville, Mississippi, is a small town in the Mississippi Delta, about a two-hour drive from Jackson, with a population of roughly 3,000 people, 37.7 percent of them living in poverty. African Americans account for more than 80 percent of the town's population and more than 80 percent of those living in poverty.[16] Many of the townspeople do their grocery shopping at the local gas station, where the foods sold are chosen for shelf life, not healthfulness, and are loaded with sugar. In 2014, the town's extraordinary diabetes rate of 13.2 percent was one of the highest in a state that had one of the highest incidences of diabetes in the country.[17]

That same year, Ruleville was chosen for a pilot program that extended the spokes of the UMMC telehealth network to the homes of people suffering from chronic diseases, starting with diabetes. The program, backed by Governor Bryant, partnered UMMC with Intel-GE Care Innovations, C Spire, and the critical-access hospital in Ruleville.

Like most chronic diseases, diabetes is expensive to treat. Two years earlier, in 2012, the 12 percent of Mississippi's population with diabetes cost the state $2.74 billion in diabetes-related medical expenses. And according to the American Diabetes Association, the United States as a whole spends about $176 billion each year on direct medical care for diabetes. The association puts the annual cost of productivity lost to diabetes at $69 billion.[18] And worldwide, according to the Harvard T.H. Chan School of Public Health, the cost of diabetes is $825 billion per year, and growing fast.

Because chronic conditions such as diabetes typically require daily monitoring, they are hard to treat in patients who don't often see their doctor, a cohort that includes most people living in the rural South. Diabetes is particularly hard to treat, because the information patients self-report about their eating and exercise habits is famously unreliable. Sometimes patients misread their numbers. Sometimes they misremember. Sometimes they flat-out lie. The Diabetes Telehealth Program, as the UMMC-driven partnership was known, eliminated that kind of error by giving two hundred diabetics in its pilot program tablet computers connected by the internet to UMMC. Each day, participants entered their glucose levels, blood pressure, and weight into software on the tablet, and the progress of their disease was tracked remotely by specialists. That data didn't lie.

"When patients checked their glucose levels, it was Bluetoothed up to our team," says Henderson. "If the numbers caused concern, a diabetes educator or a nurse would call the patient and say, 'Hey, I see your glucose is low, get something to eat and I'll call you back in a little bit, and then let's talk and see how we can make sure this doesn't happen again.'"

In a move that reminds us of Narayana Health's training of patients and patient family members to perform tasks normally done by hospital staff, the telemedicine team at UMMC distributed educational materials, including a series of two-minute videos that could be viewed on tablets.

And like Indian exemplars who enlisted the services of community health workers, the team trained other Ruleville residents to serve as counselors to their neighbors. "The local counselors could tell them, 'Go down to such-and-such grocery where you can get these foods to eat healthy,'" Henderson explained. "This was a pivotal point in our program."

Each participant was assigned to a nurse, who was supported by a team of diabetes educators, pharmacists, and dieticians. Because most chronic-disease patients have comorbidities, the teams were designed to manage more than diabetes alone.

"So much of the difficulty managing chronic diseases is related to lack of medication adherence, and this really made a huge difference," says Henderson. "We were able to get incredible compliance by having people answer questions daily and also by doing vital signs daily."

From our perspective, UMMC's Diabetes Telehealth Program mirrored Deccan Hospital's home-based peritoneal dialysis for patients with end-stage renal disease in India. And its results were equally impressive.

The Value of Telehealth Delivery

All ninety-three of the first participants in UMMC's diabetes program believed that they had their disease under control for the first time. All lost weight, and all reported feeling better. The sponsors had hoped to achieve reductions of hemoglobin A1C levels of 1 percent in 75 percent of patients over the course of one year. After only six months, they found an average reduction of A1C of almost 2 percent. With the exception of one patient, who was hospitalized at the time of enrollment, not a single participant required a hospital visit for diabetes. The compliance rate for medication was an astonishing 96 percent.

Financial results were equally winning, especially considering that 30 percent of participants were uninsured and another 30 percent were underinsured. Even if the services were unpaid and the tablet was never returned, the state still saved money.

"Part of our analysis was to ask, 'If I give these people this technology, how badly will I lose my shirt?'" says Henderson. "What we found was we saved money because we kept them out of our emergency rooms. These were people who were coming in to the emergency room four to six times a year and using our resources, and they were not able to pay. Now they were supported by a simple kit in their homes."

Adcock estimates that downstream savings in emergency-room costs in the first six months were $3,300 per patient. An independent study predicted that if just 20 percent of Mississippi's uncontrolled diabetics on Medicaid were enrolled in such a program, the state would save $189 million a year.[19] The pilot program also saved 9,454 miles of driving by patients and uncovered nine new cases of diabetic retinopathy that otherwise might have gone untreated.[20] It is in unconventional metrics like these that some of the latent values of value-based health care are revealed.

In 2014, Kristi Henderson was a local hero, the champion architect of a hub-and-spoke, value-based health-care program that was so undeniably effective that it set the stage for national policy changes. Henderson's success brought her to the attention of Mississippi's congressional delegation, which that year helped to start the Alliance for Connected Care, a telemedicine lobbying group, and which introduced bills to expand payments for telehealth delivery. In 2015, Henderson was invited to testify before two United States Senate committees considering federal-level policy changes.

"What we did in Mississippi can absolutely be replicated," says Henderson. "But it is important to understand that it's not about the technology. It's about people and process." It takes nurturing. It takes relationships and partnerships. And you've got to have buy-in across the key stakeholders. It's not an easy journey, but it can be done.

"We have health-care reform that's forcing our systems to be value-driven," says Henderson. "We are moving towards capitation payment. We also have consumers getting more involved in their care. In the next five years we will see increased use of wearable devices, ingestibles, dissolvables, robots, artificial intelligence, precision medicine—all of that. Watching to see how it all fits together to transform the health-care system is going to be pretty remarkable. We are on the cusp of that now."

The Future of Telehealth

In 2017, under the guidance of Michael Adcock, UMMC's model program continued to grow. The Center for Telehealth adopted a technology to monitor patients coping with chronic obstructive pulmonary disease, hypertension, kidney disease, and a number of other conditions that require chronic-disease management.

Mississippi was one of only seven states to get an A rating from the American Telemedicine Association for its telehealth policy and legislation. UMMC satisfaction surveys showed that 93 percent of patients were comfortable or very comfortable with the system and 85 percent rated the care as good or excellent. Among hospital administrators, 100 percent felt that the level of care had increased or remained the same.[21]

While access to medical care in the United States has improved since 1999, when Henderson first imagined a telemedicine network that could distribute quality care to underserved populations, there are still many places with too few doctors and too much chronic disease. In Texas, for example, in 2015, thirty-five counties did not have a single physician. And in all of the United States, sixty million people, or one-fifth of the population, live in an area designated by the federal Health Resources and Services Administration as a Health Professional Shortage Area.

All of them could benefit from health-care delivery innovations like those that we observed among the Indian exemplars, and those that Kristi Henderson brought to fruition in the state of Mississippi. There is no need to reinvent the wheel.

Lessons from UMMC

Why worth replicating?

- Sixty million people in the United States (one-fifth of the population) live in places where there are shortages of health-care professionals. In addition to helping serve these underserved areas, telemedicine can be used by urban hospital networks to connect city hubs with suburban or satellite hospitals and facilities.

- Telemedicine not only lowers cost but also improves convenience and patient satisfaction, and throws a lifeline to rural hospitals that might otherwise have to shut down.

How to replicate?

- *Create a demand-driven network shaped by grassroots need:* Create a truly bottom-up (grassroots) approach that is demand-driven, not one that is top-down. Also, don't use a one-size-fits-all approach but, rather, customize to the needs of each geographic and demographic situation. Don't offer telehealth services for every specialty in every spoke. Tailor the offerings to the needs of the rural areas.

Also, do not cannibalize or compete with services already available in a spoke's neighborhood. UMMC found that rural hospitals were referring too many patients to UMMC for cardiology checkups, so that was an ideal candidate for teleconsults. But where specialists were already practicing near a rural hospital (say, dermatologists), UMMC didn't offer telehealth in that specialty.

- *Make telehealth affordable (so don't overinvest in technology):* Make telehealth financially viable under the prevailing regulatory framework, which may not reimburse teleconsultations. UMMC charged the spoke hospitals an affordable "availability fee" for use of teleservices but demonstrated that the benefits would exceed that fee.

- *Build relationships between specialists at the hub and staff in the spokes:* UMMC brought nurse practitioners from rural clinics to Jackson and put them through a rigorous training program so that they would know how to use telehealth. This also created strong relationships and trust between UMMC doctors and nurses in rural clinics, made it easier to share information across the network, and improved handoffs when patients had to be moved from spokes to UMMC. All this led to greater utilization of teleservices. (Keep in mind that the hospitals in Mississippi were independent operations, with some being private and others public, yet Kristi Henderson was able to create a smoothly functioning network.)

- *Pay attention to the human side of technology:* Telehealth is not just about mastering technology. It is more about organizational change. It is important to create win-win for everyone in the system so that they will embrace change. UMMC overcame several obstacles: doctors' concerns about quality control in remote consultations, rural hospitals' fear of losing their patients, doubts about the capabilities of nurse practitioners in rural hospitals, etc.

- *Use success with bottom-up innovations to catalyze top-down regulatory changes:* Build support with different stakeholders (hospitals, citizens, insurers, regulators, and local communities) to change legislation at the state level for reimbursement for teleconsults. Kristi Henderson approached legislators after establishing a track record of success, identifying pet projects of key legislators, and demonstrating how telehealth improved outcomes in those projects.

6.

Expanding Access for the Uninsured
Ascension Health

We currently have a US health-care system designed for middle-class America. I hope we can be part of redesigning that system to support everyone, including the most poor and vulnerable.[1]

–Anthony R. Tersigni, President and CEO, Ascension

In 1828, the Bishop of St. Louis sent a request to the Sisters of Charity in Emmitsburg, Maryland, a society of Catholic women that had been serving the sick and the poor since it was founded in Paris nearly two hundred years earlier. The bishop was concerned. He had seen the population of St. Louis triple in the past ten years to more than five thousand people, but there was no place to cure the sick or heal the injured. Would any of the Sisters of Charity consider taking their mission to the far side of the Mississippi?

As it turned out, four Sisters were willing to hazard the nearly 800-mile journey, and they set out with little more than a prayer and a wagon. The infirmary they founded was not only the first hospital west of the Mississippi; it was also the first Catholic health-care institution in the country, and the first hospital run by women. True to the mission of the Sisters of Charity, it promised to serve the sick regardless of their ability to pay.

The Sisters of Charity, later the Daughters of Charity, have since merged their St. Louis hospital with other Catholic hospitals, and a 1999 transaction between the Daughters of Charity National Health System and the Michigan-based Sisters of St. Joseph Health System gave birth to Ascension, a far-flung health-care system whose parental sponsor is an institution of the Roman Catholic Church known as Ascension Health Ministries. Since then, Ascension has undertaken a run of mergers and acquisitions, and the system now comprises 141 hospitals and 2,500 sites of care, making it the largest nonprofit health system in the United States and the largest Catholic health system in the world. With $32 billion in assets and nearly $23 billion in operating revenue in 2016, it was bigger than General Mills or Monsanto.

Despite this transformation, Ascension has remained faithful to the vision of the founding institution. Deeply grounded in its Catholic faith, Ascension resembles the Indian exemplars in its commitment to providing high-quality, low-cost health care especially to the poor and vulnerable, who were often uninsured. Ascension's mission statement explicitly cites the organization's duty to serve the underserved:

> *Rooted in the loving ministry of Jesus as healer, we commit ourselves to serving all persons with special attention to those who are poor and vulnerable. Our Catholic health ministry is dedicated to spiritually-centered, holistic care which sustains and improves the health of individuals and communities. We are advocates for a compassionate and just society through our actions and our words.*

And as with our Indian exemplars, Ascension's "social heart" is coupled with a "business brain" that fosters discipline and efficiency. Under the

leadership of Anthony Tersigni, Ascension's president and CEO, the organization has sought to become much more efficient at delivering health
care, not just to prepare for a future of value-based competition but also to
serve as many uninsured and underinsured people in its service areas as
possible. To safeguard continued service to the uninsured, Ascension had
to transform its operations in a scalable and financially sustainable way.

Ascension's cost innovations included merging several independent
Catholic hospitals to create national scale, devising protocols and sharing best practices, standardizing supplies across the system, centralizing
procurement and leveraging volume discounts, streamlining the supply chain, and improving equipment maintenance to extend the life of
capital investments. The resulting savings were off the charts. By 2016,
Ascension was saving $1 billion annually, or 5 percent of total revenues,
in the supply-chain area alone. It was enough to underwrite a sweeping
social-justice initiative: in 2016, Ascension adopted a policy of forgiv-
ing copayments for underinsured patients whose incomes were less than
four times the US poverty level, a strategy similar to that of the Indian
exemplars, who used a sliding scale to bill charges according to patients'
ability to pay. In both cases, an inspiring purpose motivated innovations and created a culture that sought to lower costs and improve quality in ways that the average hospital could not or did not care to match.

Ascension also sent a select group of employees to India to study the
practices of Narayana Health, and it joined Narayana in the Cayman
Islands venture to learn how to improve quality and lower costs dramatically. Ascension understood well the promise of reverse innovation.

In the Beginning

Ascension emerged at a complicated time in American health care.
Organized in 1999, Ascension had sixty-two acute-care hospitals by 2001.
That was the year the Institute of Medicine published its eye-opening

Crossing the Quality Chasm, which drew attention to disparities in access to quality care in the United States and to the overall mediocrity of care throughout the system, including many unsafe practices.[2] *Quality* was the buzzword of the day.

At the same time, Catholic hospitals were also beginning to make an unexpected run on the health-care-delivery market. For-profit hospitals (the number of which increased 46 percent from 2001 to 2011) grabbed the headlines, but Catholic hospitals (the number of which increased 16 percent during that same period) were also making headway. The total number of all other nonprofit hospitals was decreasing, including public hospitals (down 30 percent) and non-Catholic religious hospitals (down 41 percent).[3] With its Catholic pedigree and commitment to quality health care for all, Ascension found itself in the sweet spot. Within a year of its founding it had created a tagline that captured the company's positioning: "Healthcare That Works. Healthcare That Is Safe. Healthcare That Leaves No One Behind, for Life."

But the fledgling organization had a long way to go. Its future president and CEO, Anthony Tersigni, then serving as Ascension's COO, envisioned working with his colleagues to create a modern, well-integrated hospital system, but what Ascension actually had was a collection of aging community hospitals. Some were critical-access hospitals—that is, small, government-subsidized, acute-care hospitals located in isolated areas. Others were large city hospitals facing health-care costs rising at twice the rate of inflation. Many had been run by devoted religious women, some for more than a hundred years. These hospitals had no shortage of purpose, but many of them were dying. How to make the transformation to a modern hospital system?

The work fell to a committed team of leaders that included John Doyle, who joined Ascension's St. Vincent Indiana system in 1996 and later relocated to St. Louis to become chief strategy officer for the newly forming system. Doyle says the first couple of years were daunting, because unlike our Indian exemplars, who mostly built their own hospitals, Ascension had to work with the legacy operations and cultures in the hospitals it had acquired.

"In the beginning, no one knew if we could drive large-scale change through a system or not," Doyle told us. "What we had was a far-flung organization of sixty-seven hospitals that were still coming to grips with the notion that scale matters, and many weren't altogether certain that they wanted to be part of a system at all."[4]

Equally daunting, Doyle didn't see many examples of effective health-care systems in the United States. What he saw was a lot of waste and inefficiency.

"This country spends a lot of money on health care—$3 trillion a year—and the value really isn't there, at least on a comparative basis," says Doyle. "The US spends too much on a per capita basis, and yet many people are excluded. There was a clear understanding that in order for us to fulfill our mission, we had to change things. We had to identify where scale and leverage would make a difference. We had to figure out how to manage what we do well. More fundamentally, we had to figure out in the beginning if there really was potential for something called a 'health system' in the United States." In India, this obstacle did not arise. The health-care market there was underdeveloped, legacy interests were few, and government regulation was light. Narayana, for example, could go from a small cardiac hospital to a full-fledged hospital system in less than ten years. In America, things were different.

Bedsores, Best Practices, and the Bottom Line

Ascension chose a quality initiative for its first exercise in systems management. In 2002, Ascension launched a series of pilot programs whose purpose was twofold: first, to eliminate preventable injuries and deaths, and second, to test the organization's capacity for system-wide change.

"Ascension has been leading with quality since the beginning," said Dr. David Pryor, the chief clinical officer for Ascension.[5]

"We had to find one brave organization to step up and to say, 'We'll take that one on,'" Doyle told us. "We surmised that if we made progress on one of our priorities of action, we could bundle up the learning and move the approach throughout the system, and then we would start behaving more like a system. It is important to note that this inaugural effort was led by the physician staff. Anthony Tersigni set the tone when he made a commitment to the clinical leadership: 'If you lead,' he told them, 'we will follow.'"

The efforts were aimed at eight priorities of action: the safety goals and core measures promulgated by the Joint Commission on Accreditation of Healthcare Organizations (JCAHO, now known as the Joint Commission), preventable mortality, adverse drug events, falls, pressure ulcers, surgical complications, nosocomial infections, and perinatal safety. The initiative required every hospital in the Ascension system to focus on the first three priorities. It then assigned the remaining five priorities to one or two "alpha" sites, where staff developed a set of best practices. Hospitals were encouraged to work with leading organizations like the Institute for Healthcare Improvement (IHI) as they went through their lists.[6]

To determine the best ways to prevent pressure ulcers (bedsores), for example, Ascension worked with experts from IHI and the Wound, Ostomy and Continence Nurses Society (WOCN). Ascension did not have a particular problem with bedsores. At 7.6 percent, its system-wide prevalence was actually a bit below the national average at the time. Rather, Ascension pursued best practices as an exercise in organizational discipline and team building, and to bridge the "quality chasm." But like our Indian exemplars, Ascension had another motive: cost savings. Bedsores, for example, were expensive, costing US health-care consumers between $2.2 billion and $3.6 billion a year in acute-care settings alone.

Ascension chose as its pressure-ulcer alpha site one of its large hospitals, the 528-bed St. Vincent's Medical Center (now St. Vincent's Medical Center Riverside) in Jacksonville, Florida, where the prevalence of pressure ulcers was 5.7 percent, even lower than the system-wide average. The hospital assembled a large, diverse team, including a chief nursing officer, a nurse manager, an educator, a pharmacist, a dietician, two staff nurses, two WOCN registered nurses, a nurse from performance improvement, and a long-term-care nursing educator. That group reviewed available literature on best practices and then met with experts from IHI and WOCN to create a blueprint for change. The outcome was a set of prescribed interventions that were reviewed at weekly meetings attended by nursing directors and managers, clinical-resource coordinators, and unit champions.

The results? The incidence of pressure ulcers at St. Vincent's dropped 71 percent (to less than one percent) in the seven months from December 2004 to June 2005.[7] Once success had been demonstrated at the alpha site, the same solution was rolled out to all sixty-seven Ascension acute-care facilities.[8]

"One of the underlying and central lessons learned was that variation was the enemy of quality," says Doyle. "If our caregivers eliminated variation, performed consistently, we could further improve our ability to deliver outstanding, high-quality, lower-cost care."

And so it went on down through the checklist, with similar improvements demonstrated for the other seven quality priorities at other alpha sites. Nosocomial (that is, hospital-acquired) infections were cut in half. Birth trauma rates were dropped to or near zero. Falls were reduced by 9.9 percent. By June of 2004, the mortality rate at alpha sites had dropped 21 percent—6 percentage points better than the target and more than three years ahead of schedule. Equally encouraging, said Dr. Pryor, was the speed of implementation across the system.

"In two and a half years we found that together we could accomplish what had been a five-year goal of statistically eliminating preventable injuries and deaths," he says. "What happened was that when one brave hospital began making progress, its leaders would start talking to the others, and soon Ascension had a viral spread through the organization."

Cost savings followed soon thereafter, reaffirming an Ascension article of faith. As Rhonda Anderson, the CFO of Ascension's Healthcare division, put it, "We believe that quality really drives lower costs. The reduction of clinical variation decreases readmission rates and infection rates, which in turn lowers the cost of health care."[9] The quality improvements also reduced Ascension's risk ratings, which brought down the organization's insurance costs by about $60 million a year.

Cost Innovations, All Systems Go

The success of the quality initiative buoyed the organization, and the associated cost savings came at a good time, as health-care costs were rising again.

"This early success energized us," Doyle said. "Ascension started to think about how fragmented other aspects of our operations were, like our supply chain and our ability to care for our equipment."

Having primed the pump with the quality initiative, Ascension began a ten-year effort to transform the hospital system, pursuing strategies of centralization, standardization, and group purchasing that allowed it to streamline operations and maximize economies of scale. By 2014, Ascension's efforts had made a sizeable dent in the company's annual $4.5 billion nonpayroll operations budget.

Take purchasing, for example. In a 2010 review of its purchasing strategy, Ascension concluded that it didn't really have an effective purchasing *strategy* at all. Most of its hospitals were still buying from their own legacy suppliers, with whom they had little leverage. In food and environmental support services alone, for example, $400 million a year was going to more than a hundred different contracts. It didn't make sense to Scott Caldwell, CEO of the Resource Group, an Ascension subsidiary that had been created to tackle supply-chain problems like these.

"In our industry, a significant percentage of hospitals end the year with zero profit from operations while many vendors are making between 10–20 percent net profit," Caldwell has said.[10] "[This] creates a dynamic where the sellers of products and services, in terms of sheer financial size after years of double-digit profits, are significantly larger than the hospitals buying from them."

Caldwell calculated that Ascension could save between 10 percent and 15 percent a year by aggregating all of those contracts and negotiating from the strength of the combined operation. And he was right. Over the next two years, the Resource Group so convincingly earned its keep that Ascension decided to let it offer its purchasing expertise to all comers. In 2017, the Resource Group was overseeing a supply hub in Singapore and sourcing widely in Europe, and had become the second-largest health-care supply-chain-management company in the United States, with 2,500 participants. The savings to Ascension in supplies alone totaled $896 million a year: $676 million in supplies and $220 million in other nonpayroll expenses.

Ascension also began centralizing functions such as human resources, payroll, travel services, and finance under the Ascension Ministry Service Center in Indianapolis. "One Ascension," they called the new strategy, but the integration was easier said than done. For example, it took more than four years to move Ascension's then 131-hospital network to a single inventory-management system that used scannable bar codes.[11]

Ascension pursued efficiencies like these in every corner of its operations, leveraging its expertise as well as its national influence. For example, it convened doctors' councils to evaluate the quality of available surgical implants, and then leveraged its size to purchase the devices at the best price. It also pursued process innovations that resulted in cost savings.

Another interesting example was Ascension's approach to equipment maintenance. Ascension expanded an in-house service group at one of its hospitals into a full-service maintenance company called TriMedx, which then offered its services to all of Ascension's member hospitals, making it possible to increase the useful lives of the hospital group's medical devices and machines. TriMedx was so successful that Ascension spun it off as an independent for-profit enterprise, which in 2017 had 1,800 clients in twenty-eight states.

From the Indian perspective, Ascension's cost-cutting measures hardly seem radical, more like Business 101. But in the context of legacy American health-care systems, they were steps in the right direction—aimed at fairly obvious, low-stakes areas in which significant amounts of money could nonetheless be saved. Doyle noted that by 2017 Ascension's cost structure, relative to that of other health-care organizations, ranged from very competitive to near the top of the class:

"Ascension's supply costs are 16 percent of total revenues," Doyle told us. "That includes pharmaceuticals, even with the runaway inflation and aggressive pricing in the pharmaceutical industry. And our biomedical costs [i.e., equipment costs] are among the best in the country."

Serving the Poor and the Uninsured

As in the Indian cases, Ascension's cost-saving measures supported in very concrete ways the organization's mission to serve the poor. From its inception, Ascension spent about 3 percent of its revenues on direct charity care, a figure that was about average for the industry and which pretty much covered the need. But by 2009, just as health-care costs were rising for hospitals, insurance costs were skyrocketing for patients, to the point of unaffordability. In that year, the percentage of uninsured in the United States reached 15.7 percent, or nearly fifty million people.

The Affordable Care Act of 2010 helped drop the uninsured rate to 9.1 percent by 2015, but it also contributed to a 67 percent rise in deductibles during the same period. According to the Kaiser Family Foundation, more than half of all workers with individual coverage in 2016 had a deductible of at least $1,000. Workers in small firms actually fared worse. Overall, the percentage of workers in high-deductible plans had jumped to 29 percent from 20 percent two years earlier.[12]

The health-care landscape was looking more like that of India every day, and at Ascension, the consequences were plain to see. "We were finding that people would forgo care because they couldn't afford the deductible," Rhonda Anderson told us. "But providing care for the poor and the vulnerable is a common good. We have an obligation to carry out and sustain our mission in ways that do not perpetuate the marginalization of the poor."

Ascension's solution was to waive insurance deductibles and unpaid bills at all of its hospitals for patients earning less than 250 percent of the poverty level, and provide some level of financial support to patients earning up to 400 percent of the poverty level. The new policy added to Ascension's costs of providing relief to the poor.[13] Ascension also used cost savings to support a wide range of "community outreach" programs, such as free health-screening events in many of its communities. Ascension's outreach funds, which totaled about $500 million in 2016, supported everything from clothing drives to housing initiatives. In Detroit, its St. John Providence Hospital launched a program to improve job retention and eliminate health-care inequalities. In Mobile, Ascension's Providence Hospital partnered with a local food bank and supported community gardens. And in Baltimore, Saint Agnes Hospital began building a mixed-use community with living space for grandparents raising grandchildren.

"We are always looking for ways to improve the quality of life in our communities," Anderson says. "Our mission goes back hundreds of years: providing care for the poor and the vulnerable. It's part of Catholic social teaching."

The Passage to India

In 2009, John Doyle finally found the full-blown health-care model that Ascension was looking for, and he didn't find it in the United States. He found it in India.

Ascension's president and CEO, Anthony Tersigni, had recently returned from a business trip to Grand Cayman with some interesting news: an Indian health-care company called Narayana Health was planning to build a medical complex on the Caribbean island, about 450 miles from Miami. The Indian group was calling it Health City Cayman Islands (HCCI), and was talking about building a hospital, a medical school, and assisted-living facilities. Care was going to be first-rate, and prices would be a fraction of those charged in American hospitals. Tersigni asked Doyle and his team to find out more about it.

Doyle tracked down Narayana's founder and chairman, Devi Shetty (see chapter 4). Not surprisingly, Doyle and Shetty hit it off right away.

"We bonded based on the values of our organizations," Doyle remembers. "Both organizations have concern for the poor and vulnerable, and we both feel compelled to make services available to people in need regardless of their ability to pay, understanding the obvious difficulties of providing health care for all in a high-cost environment."

Shetty invited Doyle to come to India to see what Narayana had done there. "It was a life-changing experience," said Doyle, who at the time was serving as Ascension's general manager for transformation services. "It affirmed what Ascension's leaders had been saying for years—that if you want to see new forms of innovation, you need to talk to new people. If you keep talking to the same people, you'll keep getting the same answers. Similarly, if you want to find solutions, you have to look in places where there are extreme challenges. Places like India. As an organization, we had been pushing ourselves to be in places that are not usual for us, to find new people to collaborate with and new ideas that might work for us."

Shetty and Doyle immediately began sharing innovations. Narayana signed on with TriMedx, Ascension's medical-equipment-servicing company, and Ascension began testing iKare, Narayana's bedside clinical decision-support software. Ascension began sending physicians and administrators on trips to Bangalore, where Narayana had an open-door practice-sharing policy, to see what practices could be brought back to the United States. And in 2012, Narayana and Ascension signed a partnership agreement to build Health City Cayman Islands.

The partnership called for a $40 million equity investment split between Ascension and Narayana. For Ascension, it was a big opportunity to partner with and learn from a reputable health-care provider. The learning came fast. Accustomed to hospital construction costs in the United States, which then ranged from $1 to $2 million per bed, Ascension was interested to learn that Narayana expected to build a 104-bed hospital on Grand Cayman, an island with no native building materials, at only $700,000 per bed. Ascension spent about $1 billion on buildings each year and was looking for lessons in capex frugality, so the organization sent its building-management team to Cayman to watch and learn from the building operation there, starting from the ground up.

"That hospital building is the very model of efficiency," Doyle says. "Built to purpose, highly functional, and bright, it feels like a healing environment, and it does what it's supposed to do at half the cost we would pay here in the US. Dr. Shetty would say, 'John, we start every project as if we're poor and we're broke—*because we are!*' And every time he says that, I'm chagrined, because at Ascension we start every project like the $20 billion company that we are, and [encounter] all of the complexities that that implies. What Narayana offers is a mirror for an organization like Ascension."

Over the following few years, Ascension institutionalized the reverse-innovation process, assigning a full-time staff person to oversee the transfer of knowledge and sending more than a hundred people—doctors, administrators, and support staff—to Bangalore and Grand Cayman to see the Indian operation firsthand. By 2017, openness to new ideas, even foreign ideas, was becoming part of Ascension's DNA and leadership training.

"We hunger for innovation," Doyle told us. "We know we have to transform, and we believe ideas come from all kinds of places. When you see how people are being cared for at Narayana and having great outcomes, it opens your mind to another set of possibilities."

Chasing Value

Like the Indian exemplars, Ascension was an enterprise with a social heart and a business brain, and it was making its way toward value-based health care. Having laid the foundation in 2001, Tersigni and Ascension were ready to undertake new experiments to realize the vision of transforming US health care.

"We know that many of our communities struggle with the rising cost of health care," Anderson told us, "so we have to be on the cutting edge of new and inventive ways to manage the health-care dollar while providing quality care."

In 2015, Patricia Maryland, then Ascension's president of health-care operations and chief operating officer, led an initiative to identify "value-creation opportunities" to maximize economies of scale and improve quality of care. Maryland asked hospitals in several different markets to come up with a list of best practices in six areas of operation: facilities, clinical-process reliability, revenue cycle, physician-enterprise optimization, labor optimization, and IT optimization. The idea was to standardize those operations across the system and save the company $5.2 billion over five years.

Like Ascension's earlier quality initiatives, this value-creation effort exceeded targets, saving $78 million more than expected in the first year. Encouraged, Maryland expanded the scope of the initiative to five more, patient-centered areas: physician's practice, behavioral health, cardiology, oncology, and orthopedics.[14] Maryland's work was fast-tracked, and in July 2017 she was promoted to CEO of Ascension Healthcare.

This value orientation reflected the priority of Ascension's president, Anthony Tersigni. Long a proponent of affordable, high-quality, and accessible health care, Tersigni advocated for continued access to such care after the 2016 elections, taking his case directly to the transition team of incoming President Donald Trump. Chief among his proposals for bipartisan action was the goal to "accelerate the transformation of the health system from one that rewards volume to one that rewards value, which is necessary for reducing our system's unsustainable costs."[15] That same year, as the company was looking hard at various bundled-pricing options, Tersigni announced a goal of having 75 percent of Ascension's business operating under value-based payment arrangements by 2020.

As Tersigni took an increasingly public role in the American health-care debate, Ascension continued to make its health-care solutions available to other health systems through traditional information sharing in the press and at professional events, and through its many for-profit subsidiaries (such as the Resource Group) and spin-offs (such as TriMedx). Ascension also ramped up the work of its venture-capital subsidiary, Ascension Ventures, which in 2016 managed more than $800 million for a group of fifteen limited partners, all nonprofit health networks committed to providing care for the poor and vulnerable. The fund invested in biomedical and health-care-delivery companies, mostly startups, and shared the portfolio's research and innovations across the fund's partner base. The portfolio included such companies as ISTO Technologies, which used bone-regeneration technologies to rebuild aging knees and spines; Neurolutions, which developed brain-controlled devices to help stroke victims; and Atigeo, a big-data analytics company.

"Early on, the idea of a venture-capital fund inside a faith-based organization drew a lot of skepticism," said Doyle, who helped launch Ascension Ventures and who today is the president and CEO of Ascension Holdings and Ascension Holdings International. "But today Ascension Ventures is in the fourth funding and it currently demonstrates excellent performance on the financial side. The fund stimulates innovations that we think are important to the future. We see trends and solutions before others do, and we share them with our partners. Any initial skepticism has been replaced by enthusiasm, because it really does bring value to the organization."

"Matt Hermann, managing director of Ascension Ventures, under the leadership of Tony Speranzo, Ascension's chief financial officer, has created an incredible asset for our organization, partners, and health care more broadly to foster true innovation and development of new solutions for the future," said Tersigni.[16]

Still, like the four Sisters of Charity who struck out for Missouri in 1828, Ascension remains dedicated to Christ's call to a healing ministry that serves the poor and vulnerable, all and everywhere. A prayer, a wagon, a venture-capital fund—whatever it takes.

There is good evidence that Ascension has not let the good sisters down. In 2016, the Vatican asked Tersigni, who was the president of the International Confederation of Catholic Health Care Institutions, to help organize an International Conference on Global Health Disparities in 2017 at the Vatican. Tersigni considered this whole-new-world request, and humbly accepted the call.

In the next chapter, we turn to the challenge of improving quality, and how innovative thinking reinvented practices in a hospital called Iora Health.

One Way to Serve the Uninsured?

In India, several of the exemplars took into their own hands the problem of providing health care to the middle class and the poor. Rather than wait for the government to meet this need, they pursued a strategy of cost innovation that enabled them to generate higher margins on serving the well-to-do at prevailing prices, which then allowed them to provide free or subsidized care for many poor people. Ascension was doing exactly the same thing. In both India and the United States, the strategy worked because the organizations' inspiring purpose led employees to find innovative ways of improving quality, lowering cost, and expanding access—all at once.

Pacific Vision Foundation: Seeing Is Believing

In California, another nonprofit, Pacific Vision Foundation (PVF), was taking a leaf from the book of another Indian exemplar, Aravind, to bring free eye care to the poor and uninsured in the San Francisco Bay Area. The Robert Wood Johnson Foundation, which supported PVF's experiment with a $10 million loan, was hoping that if PVF succeeded in its efforts, the Aravind model could be applied to treat other medical conditions afflicting the uninsured poor.

Dr. Bruce Spivey, founder of PVF and founding president of the American Academy of Ophthalmology, was inspired by the vision and compassion of Aravind's founder, Dr. Govindappa Venkataswamy (known as Dr. V), whom he first met many years earlier during one of Dr. V's visits to the United States. During those visits, Dr. V would often say to surgeons, "Intelligence and capability are not enough. There must be the joy of doing something beautiful." Spivey wanted to bring that spirit and the Aravind model of ophthalmological care to the San Francisco Bay Area.

The Robert Wood Johnson Foundation (RWJF) helped launch Spivey's Pacific Vision Foundation with a $10 million low-interest loan in 2016.

RWJF expected the Pacific Vision Foundation to adopt two key elements of the Aravind model:

1. Maintain "very high efficiency . . . with surgical services located in a central facility, capitalizing on high patient flow, and systematically reducing and eliminating inefficiencies both inside the operating room and out;" and

2. Maintain "a keen focus on quality, customer satisfaction and value such that paying patients are attracted to the program, thereby generating revenues that can be used to subsidize low-income patients."[17]

PVF's plan was to integrate its operations with federally qualified community health centers in nine counties throughout the Bay Area in a hub-and-spoke pattern. The community health centers, which provided only primary care, had long referred patients with cataracts and other eye problems to area hospitals, but no one knew how many patients actually followed through with treatment. PVF planned to set up an eye clinic in one of these centers and send an ophthalmologist to visit on rotation. Taking a leaf from Aravind's book, PVF would arrange free transportation to and from the hub hospital for patients who needed surgical care, because most poor patients could not afford to spend the three or four hours it would take (each way) to get to and from the hospital using public transportation. Like Aravind, PVF also planned to create telemedicine links between PVF and the community clinics so that ophthalmologists could consult with patients remotely.

Spivey estimated that PVF's costs, including nursing care and OR expenses (but excluding the surgeon's fee), would be about $500 for each free surgery. He was hoping to engage eager ophthalmology residents and junior surgeons to perform the surgeries for free. These free surgeries were projected to total from five hundred to seven hundred a year, or 10 percent of all surgeries performed at PVF. In due course, PVF might hire junior ophthalmologists on its own payroll to perform free surgeries.

Spivey knew that some of Aravind's practices, such as simultaneous surgeries, wouldn't fly in US hospitals, but he believed other practices would be transferable. He was confident, for instance, that he could steer a large volume of cases to PVF, reduce the turnaround time between surgeries, and reduce the time required to prepare patients for surgery.

"Our model is really a cross between Aravind and LV Prasad Eye Institute," Spivey told us.[18] Like LV Prasad, Spivey's PVF would rely on donations, government support, and the community-care obligations of a leading local hospital rather than on self-financing, as Aravind did. But like Aravind, PVF would strive for high operational efficiency.

The Robert Wood Johnson Foundation had a much bigger idea. It saw PVF as a test case for Indian health-care innovations that could address a wide range of other medical conditions and remedy the current societal condition of separate and unequal care for the poor. If the Aravind model worked for eye care for the uninsured, RWJF hoped to replicate that model to treat poor and uninsured patients with other problems, ranging from orthopedic to dermatologic to psychiatric.

Universal Health Care Is within Reach in the United States

The Ascension and PVF examples should make us rethink the direction of US policy. Debates about health-care reform in Washington, DC, tend to focus on how health insurance can be extended to the uninsured. While this is a laudable effort, it does little to control the spiraling cost of health care in the United States, which has become increasingly unaffordable even to those with health insurance. Ascension and PVF demonstrate an alternative solution to the problem—one in which hospitals can strive for greater efficiency in serving the insured in order to free up resources to care for the uninsured.

To put the US challenge in perspective, keep in mind that the Indian exemplars were able to treat one or two free patients for every paying patient and still be profitable—despite charging ultra-low prices. In contrast, in the United States, the uninsured account for roughly 10 percent of the total population and prices for medical care are among the highest in the world. Surely, US hospitals can find enough opportunities for cost savings to subsidize one patient in ten.

The real challenge in the United States, in our view, is to imbue American health-care organizations with the kind of purpose that inspired the Indian exemplars and organizations like Ascension and Pacific Vision Foundation. US health-care organizations need to rediscover the values and sense of purpose that attracted many employees to the health-care profession in the first place.

Lessons from Ascension

Why worth replicating?

- US hospitals are laggards in operations management, including supply-chain management. Modifying processes to improve outcomes can save billions of dollars that can be used to care for the uninsured and to provide relief on copays and deductibles for the underinsured—or just to prepare for a future of value-based competition where efficiency and cost will matter a great deal.

- If all big hospitals adopted Ascension's approach to operational excellence and efficiency, the resulting savings would be more than enough to care for all the uninsured in the United States and then some.

How to replicate?

- *Use an inspiring purpose to drive innovation and collaboration:* Health professionals and nonprofit organizations have a strong commitment to serving people. Leverage these traditions to turbocharge organizational collaboration and to drive breakthrough innovations that can free up resources for taking care of more uninsured and underinsured patients.

- *Lead with physician staff:* Doctors and nurses are key change agents. If they are involved in and committed to finding solutions, they can smooth the way for effective execution. Don't work around these groups. Work with and through them.

- *Use scale not just for market power but also to dramatically lower cost:* Many hospital mergers are motivated by the desire to build bargaining power vis-à-vis insurers, but scale should also be used to improve efficiency, by standardizing protocols and procedures and by centralizing functions such as procurement and support services.

- *Start small, and then spread what works:* Find volunteer alpha sites with multifunctional teams to take on new initiatives, improve processes, reduce complications and readmissions, etc. Then spread across the entire system those things that work. Small wins can lead to big wins.

- *Create an independent venture group:* Consider creating a separate unit to pursue new ventures and radical ideas that may not fit with or take root within the core organization but that can nonetheless help improve performance and prepare the organization for the future. Consider spinning off successful new ventures so that they can serve external as well as internal customers.

7.

Improving Quality
Iora Health

In 1902, the fastest ship took more than a month to cross the Atlantic. Suppose you wanted to travel faster. The conventional approach would be to ask the boat builders to study the tides and streamline the hull or build bigger and faster engines. Even after a hundred years of doing that, the fastest ship today takes four days. What we would have needed was an entirely new solution—an airplane. I would postulate that we are in exactly the same situation with US health care. The redesign must be very different than the current model, because you can't build an airplane by sticking wings on a ship.

—Rushika Fernandopulle, Founder and CEO, Iora Health

Sharon Callahan was fifty-five, and she was sick and tired of feeling sick and tired. Forty years of smoking had left her with a case of chronic obstructive pulmonary disease (COPD) so severe that to be on time for a 10:30 doctor's appointment, she would have to start getting ready at 6:30. Just getting out of bed often left her short of breath, and getting fully dressed could take an hour. Walking to her car took another hour, and then she had to drive into Boston and sit in the waiting room until the doctor could see her. In Sharon's world, a doctor's appointment was an all-day affair, and there were way too many such appointments.

Over the years Sharon had accumulated a dispensary's worth of treatments to help her breathe more easily: inhalers, steroids, an oxygen tank in her living room. If those treatments helped at all, it wasn't apparent to Sharon, who had also been diagnosed with diabetes, hypertension, acid reflux, and osteoporosis. She had twenty-seven open prescriptions and was taking more than a dozen pills a day. She had survived a minor heart attack and a blood clot in her lung, and her doctors were now concerned about squamous cell lung cancer.

That year, Sharon spent nine months in hospitals and rehab and bounced around from cardiologist to pulmonologist to endocrinologist to internist to gastroenterologist—twelve specialists in all. None of these specialists conferred with the others, and her primary care physician seldom saw her anymore. Like many of the chronically ill, Sharon was stumbling through the hallways of specialty care, pretty much on her own, racking up $200,000 in medical bills a year.

It was Sharon's daughter who recommended that she try Iora Health, a new primary care practice that took a different approach, one that borrowed liberally from the task-shifting practices observed in developing nations by company cofounder and CEO Rushika Fernandopulle. In Fernandopulle's view, reducing unnecessary emergency-room visits, surgeries, and medications—all of which resulted in overutilization of health care by patients like Sharon—was the key to simultaneously improving the quality of health care *and* lowering costs dramatically.

A Doctorpreneur Is Born

As a student at Harvard Medical School, Fernandopulle was frustrated by the inefficiencies and outright failures he saw in the American medical system. How could the United States spend more than twice as much on health care as other free-market democracies and yet have worse outcomes?

Most galling was a number so small it was frequently overlooked: 4 percent. That was how much of every US health-care dollar was spent on primary care, Fernandopulle's chosen field of medicine. *Four percent.* To Fernandopulle this meant that 96 percent of every health-care dollar was being spent on problems that primary care failed to address. The conventional primary care model seemed ridiculous: greet patients, ask a few questions, run some simple tests, and then pass the patients on to higher-paid specialists who collected a fee for every service they performed. It was the same system that left Sharon wandering the hallways of secondary and tertiary care. No wonder primary care was low paying, carried little prestige, and was chronically short of doctors.

And yet Fernandopulle knew that many of the chronic conditions that so overburden secondary and tertiary care—obesity, diabetes, hypertension, alcoholism, heart disease, emphysema, and others—can be addressed very powerfully by education and prevention efforts at the community level and in the primary care office. He had seen intensive interventions work in health-care systems outside the United States—in the Caribbean, in Africa, and in Southeast Asia. A big-picture thinker by nature, Fernandopulle resolved to put the *primary* back in US primary care. He was twenty-five.

According to Fernandopulle, "I went into health care to help people, and it was clear that our current system doesn't allow us to do this. Indeed, I think it is immoral that we allow such crappy care despite spending such an obscene amount of money. Our goal isn't just better care for our patient, but to raise the bar and challenge everyone to dramatically up their game."[1]

Not yet a doctor at the time, Fernandopulle was already thinking like an entrepreneur and challenging the competition. His goal was not just to carve out a bigger niche for primary care physicians but to *disrupt* the system, to wrest control of some of the dollars currently tied up in the overbuilt, overbilled, and overmedicalized segments of the US health-care system—secondary and tertiary care—and reinvest those dollars in primary care in ways that could save significantly on downstream spending.

For the past seven years he has done just that, building Iora Health as a network of primary care practices that caters both to the healthy and to the chronically ill, using a model that relies on (1) intensive task-shifting from doctors and nurses to health coaches, (2) a capitated flat-fee payment system, and (3) a custom-built IT platform that puts patients' needs over billing codes. Fernandopulle predicted that if participating health plans would double their spending on primary care, they would save three to ten times that on specialist visits, diagnostics, procedures, drugs, emergency-room visits, and hospitalizations.

And he was right. Five years after its launch, in 2011, Iora had reduced hospitalizations for its members by 40 percent and cut total health-care spending by 15 percent to 20 percent—far beyond the 4 percent needed for breakeven. Other measures of success—including clinical outcomes and patient and staff retention—were equally impressive. In late 2017, Iora had twenty-four locations in eight cities, employed four hundred people, and had attracted nearly $125 million in venture capital. It was a fast-moving enterprise that sought to turn the American health-care-delivery system on its head, putting primary first.

Purpose

Similar to the Indian exemplars, Iora Health embodies the principles of task-shifting, leveraging technology, and moving toward a hub-and-spoke network. Most remarkably, Rushika Fernandopulle is one of the most purpose-driven individuals we've met. Under his leadership, Iora has the potential to disrupt the American health-care system more force-fully than any of the established US health-care players.

Born in Sri Lanka and raised in Baltimore, Fernandopulle had a cosmopolitan upbringing. A government major at Harvard College and a self-proclaimed "systems guy," he studied ethnic conflicts in Sri Lanka and Northern Ireland. Later, at Harvard Medical School, he saw similar conflicts arising between the entrenched American medical establishments and increasingly pressing demands for cost-cutting and for patient-centered health care. A bell went off.

"I went to medical school when managed care was sweeping through," Fernandopulle told us. "Doctors were sitting around complaining, and I realized that this was a systems problem, too, like ethnic conflict. I also knew we could fix this problem, but it would take some kind of system-level change."[2]

Instead of complaining, Fernandopulle began a dogged search for solutions. He studied the work of two people he greatly admired, Paul Farmer and Jim Kim, the cofounders of Partners in Health, which had delivered quality health care at ultra-low cost in Haiti and several other developing countries. He went on medical missions of his own to developing countries, such as the Dominican Republic and Malaysia, where he took special note of the role of village-based community-health workers. Subsequently he interacted with a couple of Indian doctorpreneurs, Dr. Aravind Srinivasan and Dr. Devi Shetty, and was impressed by how their models focused on low-income patients, how they created new classes of health workers, and how they never stopped looking for better ways of doing everything.

Fernandopulle noted that as in India, health workers in the Dominican Republic and Malaysia were not doctors. In fact, they had little medical training. They were just local people, mostly women, who checked in with their neighbors periodically to advise them on how to manage a pregnancy, treat common ailments, or eat healthfully. When they visited families, they might bring along a chalkboard or some pamphlets. As Fernandopulle saw it, they had two assets that were every bit as valuable as medical credentials: interpersonal skills and the community's trust.

They didn't *deliver* health care so much as *facilitate* it. They were changing health care from the bottom up.

But how also to effect change from the top down? To answer that question, Fernandopulle took a leave of absence from medical school, went back across the Charles River, and got a master's degree in public policy from Harvard's Kennedy School of Government. He then returned to medical school to finish his MD. As his training progressed, he continued to travel the world, exploring medical practices in South Africa, Russia, and Sri Lanka. Everywhere he went, he watched and listened, considering the possibility that novel health-care practices from the unlikeliest corners could be carried by reverse innovation into the most advanced reaches of the developed world.

"Having a broader perspective is useful," Fernandopulle said. "You come to know that the typical US acute-care model is not the only one out there. There are other ways to do this. And the learning isn't always unidirectional, where we in the West teach other people how to do things. Many things happen in places that don't have the constraints or the resources that we have, and we can learn from them."

Fernandopulle's wide-ranging curiosity and Mr. Fix It determination carried him to, and up the ranks of, the Advisory Board Company, the Washington-based health-care consulting group, from which he was recruited to lead the Interfaculty Program for Health Systems Improvement at Harvard. There his personal mission became clear. He wanted to do what doctors, he says, are *supposed* to do: keep people healthy by building long-term relationships, not just treating them when they are sick, in seven-minute increments, on a transactional fee-for-service basis.

Translated to a systems level, that personal mission became a fiercely disruptive resolve. When asked for a moonshot statement for Iora Health ten years out, Fernandopulle was characteristically bold. "Our mission is to transform US health care, and we will do that through consumer-centric, value-based care," he told us. "And we're going to do it everywhere."

Taking a Chance on Casino Workers

Change everywhere had to start somewhere, and for Fernandopulle it meant looking for a loose brick in the ossified health-care system—some player willing to take a chance with a new way of providing health care. He found it in 2006 with a group of self-insured casino workers in Atlantic City. The year before, he had launched a pilot project called Renaissance Health using $250,000 in angel money from David Bradley, founder of the Advisory Board. Renaissance targeted self-insured employers in struggling economic communities because they cared about cost control and would give Fernandopulle room to innovate. The casino workers union, Local 54, fit the bill, and so did a local hospital, AtlantiCare.

Fernandopulle asked for their sickest members—the ones with the highest health-care costs, the housekeepers with hypertension, the bus-boys with drug problems—to serve as a test group for a new model of primary care, and then set out to verify his ideas. He hired community-based "health-care partners" to educate patients and monitor their care in outpatient settings. He experimented with a hybrid payment system that charged both a flat monthly "care-coordination fee" and fees for certain services. He did the best he could by adding onto the IT system used by the local hospital.

The goal was to provide intensive and compassionate primary care to vulnerable populations while saving on downstream costs, and the outcomes were impressive. Twelve months in, data showed that high-needs patients had 40 percent fewer emergency-room visits and 25 percent fewer medical procedures, as compared with a control group. Fernandopulle had his proof of concept, but he was encountering resistance, especially from his hospital partner, which was uncomfortable with the health coaches (who had no medical training) and was worried about loss of income for its own ER and physician specialists. They felt Fernandopulle was too ambitious, that he was trying to change too many things at once.

Fernandopulle, typically, worried that he was thinking too *small*. He pulled up stakes and headed back to Boston, looking for bigger imaginations and deeper pockets. There he teamed up with Chris McKown, a cofounder of the health-data-analysis company Health Dialog. Together they raised $6.25 million from three venture-capital firms and, in early 2011, launched Iora Health.

"Rushika is exceptional in a bunch of ways," said Liam Donohue of .406 Ventures, one of those investors. "He is so passionate about what needs to happen. He's incredibly smart, and he really doesn't compromise. He will say, 'We don't have to do things this way. Let's do it the right way,' and he won't quit till he's done it. That's important."[3]

Fernandopulle explained why it was important to create a for-profit venture to realize his dreams. "Ten years ago, when I started doing this, I was thinking of it as a nonprofit," he said. "I went to all the nonprofit funders and they said, 'This is too ambitious. You're changing too many things. We'll give you a little money to study it.' But too many people trying to innovate have messed around on a small scale, with little pilots. The game changer here is that people like us are now able to attract venture capital and private-equity money. Our model of change is not to change doctors directly. It's to get patients to vote with their feet. When that happens, all the others will wake up."

Like Devi Shetty of Narayana Health, Fernandopulle realized that charity was not scalable. To make his vision a reality, Iora needed not only a "social heart" but also a "business mind."

Cost Savings, Frugality, and Capitation

Fernandopulle used his $6.25 million to perfect the business model for Iora Health. He opened four flagship offices, each in partnership with a self-insured employer or union-benefits manager. The offices were in Hanover, New Hampshire (in partnership with Dartmouth College); Las

Vegas, Nevada (with the Culinary Health Fund); Brooklyn, New York (with the Freelancers Union); and Boston, Massachusetts (with the New England Carpenters Benefits Funds). To staff Iora, Fernandopulle recruited physicians who shared his values (he was flooded with applications from doctors equally frustrated with the current model), and brought in some nontraditional staff—nurse practitioners, social workers, nutrition counselors, and a new category of worker called health coaches—on the theory that primary care must be waged as a team effort.

The biggest challenge was the payment system. Fernandopulle loathed the American fee-for-service system—not just the paperwork, the coding games, and the endless pressure to order unnecessary tests, but the waste of money. In his view, the fee-for-service system rewarded doctors for keeping people sick. He had tried a hybrid payment system in Atlantic City, but it hadn't worked, so at Iora he went all out—no fees, no coinsurance, no copays, nothing to stand in the way of a patient receiving care. Instead, he charged the health plans a flat monthly fee per member, the total pegged at twice the insurer's historical spending on primary care, which was typically from 4 percent to 5 percent of the insurer's annual outlay per member.

This capitated payment system saved money immediately on administrative costs, and it also encouraged cost-saving measures to make the most of the flat-fee dollars. Iora clinics, for example, performed many of their own lab tests and processed their own blood work, which was cheaper and faster than sending samples out. But the big savings came later. In instituting the capitated payment system, Fernandopulle was betting that intensive, creative, frugal-minded primary care would pay off in the long run—small money down, but big savings in downstream costs. For high-needs patients with chronic conditions, he expected to see returns in the first year. The return for healthier patients would take longer.

"For many years, the discussion in US health-care delivery was all about patient satisfaction and health-care quality, but cost was not to be discussed," said Eric Wadsworth, codirector of the Master of Health Care Delivery Science program at Dartmouth and a longtime observer of Iora. "The truth is, there is no cost accounting in health care in the United States. The doctor and the nurses usually can't tell you the costs of the services they order. They can't even tell you how much they charge for their own procedures. Somebody has to look that up for you."[4]

But Fernandopulle knew. Why? Because every dollar he could save his partners in fees for ultrasounds, dialysis, bypass surgeries, and other secondary and tertiary care was a dollar of buy-in for his capitated fee. In fact, Fernandopulle had shined a light on costs in ways that made his specialist colleagues and local hospitals uncomfortable. After a presentation to a group of community hospitals, an audience member angrily demanded to know how Fernandopulle intended to "make him whole" for the loss of admissions in his hospital beds. Fernandopulle just laughed.

"That's not my problem, and it shouldn't be any of our problem," he told us. "The purpose of the health-care system is not to prop up hospitals. The purpose of the health-care system is to serve patients and keep them healthy. We forget that at our peril."

To bolster the organization's commitment to primary care, Fernandopulle resolved not to mix capitation patients with fee-for-service patients. Other organizations did so, using a hybrid model in which the two types of patients could be comingled. But Fernandopulle believed that doing so would muddy the culture and confuse caregivers. He felt that to do primary care right you had to go all-in for the capitation payment model. This was not an easy decision, because taking on fee-for-service patients would have improved Iora's finances in the short run—but destroyed its distinctiveness in the long run. Accordingly, Fernandopulle sought investors who understood this strategy and were willing to wait patiently for long-run returns.

Task-Shifting: Health Coaches

The most novel members of the Iora team were the health coaches, the cheerleaders and facilitators who helped to execute the doctor's treatment plan in frequent, personalized, one-on-one encounters with patients. They were the face of the practice, encountering patients dozens of times a year. Their job was to proactively manage each patient's health and intervene the moment trouble arose, especially with chronic-care patients, whose biggest—and costliest—issue was compliance (or, really, health problems associated with noncompliance). And while some competitors assigned health coaches only to their sickest patients, Iora assigned one to every patient. Fernandopulle wanted each patient to be as healthy as he or she could be in the long run.

Similar to the rural women who made up 64 percent of Aravind's workforce and to the community-health workers ("vision guardians") trained to carry out basic vision tests for LV Prasad, Iora's health coaches typically came to patient care with no prior medical training at all. In their previous lives they worked at places like Sears and Home Depot and Dunkin' Donuts. And, like the Indian exemplars, Iora surrounded primary care physicians with health coaches, freeing the physicians up to do well the things that only doctors can do.

To members of the medical establishment, these health coaches might look like losers. Some had only high school degrees. But they had cultural fluency. They lived in the neighborhoods where they worked, they spoke the patients' languages, and they understood the patients' difficulties. They had "emotional intelligence," and to Fernandopulle, that was what mattered. He recruited for empathy and trained for skill, and he set a very high bar. In fact, of the 25,000 applicants for health-coach jobs, Iora hired only about 250. "It's a 1 percent acceptance rate," Fernandopulle pointed out. "It's harder than getting into Harvard!"

The work was hard, too. It required imagination, compassion, humor, and doggedness, and it defied an easy job description. Health coaches did some work that doctors did, like reviewing charts and meds. They did some work that nurses and techs did, sometimes taking vital signs or drawing blood. But mainly they did work that no one else in primary care did. They developed a "worry score" for every patient. They followed up on every sick visit. They took diabetic patients to the grocery store and helped them shop for food. They did med checks, led Zumba classes, and ran smoking-cessation clinics. They served as confidants, cheerleaders, and friends—dispensing high fives and tough love in equal measure.

Fernandopulle loved to tell their stories. In Atlantic City a coach programmed the clinic's phone number into all the patients' phones, so they wouldn't make needless calls to 911. A patient in the same practice came in with out-of-control diabetes and such severe hypertension that she wasn't even going to work. Six months later, everything looked fine. When Fernandopulle asked if his medical skills were responsible for the improvement, she told him he had nothing to do with it: she just didn't want to let her health coach, Millie, down. In Las Vegas a health coach helped a hypertensive teenager give up Cheetos and lose fifty pounds before football tryouts.

And in Revere, Massachusetts, a health coach visited Sharon Callahan at home and helped her throw out most of her meds. Fernandopulle had reviewed Sharon's voluminous medical chart and determined that twenty of her twenty-seven medications were costing her money but doing her little good. She could also reduce the number of specialists she was seeing from twelve to two, eliminating most of the medical appointments she so dreaded. Fernandopulle persuaded the remaining specialists to call him with an update after each appointment with Sharon, and Sharon trusted the coach to manage the rest. For the first time in years, Sharon felt comfortable with her medical care.

Iora hired four health coaches for every doctor, paying them a fifth of a doctor's salary and half a nurse's. Because some of the more menial tasks were handed off to the health coaches, doctors and nurses could be more productive. As the task-shifting practices of the Indian exemplars had demonstrated, there were cost savings here, to be sure, but that was not why Fernandopulle did it. He did it because the coaches were better at what they did than anyone else on the team—and because they loved it. Iora's approach was not just cheaper. It was also better.

Liam Donohue told the story of an Iora holiday party at which health coaches stood up to speak about the personal rewards of their job. "These people were so excited that their skill set could have relevance in improving someone's life in a really meaningful way," recalled Donohue. "People got up and wept. They were literally crying as they described patients they had helped. It was incredibly moving and very different from a lot of [health-care] companies I've seen. The sense of purpose and reward from primary care just flows through the company."

Task-Shifting: The Big Picture

Fernandopulle saw the health coaches as Iora's pivotal players, levers that switch the tracks for all that follows. In fact, Iora was all about task-shifting. Fernandopulle thought primary care was caught in a downward spiral—accorded just 4 percent of total health-care spending and with insurers ratcheting down payments, which meant that primary care visits would have to be even shorter, making care worse and hospitalizations higher. It made no sense. Iora's strategy was to turn this vicious cycle into a virtuous cycle, by investing more in primary care with well-designed systems, IT, and culture. He wanted to keep specialists away from routine cases and people away from hospitals, thereby lowering total health-care costs and freeing up even more resources for primary care.

In other words, at the system level, Iora shifted much of the work of patient care from the secondary and tertiary segments of the delivery system back to the primary care office. Within that office, Iora also shifted work, from the primary care physician to a care team that included not only a doctor and nurse but also, typically, a health coach and a social worker, and perhaps also a mental-health counselor, a nutritionist, and a patient advocate. These were examples of "down-shifting" and "share-shifting" of tasks, and they served to make Iora Health practices less hierarchical and more collaborative than most physicians' practices, as well as more cost-efficient.

The health coaches added something like "in-shifting" to the mix, bringing traditional community-health supports into the doctor's office. Their job titles were new, but much of what the health coaches offered was like old-fashioned advice from the corner grocer, or the old family remedy your auntie talked about, or the gruff encouragement of a high school coach, or the reassurance of a rural general practitioner during a house call. Iora was recapturing the social context of health as experienced by earlier generations in America—and by many in developing countries today—and recreating that social connection within the primary care physician's orbit. The shifting of tasks added cultural capital to the Iora primary care tool kit, while also contributing to local job creation, just as it did for Aravind's village women in India.

Another task-shifting practice at Iora mirrored what we saw at a Narayana Health hospital in Mysore, where patients and family members were trained to help with postoperative nursing care. At Iora, patients were increasingly asked to manage some of their own care. Coaches taught patients how to monitor their own blood pressure and insulin levels and then how to teach those same skills to others. This empowered patients and cut delivery costs. Fernandopulle's philosophy was to engage patients in medical decision making and enable them to "own" responsibility for their health.

The effect of all this task-shifting at Iora was a reduction of overall costs for the payers, better delivery of care and better job satisfaction for the providers, and improved health outcomes for the patients.

It was just the kind of high-quality, low-cost dynamic we saw in the Indian exemplars, with equally beneficial results for the most vulnerable populations.

Leveraging Technology

Like Narayana Health and HCG Oncology, Iora leveraged technology to simultaneously improve quality and lower cost. Iora's capitated payment system allowed it to sidestep the usual model for maintaining electronic medical records, which was built on traditional billing codes. Instead, Iora built a truly patient-centered care platform, called Chirp, that alerted team members when lab results were out of an acceptable range; that allowed providers to set personal goals for patients, rather than having to follow standardized medical goals; and that accommodated flexible scheduling with more than one provider, such as a primary care physician and a health coach. Patients and their families could use Chirp to access their own medical records and to share notes through the portal with their care team, including via mobile devices.

Initially, Fernandopulle tried to add these features to existing IT systems in partner hospitals and insurance companies, but this did not work. Hospitals designed their IT systems around fee-for-service billing practices, and any modifications were shaped by Medicare's expectations for the use of electronic medical records. Fernandopulle said in exasperation that because these large players pay for lobbyists, "they get the rules written in their favor, and these things never work. So, we're building our own IT platform, and we are in a position to ignore the government rules. We do what's best for patients."

Fernandopulle invested in a clean-slate IT system that consumed a large part of Iora's startup investment. By 2016, the system was in good shape and ready to be rolled out in new centers as Iora scaled up its operations. Iora used data mining and analytics to improve its proactive interventions—for individual patients as well as for the population as a whole.

Fernandopulle also leveraged technology to improve communication links between patients and Iora. In traditional fee-for-service arrangements, consultations by telephone are not billable, but under the flat fee that Iora received, there was every incentive for doctors to use cheap, efficient communication technologies such as email, Skype, or even telephones.

Five years after Iora's launch, Fernandopulle was seeing the kind of quality results he hoped for. First there was the net promoter score (NPS), which measured customer loyalty. When patients were asked how likely it was that they would recommend Iora to a friend or colleague, Iora's NPS was consistently over 90 percent, as compared with scores in the range of 3 percent to 5 percent for other primary care centers. This loyalty was also reflected in Iora's patient-retention rate (excluding involuntary departures) of 98 percent. Second, clinical outcomes were also good. For example, 90 percent of Iora's hypertension patients got their blood pressure under control (versus the industry average of 60 percent). Third, Fernandopulle tracked downstream spending. Relative to a control group, Iora's approach led to a 40 percent drop in hospitalization and a 30 percent to 40 percent drop in ER visits, which together reduced total health-care expenditures by 15 percent to 20 percent. Fourth, Iora's rate of employee attrition was only 2.5 percent, unheard of in the industry. Finally, financial health was improving as well. After "burning through money" (in Fernandopulle's words) for several years, the four original practices were profitable by late 2016. The company as a whole had yet to enter the black, however, and it won't, says Liam Donohue, the investor, until Iora can scale up to at least forty health centers operating at capacity.

Nevertheless, even without having attained overall profitability, Iora's business model got a strong seal of approval from investors, when the company's series D funding in October 2016 raised $75 million for further expansion and investment in Chirp. The lead investor in this round was Singapore's Temasek, the government-owned investment fund with deep pockets and an excellent track record of past investments, which signaled that the Iora model might someday be adopted in other parts of the world, including possibly Singapore.

Scaling Up to Hub-and-Spoke

Some particularly good financial news was that one of Iora's biggest expenses, the several million dollars it had spent for a custom IT platform, was starting to bear fruit. The platform was capable of supporting Iora's ambitious growth plans as it scaled up rapidly. More important, it would enable Iora to build a unique hub-and-spoke system. Fernandopulle could tap the expertise of medical specialists without sending his patients to them and without bringing them in house. The idea arose in the context of diabetes management. Fernandopulle asked the head of endocrinology at Dartmouth-Hitchcock Medical Center what percentage of endocrinology-clinic patients could be managed by a primary care physician with a little expert advice by phone or email. The answer was eye-opening: 80 percent.

Going forward, Iora planned to make more use of specialists as consultants, essentially inviting cardiologists and nephrologists, for instance, to join the gig economy—that is, to work for Iora as and when needed, for a consultative fee. Iora's strategy was not to lower costs by withholding access to specialists but, rather, to call on specialists only if better coordination of relatively inexpensive primary care could not do the job.[5] It might seem like a radically disruptive practice, but from Fernandopulle's perspective, it was just common sense. When he gazed out at the landscape of US medical care, he saw an industry that was ripe for strategic deconstruction: one that was overbuilt, overstocked, and overpriced.

"We need to shut bed towers," Fernandopulle said. "And what's interesting, and a little ridiculous, is you go to any hospital in this country and you see cranes building new beds."

A more efficient system, he believed, would have fewer beds, so why not pluck particular components from overbuilt hospitals and use them as needed rather than vertically integrate into running company-owned hospitals? First up, he planned to rent hospital beds when his practice needed them, and only when his practice needed them. Think Airbnb for medical care.

"I need to control what happens to my people when they go downstream," Fernandopulle told us. "If you own the control point, which is primary care, everything else is a commodity. We're going to buy on the spot market. We're going to control the relationship to be able to optimize it, but I don't want to own it." It's a breathtaking inversion of the old order, one in which primary care calls the shots.

Iora is on the cusp of building a hub-and-spoke system from the spoke up, unlike Indian hospitals, which built such systems from the hub down. Given the surplus of beds and specialists in the United States, Fernandopulle saw no value in owning a hub's high-fixed-cost assets. He was quite happy for the tail to wag the dog.

Curiously, Fernandopulle was willing to own one thing that everyone else in health care was trying like mad to avoid: risk. Specifically, he wanted to own the risk that Iora's business model could fail, and he wanted to be well paid for taking it. Iora was already working with partners, including Humana, to capture a portion—and eventually all—of any downstream savings.

"We're saying, 'Tell you what. Why don't you just give us the whole health-care dollar and let us take care of it,'" Fernandopulle told us. "If we cost more, we pay it. But if we cost less, we keep it. That's changed our economics, because all of a sudden when we're generating these big surpluses, it's our money."

Similar to the approach of Indian exemplars, Fernandopulle extended his radical business model to save money and improve outcomes for the poor or uninsured. In 2014, Iora partnered with Grameen America (the US arm of the Bangladeshi microfinance organization started by Nobel laureate Muhammad Yunus) to offer primary care to immigrant communities in the New York City area for a low monthly charge of $49 per person.

Disruption Ahead

Beyond Iora's tolerance for risk, there still loomed one troubling question about the ability of Iora's model to effect system-level savings. Most observers agreed that major downstream savings would not materialize until hospital capacity shrank. And as Fernandopulle knew, that wasn't likely to happen until the egos of hospital CEOs shrank. No one expected that to happen soon.

In the meantime, Iora was experiencing some predictable bumps in the road as established interests pushed back against the upstart. Iora regularly received cease-and-desist letters from outfits trying to quash its recruiting efforts. In Las Vegas, a big health system required its doctors to sign three-year, ten-mile noncompete agreements, effectively boxing out Iora's two local practices. Even at Dartmouth-Hitchcock Medical Center, which had long had an academic interest in Fernandopulle's work, Iora had experienced pushback from people who claimed it was costing the hospital money.

"The regulatory environment is built to protect the incumbents," Fernandopulle observed. "Despite all the rhetoric from all these health systems, they make their money by filling beds. If you look at our numbers—40 percent drop in hospitalizations—that's a big number. If you are running a hospital, that just scares the bejesus out of you."

The good news, as Wadsworth points out, is that it's now acceptable to talk about the kind of disruption that's needed in health care. And with sufficient credibility and determination, it's now possible to muster the resources to make it happen. The path to value-based care is not through top-down reform but through bottom-up experiments such as Iora's.

Lessons from Iora Health

Why worth replicating?

- Iora's approach of doubling down on primary care, backed by a patient-centric IT system and organizational culture, could be applied nationally to save between 15 percent and 20 percent of Medicare and Medicaid spending, which in 2017 would have amounted to savings of $180 billion to $240 billion.

How to replicate?

- *Implement a clean-slate solution to industry problems:* If you are serious about disrupting health care and transforming the industry, don't try to do it on the backs of existing business models. Putting "lipstick on a pig" won't change the pig. Rushika Fernandopulle learned this lesson the hard way, after trying to implement his vision of primary care within existing organizations. Eventually he raised significant amounts of capital to create his own business model from the ground up.

- *Have a "social heart" but couple it with a "business brain":* Fernandopulle wanted to keep patients healthy rather than treat them in seven-minute transactional exchanges when they were sick. Fernandopulle never lost sight of this laudable goal (this was his "social heart"), but he realized that he could not scale up his model nationally and transform the industry if he couldn't fund his strategy with private capital (this was Fernandopulle's "business brain" speaking). So have the mission of a nonprofit but the discipline of a for-profit organization. To create a radically new business model you need capital for such things as facilities and IT systems, and to finance startup losses.

- *Create patient-centric care teams, anchored around health coaches:* If you are serious about primary care, use a team of doctors, nurses, health coaches, mental-health specialists, nutritionists, and so on to take care of patients. The most important among these is the health coach, who keeps in close touch with patients, monitors their health, and counsels them on such things as lifestyle and diet. Hire health coaches for attitude (empathy, compassion) and train them for skills (medical background not necessary). And assign health coaches to all patients, not just the sick ones. The goal is to create a close bond between patients and their health coaches.

- *Minimize specialists on your payroll and don't invest in downstream facilities such as hospitals:* Engage specialists as consultants to primary care doctors rather than as full-time employees. Most of the time, problems can be solved by having primary care physicians consult specialists on the phone, rather than referring patients to specialists. Similarly, avoid owning hospitals or hospital beds. Instead, rent hospital beds, à la Airbnb, because there is a surfeit of hospital beds, and it will only grow.

- *Operate on a capitation-only payment arrangement:* Avoid the hybrid model in which you serve both capitation patients and fee-for-service patients. These two practices are like oil and water. The fee-for-service model encourages short-term orientation, leading to too many tests and procedures, rather than focusing on what is best for the patient's long-term health. Capitation requires building a long-term relationship with patients and engaging them in their own care. A hybrid model confuses employees and muddies the organizational culture. The Iora model works best if your success depends on keeping patients healthy in the long run. Think of the patient as your customer, not the insurer, provider, or employer.

- *Invest in a customized, patient-centric IT system:* It is vital to create a customized and scalable IT system that allows the care team to focus on keeping patients healthy in the long run. Off-the-shelf IT packages are designed around the billing codes of the fee-for-service system. These are hard to repurpose for high-quality primary care, which requires the IT system to host a lot more information that the care team and the patient can access easily. Make sure the IT system is robust enough to work well in different settings, as this will be important once you expand your organization regionally or nationally.

8.

Promoting Reverse Innovation and Value-Based Health Care

How to Get Started

Having spent many years studying innovation and, more recently, the health-care industry, we predict that American health care is about to change radically. We think it will change the same way that Ernest Hemingway famously described the way he went broke: "Gradually and then suddenly."

And we think value-based innovations will drive that change.

But we also think a top-down, legislated solution *alone* is unlikely to suffice—and may not be forthcoming anytime soon. Rather, as we've shown in this book, we're convinced that the answer lies in innovations that start at the bottom and work their way to the top. Our research shows us that innovation can come from just about anywhere. In earlier chapters, we saw a telemedicine network in rural Mississippi built by the sheer determination of one emergency-room nurse. We saw a pioneering use of health coaches spearheaded by a doctor with one foot in Harvard Medical School and the other in medical missions to the Dominican Republic, Haiti, and Malaysia. And we saw dozens of incremental steps taken toward greater access, higher quality, lower costs, and greater profits in a giant health system built from once-struggling Catholic community hospitals in the Midwest.

If bottom-up change can come from anywhere, maybe it can come from you.

It Always Starts with a Visionary Leader

Why isn't more value-based health care already happening here? We've heard many explanations. The usual formulation goes like this: "US health care has many competing self-interests, which are locked in an escalating zero-sum game. Change is hard because no one feels empowered to change the entire system, and everyone thinks an advance in one sector of the industry will entail losses in other sectors. The result is protectionism and inertia."

We think that's half right. Certainly, many people are overawed by the complexity of the system. They think they can't change it. Others never doubt that they can. They see their goal, and they march right toward it. They are the doers, people like Kristi Henderson, a Mississippi-bred force of nature, who drove thousands of back-road miles to sell small-town nurses and state legislators on a telemedicine network. People like the leaders of Ascension, who flew halfway around the world to Bangalore to find better ways to run a Catholic health system in America. People like Rushika Fernandopulle, who reinvented primary care to save hundreds of thousands of dollars in secondary- and tertiary-care costs. And of course Devi Shetty, whose single-minded mission to serve the poor reaches every corner of Narayana Health and its Cayman operation, HCCI.

All the innovative companies we studied, both in India and in the United States, had that one thing in common: a visionary leader who was thoroughly committed to the cause. Purpose, we are convinced, is the most important of the five principles of Indian value-based health care that we identified in chapter 1 and illustrated throughout this book. It is the alpha driver, and you cannot innovate without it. The good news is that there is plenty of purpose to be found in health care, an industry that literally deals with life and death.

Finding the Loose Bricks

Of course, there are obstacles. To start, the markets in India and the United States are very different.

For example, in India, medical care and reimbursement usually happen like this: hospitals treat, patients pay cash. Both providers and patients can usually tell you exactly how much a particular procedure costs. That transparency does some very good things. It speeds payment, reduces confusion and anxiety, and makes medical bankruptcy less likely. It also encourages extremely competitive pricing. In fact, innovations in India are most often driven by concerns about cost. In the United States, on the other hand, medical innovations have historically been driven by efforts to improve quality and safety. Cost-savings, if any, have been seen as a bonus.

Some people see this difference and think that the American and Indian health-care systems are fundamentally incompatible, so reverse innovation cannot work. We disagree. The difference is interesting, to be sure, but times are changing, and costs are now front and center in the American health-care debate. In any event, for the innovator intent on transforming the health-care system, the distinction is inconsequential. Why? Because, as we have shown time and again, the three elements of value-based health care—lower costs, better quality, and greater access—all drive and reinforce each other. It is a virtuous cycle, and it doesn't matter where you step in.

More daunting for the innovator is the regulatory landscape in US health care. Try to do the kind of task-shifting that is routinely practiced by Narayana, LV Prasad, and Aravind and soon medical boards, unions, professional societies, and government regulators will appear in your waiting room, armed for combat. In India, by contrast, the industry has more freedom to innovate, because government regulation has been much lighter, and professional associations are less organized to block innovative practices. Owing to those differences and others, Indian providers turn squarely toward value-based competition, while US providers are mired in a strange market dynamic called "regulated competition," a system that serves special interests first and patients second.

Remember that until recently few enterprises were as regulated as the US postal system or the taxi service, yet FedEx and Uber found ways around regulatory barriers. What holds US hospitals back is not regulation. It's a lack of will and leadership and an organizational culture that is indifferent to costs. As Ellen Zane, CEO emeritus and vice chair of Tufts Medical Center, told us: "We simply cannot sustain these kinds of year-over-year increases in insurance premiums—we need an Uber of health care!"[1]

On the bright side, US health care is an ill-built system full of "loose bricks," and each one presents an opportunity for change.

Rushika Fernandopulle found one in Atlantic City, where casino workers with chronic, high-cost health problems like hypertension, diabetes, and emphysema strained the resources of their union-provided health care. The union, Local 54, was self-insured and cared a lot about cost control, so it gave Fernandopulle room to innovate. We have seen how Fernandopulle wiggled that loose brick and removed it, and its neighbors, replacing an expensive system of referrals to medical specialists with a primary care practice that delivered much of its care through frontline health coaches who had no prior medical training. This is an example of a direct reverse innovation: Fernandopulle had seen community health workers like these on medical missions abroad, and he took the innovation and adapted it, addressing regulatory issues and insurance requirements as they arose.

In some ways, Fernandopulle had it easy. He could implement a practice of radical task-shifting because Iora was his company and he made the rules. The physicians who signed on with his practice came with a commitment to a new kind of health care. Fernandopulle didn't attempt to change a company's culture. He invented a new one.

Changing an entrenched medical culture is much harder. Just ask Gary Kaplan, CEO of Seattle's Virginia Mason Medical Center, one of the earliest health-care innovators in the United States. Back in 2000, when Virginia Mason was struggling financially, Kaplan set out to turn his physician-driven organization into a patient-driven organization with the then-radical goal of providing high-quality care at low cost. Eighteen months later, Kaplan was still negotiating with physicians—one recalcitrant doctor at a time. Resistance to Kaplan's effort wasn't subtle, either. When the CEO asked one of his surgeons to go to Japan to learn about Toyota's highly regarded system for quality control, the surgeon flatly refused to go. The doctor saw himself as an artisan-practitioner. Assembly-line medicine and penny-pinching were beneath his dignity. Many doctors still feel that way.

Kaplan knows from experience that changing a big US hospital is hard even before the effort really gets started. It's not just legacy cultures that create difficulty but also the absence of organizational thinking. When he first looked for a good model of value-based health care, he surveyed the best of the best: The University of Michigan, Johns Hopkins, Mayo Clinic, Mass General, and Stanford. "Nobody even had a management system," he told us.[2] That's how Kaplan ended up in Japan, taking lessons from Toyota. John Doyle tells a similar story, recalling that Ascension searched far and wide for an American health-care network that functioned as any kind of true system—for example, with a centralized supply chain, sophisticated inventory control, or coordinated quality-control protocols. Ascension created its own systems and ended up going to India, where it borrowed ideas from Narayana.

These stories are important not only because they point out cultural and organizational barriers to value-based health care but also because they show us that those barriers can be overcome. Gary Kaplan finally did change the culture at Virginia Mason (only ten of the medical center's four hundred doctors left the group), and he improved the productivity of Virginia Mason by 44 percent.[3] And we have seen the impressive gains that Ascension has made in quality, efficiency, and cost control.

These successes are heartening, because there are so *many* obstacles to health-care reform in the United States: government regulation, the fee-for-service payment system, skyrocketing insurance premiums, opaque billing practices, malpractice litigation, overbuilt hospitals, patent and drug protections, the FDA approval process, union rules and benefits costs, protectionist professional associations, the high cost of medical school—the list goes on and on. But if Virginia Mason and Ascension and Iora and the University of Mississippi Medical Center can effect changes, so can others, one loose brick at a time.

We like the loose-brick analogy because it captures something else we have noticed about these early efforts at value-based health care. All of our innovators faced obstacles, and all found ways to get over them, *but they didn't do it by blowing things up.* They worked within the system. They collaborated with the vested interests. They co-opted and cajoled. And they planned like crazy. In Mississippi, Kristi Henderson took care, while expanding her telemedicine network, not to cannibalize the practices of rural doctors, and when she lobbied state legislators for insurance coverage for telemedicine consults, she made sure the pitch touched every legislator's agenda and benefited every district. At Virginia Mason, Gary Kaplan literally spent years talking to his staff about change, and assuring them that no one would be left without a job.

We can't guarantee our innovators a bright and profitable future. It's far too soon to declare victory. The current crop of value-based health-care experiments are but green shoots, glimpses of what might yet come. We think of them as faint signals coming to us from the future. Our goal for this book is to amplify those signals to embolden others to launch new experiments.

What would a fully value-based health-care system look like in America, one that embodied all five of the principles from the Indian exemplars? We don't really know, but we believe such a system will arise from promising "next practices" like those we've seen in this book, and will culminate in sustainable best practices that will be adopted by health-care systems all around the world. That is the nature of innovation in the global economy: it emerges, is disseminated, is reversed, and is spread again, reaching ever wider markets and creating ever greater good.

Opportunities for Change: It's Already Happening

We'll end this book with a prediction and with an appeal. First, the prediction: the status quo will not persist. As care becomes less and less affordable in the United States, stakeholders will exert increasing pressure on the health-care system, forcing it to become more value conscious. It is the nature of the free market to do so, and it is in the interests of all parties to do so. As we have seen over and over again, *change can come from anywhere*, and all of the stakeholders are positioned to play important roles.

Here are just some of the opportunities we see (figure 8-1).

FIGURE 8-1

Key actors in promoting value-based competition in the United States

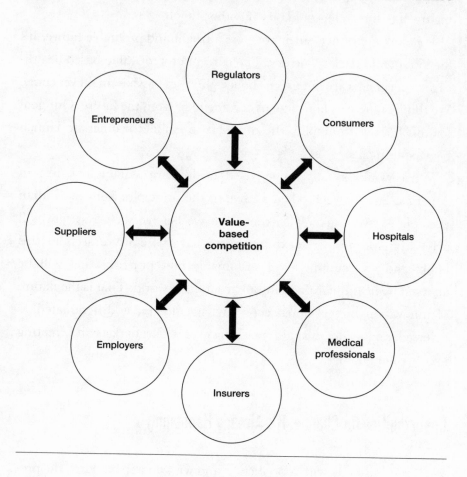

Regulators

The federal government is the biggest spender in US health care, and it is the most powerful influencer. While it's often hard to know where government regulations and expenditures are headed, there is already a trend toward value-based health care. The Centers for Medicare & Medicaid Services (CMS) has been experimenting with risk-sharing arrangements and alternatives to the fee-for-service payment model, including bundled pricing and capitation, strategies that promise a move toward value-based competition.[4] Other changes under the Medicare Access and CHIP Reauthorization Act of 2015 offer incentives for providers to lower costs, improve quality, and upgrade information technology. Value-based experiments are under way at the state level as well. For example, Arkansas has aligned bundled payment reforms across both private and public payers, including Walmart (which is self-insured). California offers state workers price lists detailing what different insurers will pay for selected procedures. And Maryland has set goals to limit per capita health-care spending.[5]

These are important steps. Perhaps governments can also turn their attention to developing national telemedicine networks and encouraging task-shifting. The United States has already accepted the roles of paramedic, nurse practitioner, and physician's assistant. Why not community vision screeners and junior surgeons, as we've seen in India, or the wider use of health coaches, as Rushika Fernandopulle has pioneered in primary care? Certifying new professional and paraprofessional roles would not only reduce health-care costs but also create thousands of new midlevel jobs. Through such reforms, we think it's reasonable for regulators to aim for overall cost reductions of 30 percent to 40 percent over the next decade, and we see a plum role for government in developing national telemedicine networks.

Consumers

With rising insurance copayments and deductibles, American consumers have already begun to shop around for health-care services based on value—just like their Indian counterparts. In the future, we see value-conscious consumers driving change by demanding price transparency, asking more questions about risks and outcomes, leveraging new consumer tools, being open to care from new kinds of health workers, and embracing novel delivery methods (e.g., home-based health, telehealth, and mobile apps).

We also see consumers taking more responsibility for their health and disease management, through self-care, as a way of avoiding downstream costs. Patient advocacy and class-action lawsuits are other avenues consumers might turn to as they seek to move the system in a more patient-centric direction. We believe that patients are the greatest untapped resource in health care, and that their potential will be realized only when health care becomes more patient-centric, a key goal of value-based care. Gary Kaplan, CEO of Virginia Mason Medical Center, told us: "Health care still is designed around doctors and nurses and not around patients. If you think about it, what are waiting rooms, really, but places for patients to be on time, and then *wait for us*!"[6]

Hospitals

American hospitals today are too big, and way too expensive. We see several value-driven solutions that hospitals can adopt. First, hospitals must look to drastically reduce their capital expenditures on buildings and facilities; too many hospitals look like seven-star hotels, with luxuries that have no bearing on medical outcomes. Second, they should look for ways to convert fixed costs to variable costs, as Children's Hospital of Philadelphia did by sending specialists to community hospitals, and by renting beds when needed. Third, hospitals could be a lot more efficient in their use of fixed-cost resources, as Mayo Clinic was when it created a "focused factory" for adult cardiac surgery.[7] Fourth, they can extend the life of expensive equipment through meticulous maintenance, as the Indian exemplars are doing. Finally, they can reduce downtime in expensive resources such as operating suites, by moving patients in and out much more quickly.

American hospitals' fixed costs are so high that dramatic improvements in utilization and efficiency, as indicated by the above strategies, won't bring spending within bounds. Such efficiencies will, however, create additional capacity in a system that is already overbuilt. "Under fee-for-service, hospitals were better off keeping people in their beds and getting more people into hospital," says Diane Daych, a partner at health-sector venture-capital firm Apple Tree Partners, "but under value-based purchasing they're going to make money by keeping healthy people out of the hospital—and it's going to be hard to get there."[8]

How can hospitals deal with impending excess capacity? Some, but not all, of that capacity should be absorbed as the aging population increases demand for health care. It's also possible that millions of low-income, formerly uninsured Americans will be covered by health insurance. Hospitals should manage this new favorable demand environment wisely, finding new ways to absorb the industry's excess capacity. Mothballing hospital beds is a last resort, but it's a far better solution for society than admitting patients who don't need to be in a hospital. Like any industry with high fixed costs, hospitals must stop chasing volume and start thinking about right-sizing. Visionaries who can turn excess capacity to profit—and to the common good—will be tomorrow's health-care heroes.

Medical Professionals

American physicians get a lot of heat from health-care reformers and are often cast as obstructionists for their once widespread resistance to any change that might threaten their authority, independence, or income. But we have seen the extraordinary work of doctor-crusaders and doctorpreneurs in India and the United States, and we have recently seen doctors and nurses marching in demonstrations for health-care reform in America, wearing their scrubs and white coats. We see medical professionals moving to the vanguard.

The successful enterprises we present in this book were launched by medical professionals who had four things in common: an extraordinary commitment to medical excellence, an entrepreneurial outlook, a real interest in teamwork, and a genuine compassion for patients. Many— maybe most—American medical students start out that way. Many are frustrated by the status quo and would like nothing better than to focus on their profession rather than on red tape and paperwork. Let's leverage *that* spirit. We believe that when physician leaders get the model right, other medical professionals want to work with them, and a positive chain reaction sets in. We see doctors—and nurses and physician assistants and other medical professionals—spearheading important innovations within their own practices and hospitals, as well as through medical training, patient advocacy, and political activism.

Insurers

As insurance premiums and deductibles rise, more stakeholders will question the contribution of private health-insurance companies that take 15 percent to 20 percent off the top. Insurers must find ways to help lower the real cost of health care rather than endlessly raising premiums to preserve their margins or ignominiously leaving the market when times get tough.

Fortunately the value proposition of value-based health care—high quality, low-cost, universal care—is a win-win-win proposition for insurers, and we are seeing some interesting experiments in risk-sharing, capitation, downstream incentives, and bundled payments that can help move the system in that direction. Outside the existing system, single-payer models still have many supporters. Innovators might look harder at radically decentralized models as well—ideas like concierge practices, local mutual-aid societies, and direct prepayments to physicians groups—for ideas on how to reform the current insurance system.[9]

Employers

In the United States, more than half the population under sixty-five gets health insurance through an employer-sponsored plan. Those plans cost employers a lot of money, require specialized benefits support, and depress employee wages. Increasingly, employers are looking to contain those costs, talking with workers about health-care value and employee choice. We see increasing opportunities for employers to work with companies like Iora that prioritize prevention, and to provide incentives for employees to use select nontraditional providers, such as Health City Cayman Islands.

Fortune 500 companies, which direct large numbers of consumers to health-care providers, have the clout to encourage Indian-style innovations. When Intel educated its health-care suppliers on "lean" methodologies in 2009, treatment costs for certain medical conditions fell by anywhere from 24 percent to 49 percent.[10] The collaborative venture announced in January 2018 by three large employers—Amazon, Berkshire Hathaway, and JPMorgan Chase—has the potential to rock the boat and trigger some bold bottom-up innovations. We could use a lot more value-based thinking like that!

Suppliers

As US health care migrates to value-based competition, medical-device makers and suppliers of pharmaceuticals, surgical materials, and other medical products will all have to dramatically lower their prices. These players, who have been hiding in the forest of our overgrown health-care system, are at risk of disruption by startups. Remember Narayana's cost-saving decision to have its surgical gowns made locally, a move that drove an overpriced surgical-gown maker out of business? Suppliers can also learn an important lesson from the wireless telephony industry: When the industry signed on hundreds of millions of new users in poor countries, sales of handheld telephones swelled and profits exploded even as prices dropped sharply. It was a win-win result for producers and consumers alike. How can these dynamics be applied to the health-care industry?

Entrepreneurs

Digital technologies have already transformed many US sectors, including manufacturing, banking, retailing, and publishing. Better digital delivery of US health care is long overdue, and venture capitalists are all over it, currently investing $4 billion a year on digital health-care startups.[11] This is an important development, and Indian companies, which are very tech-savvy, can point the way. But can entrepreneurs think beyond hardware and software, medical devices and pharmaceuticals? Can they think bigger? Can they target the entire health-care ecosystem? Can they turn their attention to more disruptive *business models*, like those of Iora and offshore hospitals? We think they can, and we think they will. Doctors can play an important role in leading this charge, and we see a whole new class of doctorpreneurs emerging in coming years.

All of the above players have an important contribution to make. We do not foresee a coordinated effort happening anytime soon, but we know that innovations in any one sphere will trigger actions in other spheres, because the players in the American health-care system are interdependent. Regulators or self-insured employers may spur doctors and hospitals to change. Hospitals may persuade suppliers and insurers to change. Startups may wake up established players. Foreign entrants may disrupt local players.

We believe that change will come through a series of disruptions, some homegrown, some through reverse innovation. Over time, these changes will cascade through the system until a point is reached at which the status quo will give way and transformation of US health care will gather a sudden and significant momentum. That's how innovation works—first gradually, then suddenly—and it is sometimes painful.

"To date, doctors and hospitals have been spared the pain of disruption," Robert Pearl, the former CEO of Permanente Medical Group, said in 2017 after visiting Devi Shetty in India. "But that day is ending, and I predict that even people looking for it to happen are gazing in the wrong direction. They expect disruption to be led by companies like Google and Apple or maybe entrepreneurial start-ups. Based on my time in India, they should be looking globally."[12]

We agree, and we believe the time to start looking to make that difference is now, when value-based innovations are just getting off the ground. There are so many opportunities, so much reward. But now it's up to you. You know your segment of the industry best. You know where the loose bricks are.

So here's the appeal.

Write down one big idea, find a loose brick, think about what you've read and heard about the Indian and US models in this book, and then take one concrete step toward change. See where that takes you. Repeat.

We have been greatly inspired by the vision, compassion, energy, and business sense of all the health-care innovators we have met in India and the United States. We hope this book will inspire you to take your own bold steps. But go where *your* social heart and business brain take you. Health care is waiting for your good ideas, and so are billions of people around the world.

Appendix A

India? Really?

Countering Skepticism about Transferring Practices from India to Developed Countries

Over the last five years, as we have shared our research with colleagues, we have encountered skepticism about our thesis that India can offer lessons for health-care reform in the United States.

"India?" people ask. "Really?"

"Yes, India!" we reply, time and again.

But the question is understandable. After all, India's overall performance in the health-care sector leaves a lot to be desired, compared with the United States and even with China (see table A-1). So we would like to address some recurring doubts. Skeptics' concerns typically fall into one of two camps: skepticism about the exemplars' results and skepticism about reverse innovation. Let's take them one at a time.

TABLE A-1

Health-care statistics: India, China, and the United States

Health-care indicator	India	China	United States
Per capita total expenditure on health, 2014 (USD)	$75	$420	$9,403
Private expenditure on health as percentage of total health expenditure, 2014	70.0	44.2	51.7
—of which out-of-pocket expenditure, 2014	89.2	72.3	11.1
Infant mortality rate, 2015 (number of deaths of children less than one year of age per 1,000 live births)	37.9	9.2	5.6
Percentage of births attended by skilled health personnel, 2005–2011	58 (Rural: 37)	96	99
Physicians: total number, 2011 Density: per 10,000 pop., 2011	922,177 7.0	2,020,154 15.0	767,782 24.5
Nurses and midwives: total number Density: per 10,000 pop.	2,124,667 17.1	2,244,020 16.6	2,927,000 98.2
Hospital beds per 10,000 pop., 2014	9	42	30

Source: Compiled from World Bank and World Health Organization databases and from *World Health Statistics 2017: Monitoring Health for the SDGs.*

Skepticism about Results: Are Indian Exemplars Really Achieving High-Quality, Low-Cost Care for All, and Are They Really Making Money at It?

Here we address five frequently asked questions from economists, insurers, patient advocates, and hospital CFOs. To help with this discussion, table 1-2 in chapter 1 presented prices for a range of medical procedures in India and the United States. A second table in this appendix, table A-2, provides more in-depth information on the prices, quality, volume, subsidized care, and financial results of one of our exemplars, Aravind Eye Care System, in 2012–2013, when we began our research.

TABLE A-2

Aravind Eye Care System, FY 2012–2013

	Aravind Eye Care System	US or UK comparison
Ultra-low prices for cataract surgery		
Consultation, including comprehensive eye exam	$1	
Free patients	Free	
Paying patients, manual small-incision cataract surgery (MSICS) with rigid intraocular lens, same-day discharge, all inclusive	$100	$3,500–$9,000, depending on lens and hospital
Paying patients, phacoemulsification, intraocular lens, private suite	$247	
Access and volume		
Number of outpatients, all ailments (annual)	2.84 million	n/a
Number of cataract surgeries (annual)	349,000	28,076 (New York Eye and Ear Infirmary)
Subsidized patients, eye surgery		
Share of free patients in total	51%	n/a
Productivity		
Surgeries per senior ophthalmologist (annual)	1,000–1,400	n/a
Incidence of complications		(National Health Service, UK)
Capsule rupture and vitreous loss	2.00%	4.40%
Incomplete cortical clean-up	0.75%	1.00%
Iris trauma	0.30%	0.70%
Persistent iris prolapse	0.01%	0.07%
Anterior chamber collapse	0.30%	0.50%
Loss of nuclear fragment into vitreous	0.20%	0.30%
Loss of intraocular lens into vitreous	0.01%	0.16%
Financial results		(New York Eye and Ear Infirmary)
Total revenues	$35 million	$153 million
EBITDA margin (percent of total revenue)	40%	n/a
Net profit margin (percent of total revenue)	34%	n/a

New York Eye and Ear Infirmary was ranked no. 11 among all eye hospitals in the United States by *U.S. News & World Report* in 2012 and is the highest-ranked eye hospital for which volume and financial data were publicly available.

Indian rupees (INR) were converted to US dollars (USD) at the rate of 1 USD to 50 INR, the rate prevailing in 2012–2013.

n/a = not available

Were the hospitals' bills really that low, or were there hidden charges?

They were really that low. The prices shown in table A-2 are bundled prices—that is, they include the full price of the listed procedure, including diagnostics and follow-up care and any unanticipated tests or procedures required in a particular case. These prices were usually transparent to the patient, as they must be in India, because insurance coverage is limited and patients must pay out of pocket. Upgrades were sometimes available for nonmedical amenities such as private hospital rooms. These were typically priced separately. As you can see, the Indian exemplars didn't just charge low prices. They charged *ultra-low, comprehensive* prices.

For example, Aravind's fee for a comprehensive eye exam was only $1, which was low enough to encourage everyone to get tested (see table A-2). Its price for cataract surgery included consultations before the procedure, hospital and operating-room charges, a surgeon's fees, medications, recovery, room and board, and postoperative consultation. For poor patients, Aravind also provided free screening, free eyeglasses, free accommodations, and free transportation from their villages if they required surgery.

Similarly, Narayana Health's price of $2,100 for a coronary artery bypass graft included preoperative tests, surgery charges, a doctor's fees, medicines, and postoperative recovery. This is not a subsidized price. In fact, Narayana's cost, as opposed to price, was even lower, estimated at between $1,100 and 1,200 for each open-heart surgery.

Finally, at our maternity-hospital exemplar, LifeSpring, the price for a normal delivery was $120. That price included prenatal care (including multiple consultations with obstetricians, three ultrasounds, lab work, and an HIV test), the delivery itself, medicines, and hospital-stay charges. A cesarean delivery cost $180 more, to cover the surgery. In all cases, LifeSpring also provided one month of postnatal care, including government-sponsored vaccinations and one visit each with an obstetrician and a pediatrician. LifeSpring posted these prices prominently in its hospital lobbies so patients would know exactly how much a delivery would cost well in advance of receiving the bill.

Was the care actually high-quality, despite these ultra-low prices?

Yes, just take a look at the quality metrics in table A-3. Our hospital exemplars are exemplary for a reason. All of the physician founders of these hospitals trained to very high standards, four of them in the United States and the United Kingdom, and quality health care was their mission. Several of the hospitals were accredited by Joint Commission International (JCI) or by its Indian equivalent, the National Accreditation Board for Hospitals & Healthcare Providers (NABH). One hospital, Aravind, chose not to seek accreditation for fear that accreditation would stifle experimentation and curtail innovation, but as shown in tables A-2 and A-3, Aravind's outcomes were as good as or better than those of the United Kingdom's National Health Service. LifeSpring, the maternity hospital, was not big enough to seek accreditation.

Some of the exemplar hospitals also benchmarked themselves against international standards for medical care, including rates of complications for different procedures. The data suggests that their medical outcomes were comparable to those prevailing in the West. For example, the five-year survival rates for patients with breast cancer (stages 1 through 3 combined) at HCG Oncology averaged 86.9 percent from 2003 to 2009, compared with an average rate of 89.2 percent for such patients in the United States in the same period. Deccan Hospital patients undergoing peritoneal dialysis for kidney failure showed outcomes statistically identical to those of US patients undergoing hemodialysis, the more expensive treatment commonly used in the United States.

Aravind, the eye hospital, has come under particularly close scrutiny, perhaps because of its wildly successful run of more than forty years in India. Rigorous studies by renowned ophthalmologist David F. Chang of the University of California, San Francisco, and others have shown that

Indian hospitals: quality-of-care indicators

Hospital	Accredited by[1]	Quality-of-care indicators (where available)			

Aravind Eye Care System	• Has selectively adopted NABH processes without seeking accreditation, as that would inhibit Aravind's innovative practices		**National Health Service (UK) Hospitals**		
		Indicator	Western Eye Hospital, 2004	Moorfields Eye Hospital, 2003	Aravind's Madurai Hospital, 2008–2009
		• Vitreous loss	1.1%	0.70%	0.71%
		• Endophthalmitis	0.1%	0.0%	0.04%
		• Overall incidence of major complications	2.4%	2.4%	1.15% (0.80% for full-time doctors)

Care Hospitals	• NABH		Western norm		Care Hospitals
		• Angioplasty patients requiring emergency surgery	1 in 200		1 in 20,000
		• Mortality rate of angioplasty patients undergoing emergency surgery	50%		50%

Deccan Hospital	• NABH	Deccan Hospital patients undergoing peritoneal dialysis for end-stage renal disease showed outcomes statistically identical to those of US patients undergoing hemodialysis, the more expensive treatment commonly used in the United States. The five-year survival rate for Deccan's patients was better than the US average for hemodialysis: 50% versus 41%.			

HCG Oncology	• NABH	Five-year survival rate, breast cancer (most common condition at HCG)	US average 2003–2009 (SEER database)[2]		HCG average (2003–2009)
		• Overall survival rate, stages 1 through 3 combined	89.2%		86.9%
		• Survival rate, localized stage 1 cancer	98.6%		96.2%
		• Survival rate, regionally spread cancer (stages 2 and 3 combined)	84.4%		82.2%

LifeSpring Hospital	• Not accredited	n/a
LV Prasad Eye Institute	• NABH	n/a
Narayana Health	• JCI • NABH	Narayana's coronary-bypass mortality rate thirty days after surgery was 1.27% versus a US average of 1.2%.[3] A more recent study cited in an article in *The Lancet* suggests the rates at Narayana and in the United States were 1.4% and 1.9%, respectively. Narayana also outperformed US benchmarks for "post-coronary complication rates" (benchmark of 2%) and "post-angioplasty average length of stay" (benchmark of 2.5 days).[4]

n/a = not available

1. Joint Commission International (JCI) is the international arm of the Joint Commission, an independent, nonprofit organization that accredits more than 15,000 health-care organizations in the United States. Its Indian equivalent is the National Accreditation Board for Hospitals & Healthcare Providers (NABH). Accreditation by JCI was usually limited to the group's flagship hospitals, whereas NABH accreditation was more widespread.

2. The Surveillance, Epidemiology, and End Results (SEER) Program of the National Cancer Institute provides information on cancer statistics in an effort to reduce the cancer burden among the US population. It is maintained by the National Cancer Institute belonging to the US government.

3. Based on case study of Narayana Health by T. Khanna, K. Rangan, and M. Manocaran, "Narayana Hrudayalaya Heart Hospital: Cardiac Care for the Poor," Case 505-078 (Boston: Harvard Business School Publishing, 2005), p. 3. Also, Narayana Health's patients were probably at higher risk than US patients for four reasons: 1. As the largest cardiac hospital in India (and the world), Narayana accepted patients with complications who may have been turned down by other hospitals. 2. Indians tend to have weak hearts. 3. Indians generally go for heart surgery in advanced stages of disease. 4. Poor hygienic conditions and higher pollution outside the hospitals may increase postoperative complications and mortality.

4. Metrics used by *American Journal of Therapeutics*.

medical outcomes for Aravind's revolutionary manual small-incision cataract surgery were generally comparable to those of the costlier and more sophisticated procedure known as phacoemulsification.[1] In fact, in an editorial in the *British Journal of Ophthalmology*, Chang argued that the technique produced *better* outcomes than phacoemulsification in developing countries where cataracts are more advanced and severe (typically for having gone too long untreated).[2] In other work with Aravind colleagues, Chang found that the streamlined sterilization methods and unconventional operating-room protocols used at Aravind did not produce higher infection rates than those associated with traditional methods and protocols, and that Aravind's outcomes were as good as those of hospitals with smaller volumes and a slower pace of surgery.[3]

Did the hospitals really cater to the poor or just to the rich?

Targeting the rich is a surefire way to succeed in health care in poor countries like India. Elites, tycoons, high-ranking politicians, and expatriate managers—these people get sick and die as regularly as do the poor, and they are willing to pay handsomely for medical care. But our Indian exemplars were not concierge medical practices. As explained in chapter 1, the Indian exemplars extended care to all, often providing free or subsidized care for the poor. For instance, at LifeSpring, with its chain of maternity hospitals located in and around the city of Hyderabad, most patients were the urban poor, who paid prices that were 50 percent to 70 percent below those charged in other private Indian hospitals.

Don't most of these Indian innovations involve pretty simple procedures and practices?

Some do, some don't. We do profile three Indian hospitals that performed ordinarily straightforward interventions such as cataract surgery and maternity care, but the other four Indian exemplars dealt with many complex procedures involved in cardiac care, renal care, and cancer care. Moreover, these latter four hospitals used many of the same management innovations that we observed in hospitals tending to eye care and maternity care. Thus, the breakthrough business model for health-care delivery that we describe in chapters 2 and 3 has broad applicability to all medical procedures and hospital practices. And here's something else to think about: The field of medicine keeps improving. What was complicated in the past has become more straightforward today. We believe that as time goes on, innovations pioneered in India will become relevant to a wider swath of medical procedures and management practices.

Did the Indian hospitals really make money?

Yes, they did make money, and decent amounts of it, as we explained in chapter 1. Although it was a nonprofit hospital and served the highest proportion of free or subsidized patients among the hospitals we studied, Aravind had an EBITDA margin and a net profit margin that were the highest in our sample. LV Prasad Eye Institute enjoyed similar success since its founding, covering all its operating costs as well as its training and research expenses, with money left over each year.

So, yes, it's true. These seven Indian hospital systems have achieved what US health-care reformers have been talking about, dreaming about, and fighting about for decades: high-quality, low-cost health care for everyone, and money in the bank at the end of the day.

Skepticism about Reverse Innovation: Can US Hospitals Really Apply Indian Practices?

We noted in chapter 2 that India presented three realities that laid the groundwork for value-based competition: (1) a huge, low-income population that mostly paid for health care out of pocket, (2) a shortage of health-care resources, and (3) an unfettered industry. Conditions in the United States are exactly the opposite on each of these fronts (see the sidebar "Indian versus American Health-Care Context"): The largely middle-class population relied on third-party insurers to pick up most of its health-care costs. The country generally enjoyed a surplus of medical resources (though those resources were unevenly distributed). And health care was highly regulated.[4] For many years, the United States eschewed value-based competition in favor of "regulated competition," including the country's fee-for-service payment system, which distorted incentives for industry players. As a result, US health care evolved in entirely different ways than Indian health care.

While Indian patients shopped around for value, US patients became indifferent to price because of third-party payment for health care, which also added administrative complexity and costs to the system. Because most hospital costs (e.g., doctors' and nurses' salaries, depreciation on

---

Indian versus American Health-Care Context

India	United States
Many self-paying, low-income, price-conscious patients	Mostly insured, do not worry about cost
Severe capacity shortage	Significant excess capacity (beds, equipment) Very high fixed costs (beds, equipment, doctors)
Largely unregulated industry, resulting in value-based competition and relatively clean slate	Highly regulated, including fee-for-service reimbursement, and encumbered by legacy

---

buildings and equipment, administrative overhead, and interest expenses) were fixed, hospitals were eager to drive up volume and utilization. A built bed became a filled bed as supply drove demand. Fee-for-service reimbursement encouraged providers to perform unnecessary tests and procedures and didn't reward better care, only more of it. The net result was that US health care became extraordinarily expensive and uneven in quality.

A doubter might still note that even if our characterization of the Indian exemplars' results is accurate, won't differences between the American and Indian contexts limit what can be transferred and applied to US health care? Yes, of course there will be limitations and adaptations, but what impresses us is how much *can* be transferred to good effect.

Let's take a look at the five questions we've been asked most often about reversing the Indian innovations.

What about labor costs? Don't they account for most of the cost savings in India?

Surprisingly, no. Nurses, paramedical staff, and administrators were certainly paid less in India than in the United States, sometimes dramatically so. Some earned only 2 percent to 5 percent of what such workers in a US hospital would earn. But medical specialists, who accounted for more than half the salary bill in a typical Indian hospital, were a different story. Many Indian doctors trained and practiced in the United States or the United Kingdom before returning to work in India. They were highly skilled and financially savvy. They knew their worth on the global market. Cardiothoracic surgeons, nephrologists, ophthalmologists, and oncologists in India typically earned anywhere from 20 percent to 74 percent of what their American counterparts did.[5] For example, Aravind's ophthalmologists earned $50,000 annually compared with the $253,000 that was the average for US ophthalmologists, and Narayana's senior cardiothoracic surgeons grossed between $150,000 and $300,000, compared with $408,000, the median income for their US counterparts.

We calculated what the cost of an open-heart surgery at Narayana Health would have to be if the salaries of its doctors and other staff were adjusted to match US levels. Even with commensurate wages factored in, and no reduction in headcount to match lower US staffing levels, Narayana's cost for open-heart surgery would still be only 3 percent to 12 percent that of a comparable procedure in a US hospital (see table A-4). The labor-cost differential just isn't that important.

Moreover, our Indian hospitals faced cost drivers that American hospitals didn't. For example, imported devices such as stents, valves, and orthopedic implants, as well as high-end equipment such as CT scanners, PET-CT scanners, MRI machines, and cyclotrons were subject to transportation costs and import duties. The cost of capital in India

TABLE A-4

Open-heart surgery at Narayana Health: salaries are only part of the equation

Lower wages in India contribute to the lower health-care costs there—but not as much as you might think.

Narayana Health reports that the cost of open-heart surgery is $2,100, one-third of which goes to salaries.

**Total surgery salaries
$690**

**Plus other costs
$1,410**

Salary costs are split evenly between doctors and other staff. Assuming that US doctors are paid twice as much as their Indian counterparts, on average, and other staff twenty times as much, here's the salary cost at US levels:

**Salaries at US levels
Doctors' wages
$345 × 2
+
Staff wages
$345 × 20**

**Total salaries at US levels
$7,590**

So what is the total cost of the surgery when salaries are comparable to those in the United States?

**Narayana Health's total cost of surgery at US levels
Salaries at US levels
$7,590
+
Other costs
$1,410**

**Total cost of open-heart surgery
$9,000**

Which is still less than the total cost of open-heart surgery in the United States
$75,662–$342,087
(range in Texas, 2010 data)

could be as high as 14 percent per annum, more than double that in the United States. And the cost of land in urban areas such as Bangalore and Hyderabad was very high—two-thirds that in Manhattan. As a result, Narayana's 21-point labor-cost advantage relative to Cleveland Clinic, for example, was mostly offset by a 17-point disadvantage in its cost of supplies, pharmaceuticals, and other direct expenses (see table A-5). Overall, the result was a win-some, lose-some cost structure for Indian hospitals compared with that of hospitals in the United States.

What about volume? How can the United States ever achieve India's economies of scale?

True, India has four times the population of the United States, and Indian hospitals do enjoy cost advantages based on economies of scale. But consider three things. First, population and health-care markets can vary independently. US volumes may be lower than India's in some areas (e.g., eye care) but higher than India's in many other areas (e.g., heart disease, kidney problems, obesity-related problems, and Alzheimer's). Second, even for medical procedures for which US volumes are lower in the national aggregate, individual hospital chains or specialty hospitals might attract sufficiently high volumes to see similar economies of scale. Finally, many of our Indian exemplars achieve cost advantages in ways unrelated to volume. For this reason, countries much smaller than the United States—e.g., Finland and Sweden—have adopted Indian-style innovations with significant gains.

But aren't these Indian hospitals spared the overhead costs of running educational and research programs?

No. The higher cost position of major US hospitals cannot be explained by the fact that they often have twin missions: both treatment and research and training. Five of the seven Indian hospitals we profiled also engaged in applied research and knowledge building through clinical

TABLE A-5

Cost structure of Cleveland Clinic versus Narayana Health

Item	Cleveland Clinic, calendar year 2012, % of revenues	Narayana Health Hospitals, December 2012 (month) % of revenues
Salaries	55	34
Medical supplies	10	16
Pharmaceuticals, reagents, blood from blood banks, etc.	7	12
Other services (purchased or in-house), fees, etc.	7	7
Administrative costs	9	15
Total costs	88	84
EBITDA	11	16
Interest	2	2
Depreciation	6	5
Net operating income	3	9
Nonoperating income	9	-
Net income	12	9
Total sales	US$ 1,594 M	US$ 121.4 M
Total assets	US$ 10,200 M	US$ 145.9 M
Asset turnover (total sales/ total assets)	0.16	0.83

Notes: Cleveland Clinic categories as reported in its 2012 Annual Report. Narayana Health data matched to Cleveland Clinic categories to the extent possible. Supplies included stents, valves, etc. Pharmaceuticals included medicines, reagents, blood from blood banks, etc. Other services included radiology, power and fuel, linen/laundry, food catering, bad debt, and clinical research. Administrative costs included repairs and maintenance, housekeeping, waste disposal, traveling and conveyance, telephone, printing and stationery, rent, security, insurance, business promotion, rates and taxes, and other costs, including unspecified amortization.

Narayana Health's sales and assets, in Indian rupees (INR), converted to US dollars (USD) at a rate of 1 USD to 50 INR, the rate prevailing in 2012.

innovations, and they functioned as teaching hospitals that invested heavily in training medical staff. In fact, they graduated more medical professionals than most hospitals in India. Aravind Eye Care alone was estimated to have trained one in six ophthalmologists working in India, for example, while also training thousands of young women to serve in the newly created occupation of midlevel ophthalmic paramedic in its own hospitals and clinics across India.

The Indian hospitals also allocated resources to develop and perfect clinical innovations as doctors adapted procedures to rein in costs and deal with local problems. For example, the vast majority of coronary-bypass procedures at Care Hospitals and Narayana Health employed an unconventional "beating-heart" approach, as described in chapter 3. Given the shortage of cornea donors, LV Prasad Eye Institute developed a novel method of corneal slicing that allowed a single cornea to be used to treat two patients. Similarly, Aravind mastered manual small-incision cataract surgery, which was faster to perform and required less-sophisticated equipment than standard Western practices. In the same way, HCG Oncology perfected novel procedures for treating breast, neck, and throat cancers. All of these incubator and dissemination efforts involved overhead expenses similar to those at teaching hospitals in the United States.

But isn't regulation killing innovation in the United States? Indian hospitals don't face that problem!

It is true that Indian health care is less regulated than US health care. In fact, the Indian regulatory environment is pretty lax, although this was starting to change slowly in 2017. India also has far fewer malpractice suits, and hospitals are less pressured by unions and insurance interests. These pressures on the US health-care system certainly inhibit its efficiency and its ability to innovate. But by the same token, India is likely to be a better laboratory for health-care-delivery innovations than the United States. Not all Indian innovations will reverse easily, and some likely cannot be reversed at all. But many can be transferred directly, or with adaptations, and some will show such promise that they will invite disruption of the burdensome US system.

Unless there is a system-level change, how can US hospitals really benefit from Indian-style innovations? Can bottom-up change really work?

Absolutely. We have seen it, and we describe several Indian-style innovations under way in the United States in part two of this book. No doubt, there is a system-level problem in the United States, and one of the symptoms is inertia. But systems do change. Over time, US regulations can and will change so that innovations to lower cost, expand coverage, and improve quality will become easier to adopt. Both the market and the public good demand it. We hope this book will catalyze bottom-up changes that will encourage top-down policy reforms, so that the two will be mutually reinforcing.

So, here's the bottom line: while the Indian exemplars, vis-à-vis US hospitals, did enjoy labor-cost advantages and a lighter regulatory burden, other costs were actually higher in India and other pressures were similarly burdensome. It would be a mistake to dismiss the Indian experience as irrelevant for rich countries, just as it would have been a mistake in the 1960s to dismiss the experience of Japanese manufacturers such as Toyota.

Appendix B

Health-Care-Delivery-Innovation Diagnostics

We've developed the following set of questions to help guide strategic discussions about breakthrough health-care innovations aimed at fostering value-based care. They are designed for use by clinical and nonclinical executives of health-care companies of all sizes, including startups hoping to disrupt existing practices.

The questions serve as a set of diagnostic tools to help identify opportunities for change within your organization. They can be used in a variety of settings, including team meetings, performance reviews, mission-building activities, and off-site strategy meetings—whatever settings you imagine. We hope they help you to align your organization with value-centered goals and to find some loose bricks for change.

For convenience, we organize the questions according to the five principles of value-based innovation that define the Indian business model. You can take them in any order you wish, but we suggest beginning with Purpose, as that is the alpha driver of the breakthrough business model.

1. Pursuing an Inspiring Purpose

How can we (re)define our purpose as a health-care organization so that it inspires everyone to pursue extraordinary cost innovations *and* offer world-class medical care?

How can our organization nurture doctorpreneurs who are committed to providing affordable, world-class health care for all, and who can encourage everyone to pursue value-based care?

How can we encourage innovation at all levels of the organization, including frontline staff, and how can we foster a commitment to lean production?

How can our organization educate people about how to lead healthy lives and prevent disease, rather than simply treating them when they are sick?

How can we prevent the overutilization of health-care facilities? How can we serve the real needs of health care rather than the unnecessary conventions created by perverse incentives?

How can we care for more uninsured and underinsured patients without increasing our total costs? For example, how might we dramatically improve the productivity of our people and facilities to free up money to serve the poor?

Can we embrace transparent, bundled pricing so that patients and insurers know in advance how much a standard procedure is likely to cost them?

How can for-profit organizations develop a "social heart" and nonprofit organizations develop a "business brain" so that both have "social hearts and business brains"?

Is there a "hero" in our organization's history and story? If yes, who is it and why? Does that person's example support value-based, patient-centric health care?

Who in our organization is the most purpose-driven individual—regardless of department, title, or role? How can we help that individual to assume a greater leadership role?

Does our stated organizational mission reflect value-based and patient-centric goals? If yes, how is that mission manifested throughout the organization? If no, what would it take to get there?

Can we craft a five-year strategic goal of reducing health-care-delivery costs by 30 percent of current levels, without adversely affecting quality?

Purpose informs the reason for your existence, and strategic intent expresses a stretch goal. Topics two through five below will help you develop strategies to achieve your intent.

2. Configuring Assets in a Hub-and-Spoke Network

How can we streamline our network (or become part of someone else's network) so that we separate complex care from straightforward care?

Can we concentrate the most expensive equipment and the scarcest talent in "hubs" or "centers of excellence" to treat complex procedures, and can we house less-expensive equipment and less-scarce talent in "spokes" that can treat simpler procedures closer to where patients live?

Can we leverage our own spoke facilities (or those of partner organizations, including critical-care facilities or community hospitals) to provide quality care closer to where patients live?

When appropriate, are we using hubs and spokes as "focused factories" that perform either complex or simple procedures, but not both?

Are we using our hubs and centers of excellence to develop clinical innovations that simultaneously improve quality and lower cost?

Are we using volume to maximize utilization of expensive equipment? Are we ensuring that such equipment is used day and night? Are we "making our equipment sweat"?

Are we using the volume in "hubs" to accelerate learning and skill development by medical professionals and other staff?

Are we using high volumes to continually develop better protocols for various risk categories?

Are our volumes high enough that we can create specialists even for relatively rare conditions?

Which essential services should always be delivered in the spokes? What services should always be centered in the hubs? What services does that leave for managers to assign creatively?

How can we ease the transition for patients who must move from spoke to hub? What transportation services, family supports, or cost reimbursements might we institute?

How can the organization build brand in the spokes without replicating services that belong in the hub?

How do we ensure that workers in the hubs and spokes are "on the same page" about the organization's overall mission and approach to value-based health care?

3. Leveraging Technology

Are we using technology to link hubs and spokes and create a telehealth network?

Can we leverage technology to better monitor patients remotely and provide home-based care for those with chronic conditions, rather than treating them in hospitals?

Are we exploiting innovations in medical technology to provide better, cheaper, and more convenient care for patients?

Can we lower costs and reduce errors, while also preserving patient confidentiality, by using electronic medical records and IT systems?

Can we sponsor internal or external research to develop low-cost alternatives to expensive supplies such as medicines, instruments, and consumables?

Can we nurture frugal innovations to develop ultra-low-cost devices and tests?

Can we leverage wearable technologies, smartphones, big data, and artificial intelligence to generate earlier and better diagnoses, to customize treatments, and to improve population health?

Can we help change regulations that impede the adoption of such telehealth practices as reimbursing doctors for teleconsultations and email consultations?

What single problem that you encounter every day might have a technological solution? How would you make that solution happen? Who would you bring the problem to? Where would the resolution go from there?

If we do not have tech savvy in-house, how can we bring it to us?

What incentives and supports can we offer professional staff to pursue continual adoption of new technologies?

What outdated technologies are holding our organization back? What can we do to move past them?

4. Promoting Task-Shifting and Continuous Process Innovations

Can we leverage task-shifting to use doctors and nurses at the high end of their credentials while passing on less-skilled work to other health and service professionals?

Can we create new job categories, such as health coaches or medical intensivists, to which tasks can be shifted in ways that lower cost and improve care and patient well-being?

Can we rethink our policies for right-sizing headcount so that it doesn't overburden doctors and specialists with tasks that are best done by less-expensive and less-skilled staff?

Can our workflow and processes be improved to reduce the time required for procedures and the downtime between procedures, especially in cases where scarce expertise (e.g., specialists) and sophisticated facilities (e.g., operating rooms) are involved?

Can our patient flow be improved to make our health care more patient-centered?

Can we continually improve our processes and protocols and make sure everyone follows them to both lower costs and improve quality (e.g., by avoiding needless injuries, infections, and death)?

Can we encourage patients and their families to take on tasks normally done by nurses or other medical staff, in ways that lower cost and improve continuity of care?

How can we encourage patients to take ownership of their own health and become equal partners in their treatments?

Have we developed practices that address the psychological dimensions of well-being, such as anxiety disorders, stress, and depression? Are we clear about which workers "own" behavioral health?

Who does our organization really serve? Are we patient-centric or are we staff-centric? Or do we mostly serve headquarters and the bottom line?

Do the job descriptions in place in our organization match the work that needs to be done? Can human resources lead a review?

What barriers are there to making task-shifting changes in our organization? Regulations? Union interests? Employee training? Recruitment pools? How can we overcome those barriers?

Can we work with area schools and workforce-development agencies to train workers for new paramedical and service positions that we need?

If you could empower your closest subordinate to take over three of your current tasks, what would they be? Would that subordinate be interested in doing that work? What would the barriers be to shifting those tasks? Conversely, if you could take over three of your boss's tasks, what would they be? Are you qualified to do that work? What would it take to get there?

What work in our organization does nobody want to do? Can it be outsourced?

5. Creating a Culture of Ultra-Cost-Consciousness

Above all, how can we avoid unnecessary tests, procedures, and hospital admissions that increase costs and sometimes worsen outcomes?

Can we reuse any of our medical supplies or devices instead of throwing them away after one use? What protocols would such a policy require (related, for example, to sterilization)?

Can we implement "activity-based costing" to understand the full cost of each medical procedure during the entire care cycle: from admitting the patient to treatment to discharge to postdischarge visits?

Would bundling prices and publishing those prices help rein in our costs and improve our outcomes? How could we make up lost revenues?

How should we enforce our protocols to ensure that all required tests and procedures—no more and no less—are performed properly?

Are we minimizing capital outlays on medical facilities (e.g., by using simple and standardized hospital designs, inexpensive materials and furnishings, and multipurpose spaces where appropriate)?

Are we purchasing equipment with only the features we need, and can we avoid unnecessary duplication in our various locations?

Should we lease rather than own land, buildings, or equipment (e.g., by opting for pay-per-use arrangements)? Can we take the same approach to hospital beds, considering that there will likely be a surplus of beds in many hospitals in the future?

If we have persistent excess capacity, can we mothball some hospital beds or lease them to other users?

Can we extend the useful life of costly medical equipment through better repair and maintenance contracts?

How can we encourage doctors to consider the costs and value implications of their decisions when prescribing medicines, tests, and treatments for patients?

Are there sensible ways to share financial results and cost data with our staff so that they better understand our efforts to provide value-based care?

Are we doing all we can to identify and share best practices in value-based care across our various locations and medical departments?

What incentives and supports can we offer frontline workers to help them find cost-savings in every corner of the organization?

How can we transform cost savings into value creation for patients and for our company?

Notes

Chapter 1

1. "The National Health Service: Accident and Emergency," the *Economist*, September 10, 2016, 48.

2. "A Prescription for the Future: How Hospitals Could Be Rebuilt, Better Than Before," the *Economist*, April 8, 2017, 51.

3. Nick Wingfield, Katie Thomas, and Reed Abelson, "Amazon, Berkshire Hathaway, and JPMorgan Team Up to Try to Disrupt Health Care," *New York Times*, January 30, 2018.

4. US health-care data is from *National Health Expenditure 2016*, published by the Centers for Medicare & Medicaid Services of the US Department of Health and Human Services. Health-care inflation data is from the US Bureau of Labor Statistics (2016). We are grateful to Matt Slaughter for pointing us to this data.

5. Regina E. Herzlinger, Barak D. Richman, and Richard J. Boxer, "How Health Care Hurts Your Paycheck," *New York Times*, November 2, 2016.

6. Eric C. Schneider et al., "Mirror, Mirror 2017: International Comparison Reflects Flaws and Opportunities for Better U.S. Health Care," Commonwealth Fund, July 2017.

7. Nicholas Bakalar, "Nearly 20 Million Have Gained Health Insurance since 2010," *New York Times*, May 22, 2017.

8. Institute of Medicine, *Crossing the Quality Chasm: A New Health System for the 21st Century* (Washington, DC: National Academies Press, 2001).

9. Jeffrey R. Immelt, Vijay Govindarajan, and Chris Trimble, "How GE Is Disrupting Itself," *Harvard Business Review*, October 2009; Vijay Govindarajan and Ravi Ramamurti, "Reverse Innovation, Emerging Markets, and Global Strategy," *Global Strategy Journal* 1, no. 3–4 (2011): 191–205; and Vijay Govindarajan and Chris Trimble, *Reverse Innovation: Create Far From Home, Win Everywhere* (Boston: Harvard Business Review Press, 2012).

10. Immelt, Govindarajan, and Trimble, "How GE Is Disrupting Itself," 56.

11. Govindarajan and Trimble, *Reverse Innovation*.

12. Govindarajan and Ramamurti, "Reverse Innovation, Emerging Markets, and Global Strategy," 191. This article received the 2012 EBS Best Paper Award in Innovation Management and the 2017 *Global Strategy Journal* Best Paper Prize.

13. Amos Winter and Vijay Govindarajan, "Engineering Reverse Innovations," *Harvard Business Review*, July–August 2015.

14. "US Foreign Aid Saves Money and Lives," *Nature*, April 20, 2017, 269.

15. Govindarajan and Ramamurti, "Reverse Innovation, Emerging Markets, and Global Strategy," 191–205.

16. Pioneering work on Aravind hospital was done by several authors: V. Kasturi Rangan, "The Aravind Eye Hospital, Madurai, India: In Service for Sight," Case 593-098 (Boston: Harvard Business School, 1993); Sankaran Manikutty and Neharika Vohra, "Aravind Eye Care System: Giving the Most Precious Gift," Case BP0299 (Ahmedabad: Indian Institute of Management, 2004); Pavithra K. Mehta and Suchitra Shenoy, *Infinite Vision: How Aravind Became the World's Greatest Business Case for Compassion* (San Francisco: Berrett-Koehler Publishers, 2011).

17. For two classic publications on the Toyota Production System, see James P. Womack, Daniel T. Jones, and Daniel Roos, *The Machine That Changed the World* (New York: Free Press, 1990), and Steven Spear and H. Kent Bowen, "Decoding the DNA of the Toyota Production System," *Harvard Business Review*, September–October 1999, 96. For an illustration of how TPS might be applied to health care, see Steven Spear, "Fixing Health Care from the Inside, Today," *Harvard Business Review*, September 2005, 78.

18. Michael E. Porter and Elizabeth Olmsted Teisberg, *Redefining Health Care: Creating Value-Based Competition on Results* (Boston: Harvard Business Press, 2006); Clayton M. Christensen, Jerome H. Grossman, and Jason Hwang, *The Innovator's Prescription: A Disruptive Solution for Health Care* (New York: McGraw-Hill, 2009); Regina Herzlinger, *Who Killed Health Care? America's $2 Trillion Medical Problem—and the Consumer-Driven Cure* (New York: McGraw-Hill, 2007); Donald M. Berwick, Thomas W. Nolan, and John Whittington, "The Triple Aim: Care, Health, and Cost," *Health Affairs* 27, no. 3 (2008): 759; J. Y. Kim et al., "From a Declaration of Values to the Creation of Value in Global Health: A Report from Harvard University's Global Health Delivery Project," *Global Public Health* 5, no. 2 (2010): 181; Jim Yong Kim, Paul Farmer, and Michael E. Porter, "Redefining Global Health-Care Delivery, *Lancet* 382, no. 9897 (2013): 1060. Other notable contributions include: Richard J. Bohmer, *Designing Care: Aligning the Nature and Management of Health Care* (Boston: Harvard Business Review Press, 2009); Carolyn M. Clancy and Thomas Scully, "A Call to Excellence," *Health Affairs* 22, no. 2 (2003): 113; Denis A. Cortese and Robert K. Smoldt, "Healing America's Ailing Health Care System," *Mayo Clinic Proceedings* 81, no. 4 (2006), 492; Brent C. James and Lucy A. Savitz, "How Intermountain Trimmed Health Care Costs through Robust Quality Improvement Efforts," *Health Affairs* 30, no. 6 (2011): 1185; John E. Wennberg, *Tracking Medicine: A Researcher's Quest to Understand Health Care* (New York: Oxford University Press, 2010).

19. Michael E. Porter, "What Is Value in Health Care?" *New England Journal of Medicine* 363, no. 26 (2010): 2477.

20. Porter, as quoted on the website of the Institute for Strategy and Competitiveness: http://www.isc.hbs.edu/health-care/vbhcd/Pages/default.aspx, accessed on November 10, 2017.

21. Porter and Teisberg, *Redefining Health Care*.

22. Ibid., 98.

23. See the section on value-based health-care delivery on the website of Institute for Strategy and Competitiveness, founded by Michael Porter, at https://www.isc.hbs .edu/health-care/vbhcd/Pages/default.aspx.

24. Michael E. Porter and Thomas H. Lee, "The Strategy That Will Fix Health Care," *Harvard Business Review*, October 2013, 1.

25. An article in the British medical journal *Lancet*, citing an independent report, provides these data for Narayana Health and the US average. An older Harvard Business School case study reports the thirty-day mortality rate for Narayana as 1.27 percent and the US average as 1.4 percent. (See Tarun Khanna, Kasturi Rangan, and Merlina Manocaran, "Narayana Hrudayalaya Heart Hospital: Cardiac Care for the Poor (A)," Case 505-078 [Boston: Harvard Business School, 2005, revised 2001].) It is safe to conclude that Narayana's outcomes are comparable to those of US hospitals.

26. Company data is from annual reports or websites.

27. Biswajit Baruah and Divya Rajagopal, "Narayana Hrudayalaya IPO Over-subscribed 8.63 Times," *Economic Times*, December 22, 2015.

28. "Dubai-Based Abraaj Group Buys 72% Holding in CARE Hospitals," *Economic Times*, January 14, 2016.

29. Dr. Aravind Srinivasan, Administrator, Aravind Eye Care System, interview with authors.

30. Nigel Crisp, *Turning the World Upside Down: The Search for Global Health in the 21st Century* (London: Royal Society of Medicine Press, 2010).

31. Barak D. Richman and Kevin A. Schulman, "What U.S. Hospitals Can Still Learn from India's Private Heart Hospitals," *NEJM Catalyst*, May 25, 2017. The authors concluded that "American hospitals could learn a great deal from the organizational focus and structure of their Indian counterparts."

32. Faheem Ahmed et al., "Can Reverse Innovation Catalyse Better Value Health Care?" *Lancet* 5, no. 10 (2017).

33. Eric Wadsworth, interview with authors, June 2015.

34. Ascension website, "Mission, Vision, and Values," https://ascension.org/ our-mission/mission-vision-values.

35. John Doyle, EVP, Ascension, interview with authors, December 2016.

36. Wennberg, *Tracking Medicine*; Elliott S. Fisher et al., "The Implications of Regional Variations in Medicare Spending. Part 1: The Content, Quality, and Accessibility of Care," *Annals of Internal Medicine* 138, no. 4 (2003): 273; and Fisher et al., "The Implications of Regional Variations in Medicare Spending. Part 2: Health Outcomes and Satisfaction with Care," *Annals of Internal Medicine* 138, no. 4 (2003): 288.

37. Richard M. J. Bohmer, "Virginia Mason Medical Center (Abridged)," Case 610-055 (Boston: Harvard Business School, 2010).

38. Michael E. Porter, Carolyn Daly, and Andrew Peter Dervan, "The Children's Hospital of Philadelphia: Network Strategy," Case 710-463 (Boston: Harvard Business School, 2010, revised 2011).

39. Michael E. Porter and Elizabeth O. Teisberg, "Cleveland Clinic: Transformation and Growth 2015," Case 709-473 (Boston: Harvard Business School, 2009, revised 2016); https://my.clevelandclinic.org/departments/heart/depts/heart-vascular-affiliates.

40. David Cook et al., "From 'Solution Shop' Model to 'Focused Factory' in Hospital Surgery: Increasing Care Value and Predictability," *Health Affairs* 33, no. 5 (2014): 746.

41. Pioneer Institute, "Critical Care, Critical Choices: The Case for Tele-ICUs," July 19, 2011, http://bgc.pioneerinstitute.org/critical-care-critical-choices-the-case-for-tele-icus/, and UMass Memorial Medical Center, eICU, https://www.umassmemorialhealthcare.org/umass-memorial-medical-center/services-treatments/critical-care/services-we-provide/eicu.

42. See www.mercyvirtual.net.

43. Minnesota Department of Health and Minnesota Board of Dentistry, "Early Impacts of Dental Therapists in Minnesota," Report to the Minnesota Legislature 2014, February 2014, http://www.health.state.mn.us/divs/orhpc/workforce/dt/dtlegisrpt.pdf. The Pew Charitable Trusts, "The Oral Health Crisis Among Native Americans," Fact Sheet, July 23, 2015, http://www.pewtrusts.org/en/research-and-analysis/fact-sheets/2015/06/the-oral-health-crisis-among-native-americans.

44. Eric R. Yoo et al., "The Role of e-Health in Optimizing Task-Shifting in the Delivery of Antiviral Therapy for Chronic Hepatitis C," *Telemedicine and e-Health* 23, no. 10 (2017): 870.

45. James L. Heskett and Roger H. Hallowell, "Shouldice Hospital Limited (Abridged)," Case 805-002 (Boston: Harvard Business School, 2004, revised 2005).

46. Anssi Mikola, interview by authors, September 28, 2017.

47. Diane Daych, interview by authors, August 10, 2016.

48. Rick Tetzeli, "How Former Apple CEO John Sculley Reinvented Himself in Health Care," *Fast Company*, November 30, 2016. https://www.fastcompany.com/3065143/how-former-apple-ceo-john-sculley-reinvented-himself-in-health-care.

49. For a roundup, see "The Future of Mental Health Therapy," *On Point*, with guest host Jane Clayson, WBUR, June 20, 2017, http://www.wbur.org/onpoint/2017/06/20/the-future-of-mental-health-therapy.

50. Dr. Richard Friedland, interview with the authors.

51. See https://www.globaltolocal.org/about-us/.

52. Crisp, *Turning the World Upside Down*.

53. Rushika Fernandopulle, Iora Health founder, interviews with the authors, August 2016.

54. Paul Wafula, "Top Indian Hospital Sets Foothold in Nairobi," *Standard Digital*, June 7, 2016.

55. Thulasiraj Ravilla and Dhivya Ramasamy, "Efficient High-Volume Cataract Services: The Aravind Model," *Community Eye Health Journal* 27, no. 85 (2014): 7.

56. Landon Thomas Jr., "An Investor's Plan to Transplant Private Health Care in Africa," *New York Times*, October 8, 2016.

Chapter 2

1. Unless otherwise noted, quotes from Dr. Devi Shetty are from an interview with the authors, February 2013.

2. Kounteya Sinhai, "India Doesn't Have Even 1 Hospital Bed per 1,000 Persons," *Times of India*, October 10, 2011.

3. Pavithra K. Mehta and Suchitra Shenoy, *Infinite Vision: How Aravind Became the World's Greatest Business Case for Compassion* (San Francisco: Berrett-Koehler Publishers, 2011).

4. Aravind Eye Care System, Activity Report 2016–17, pp. 16–17.

5. Email communication by Dr. N. Krishna Reddy, CEO, Care Hospitals.

6. "Dubai-Based Abraaj Group Buys 72% Holding in CARE Hospitals," *Economic Times*, January 14, 2016.

7. LV Prasad website: http://www.lvpei.org/eye-health-pyramid.php.

8. Gullapalli N. Rao et al., "Integrated Model of Primary and Secondary Eye Care for Underserved Rural Areas: The LV Prasad Eye Institute Experience," *Indian Journal of Ophthalmology* 60, no. 5 (2012): 396.

9. See http://www.lvpei.org/aboutus.php.

10. Aravind Eye Care System, Activity Report for FY 2016–17, pp. 16–17.

11. Atul Gawande, "Big Med: Restaurant Chains Have Managed to Combine Quality Control, Cost Control, and Innovation. Can Health Care?" the *New Yorker*, August 13, 2012.

12. Aravind Eye Care System, Madurai, February 2013, and follow-up interview with Dr. Aravind Srinivasan, January 2017.

13. Unless otherwise noted, quotes from Dr. Ajaikumar are from an interview with the authors, December 2012.

14. Nikhil R. Sahni et al., "Surgeon Specialization and Operative Mortality in United States: Retrospective Analysis," *British Medical Journal* 354 (2016): i3571.

15. Unless otherwise noted, quotes from Dr. N. Krishna Reddy, CEO, Care Hospitals, Hyderabad, are from an interview with the authors, February 2013.

16. Andrew J. Epstein et al., "Coronary Revascularization Trends in the United States, 2001–2008," *JAMA* 305, no. 17 (2011): 1769–1776.

17. Aditi Nayak et al., "Use of a Peritoneal Dialysis Remote Monitoring System in India," *Peritoneal Dialysis International* 32, no. 2 (2012): 200; K. S. Nayak et al., "Telemedicine and Remote Monitoring: Supporting the Patient on Peritoneal Dialysis," *Peritoneal Dialysis International* 36, no. 4 (2016): 362.

18. Pavithra K. Mehta and Suchitra Shenoy, *Infinite Vision: How Aravind Became the World's Greatest Business Case for Compassion* (San Francisco: Berrett-Koehler Publishers, 2011).

19. Communication with Dr. K.S. Nayak, November 2016.

20. See https://www.indiamart.com/aurolab/profile.html.

21. Vivek Wadhwa, "This Indian Start-Up Could Disrupt Health Care with Its Powerful and Affordable Diagnostic Machine," *Washington Post*, November 18, 2014.

22. Myshkin Ingawale, "ToucHb: The Story of Prick Free Blood Testing," video, TED conference, Long Beach, California, February 2012: https://www.youtube.com/watch?v=RyeQt0GodsE.

23. Unless otherwise noted, quotes from Eric Wadsworth are from an interview with the authors, March 2013.

24. Atul Gawande, *The Checklist Manifesto: How to Get Things Right* (New York: Metropolitan Books, 2009).

25. Unless otherwise noted, quotes from Dr. Raghuvanshi, Vice Chairman and CEO, Narayana Health, Bangalore, are from an interview with the authors, February 2013.

Chapter 3

1. Unless otherwise noted, all quotations from Devi Shetty are from interviews with the authors, conducted in February 2013 and January 2017.

2. Pioneering work on Narayana Health includes Tarun Khanna, Kasturi Rangan, and Merlina Manocaran, "Narayana Hrudayalaya Heart Hospital: Cardiac Care for the Poor (A)," Case 505-078 (Boston: Harvard Business School, 2005, revised 2011).

3. Ibid.

4. Mayo Clinic financial statements (January–June 2016) and Cleveland Clinic's Annual Report for calendar year 2016.

5. Draft Red Herring Prospectus, September 2015.

6. Unless otherwise noted, all quotations from Ashutosh Raghuvanshi are from interviews with the authors, conducted in 2013, 2016, and 2017.

7. Seema Singh, "Magnificent Obsession," *New Scientist*, February 2, 2002.

8. From Al Jazeera production *Indian Hospital*, Part 1, 2012.

9. Prabakar Kothandaraman and Sunita Mookerjee, "Healthcare for All: Narayana Hrudayalaya, Bangalore," case study (New York: United Nations Development Programme, 2007).

10. Geeta Anand, "The Henry Ford of Heart Surgery: In India, a Factory Model for Hospitals Is Cutting Costs and Yielding Profits," *Wall Street Journal*, November 25, 2009.

11. Budhaditya Gupta, Robert S. Huckman, and Tarun Khanna, "Task Shifting in Surgery: Lessons From An Indian Hospital," *Healthcare: The Journal of Delivery Science and Innovation* 3, no. 4 (December 2015): 245–250.

12. Khanna, Rangan, and Manocaran, "Narayana Hrudayalaya Heart Hospital."

13. See http://extreme.stanford.edu/projects/noora-health-formerly-care -companion.

14. Priti Salian, "Poor Country, Top Doctors: A Hospital in India Shows How to Separate a Nation's Wealth from the Quality of Its Health Care," *TakePart*, March 18, 2016.

15. Aravind's strategy for high-quality surgery at ultra-low cost is described very well in the following sources: V. Kasturi Rangan, "The Aravind Eye Hospital, Madurai, India: In Service for Sight," Case 593-098 (Boston: Harvard Business School, 1993); and Pavithra K. Mehta and Suchitra Shenoy, *Infinite Vision: How Aravind Became the World's Greatest Business Case for Compassion* (San Francisco: Berrett-Koehler Publishers, 2011).

16. Anand, "The Henry Ford of Heart Surgery."

17. "Narayana Hrudayalaya: A Model for Accessible, Affordable Health Care?" Knowledge @ Wharton, July 1, 2010, http://knowledge.wharton.upenn.edu/article/ narayana-hrudayalaya-a-model-for-accessible-affordable-health-care/.

Chapter 4

1. Wayne Wright, interview with authors, April 20, 2017.

2. Unless otherwise noted, all quotations from Devi Shetty are from telephone interviews with the authors, conducted in February 2013 and January 2017.

3. Robert Pearl, "U.S. Health Care Needs a Wakeup Call from India," *USA Today*, January 29, 2017.

4. Unless otherwise noted, all quotations from Viren Shetty are from telephone interviews with authors, conducted in February 2013 and February 2014.

5. Tarun Khanna and Budhaditya Gupta, "Health City Cayman Islands," Case 714-510 (Boston: Harvard Business School, 2014, revised 2016); John Doyle, interview with authors, December 2016.

6. Unless otherwise noted, all quotations from John Doyle are from an interview with the authors, December 20, 2016.

7. Jim Doyle, "Ascension to Build $2 Billion 'Health City' in Caymans," *St. Louis Post-Dispatch*, April 10, 2012.

8. Khanna and Gupta, "Health City Cayman Islands," Exhibit 7, "Nine Point Request by Dr. Shetty to Cayman Government."

9. Ibid.

10. Fred Goldstein, "Health City Cayman Island—Medical Tourism May Be One Way to Lower Healthcare Costs," *Accountable Health* blog, January 13, 2016, https://

accountablehealth.wordpress.com/2016/01/13/health-city-cayman-island-medical-tourism-may-be-one-way-to-lower-healthcare-costs/.

11. Khanna and Gupta, "Health City Cayman Islands."

12. Shamille Scott, "Health City Set to Install Solar Farm," *Loop*, June 1, 2015.

13. HCCI company data.

14. Pearl, "U.S. Health Care Needs a Wakeup Call."

Chapter 5

1. David Grubin Productions and WTTW Chicago, *RX: The Quiet Revolution* (Public Broadcasting Service, 2015), http://www.pbs.org/program/rx-quiet-revolution, and Janis Quinn, "TelEmergency Network Provides Vital Link to Rural Hospitals during Times of Trauma," *CenterView*, May 16, 2011.

2. These criteria were spelled out in HRSA's call for proposals for creating national Telehealth Centers of Excellence. See https://www.hrsa.gov/ruralhealth/program opportunities/fundingopportunities/default.aspx?id=347d8709-69bb-493c-bfc5-0b0a655dbd6a (accessed on Nov 26, 2017).

3. David Pittman, "Mississippi Emerges as Telemedicine Leader," *Politico*, February 26, 2015; "Telemedicine Receives A-Rating in Mississippi," North Sunflower Medical Center, http://northsunflower.com/nsmc-news/telemedicine-receives-a-rating-in-mississippi.

4. Unless otherwise noted, all quotations from Kristi Henderson are from interviews with the authors, conducted in August 2016 and February 2017.

5. See https://www.umc.edu/news/News_Articles/2016/October/UMMC-telehealth-enters-next-chapter-of-remote-patient-monitoring.html.

6. Henderson Testimony before US Senate Committee on Commerce, Science and Transportation, April 21, 2015.

7. For median income, see US Census Bureau, "Median Household Income by State," 2012–2016 American Community Survey 5-Year Estimates, https://www.census .gov/search-results.html?q=median+household+income&search.x=0&search.y=0&sear ch=submit&page=1&stateGeo=none&searchtype=web&cssp=SERP. For poverty level, total population, and rate of educational attainment, see US Census Bureau, Quick Facts: Mississippi, https://www.census.gov/quickfacts/table/PST045215/28. For children in poverty, see Jerry Mitchell, "246,000 Mississippi Children Living in Poverty," *Clarion-Ledger*, July 21, 2015. For percentage of rural dwellers, see the Rural Health Information Hub webpage for Mississippi: https://www.ruralhealthinfo.org/states/mississippi.

8. United Health Foundation, "America's Health Rankings: 2016 Annual Report," http://www.americashealthrankings.org/explore/2016-annual-report/state/MS.

9. For overall ranking, see the Commonwealth Fund, "Overall Ranking, 2017," http://datacenter.commonwealthfund.org/#ind=1/sc=1. For percentage of primary doctors, see the Association of American Medical Colleges, "2017 State Physician

Workforce Data Report," https://members.aamc.org/eweb/upload/2017%20State%20 Physician%20Workforce%20Data%20Report.pdf, 11. Number of uninsured is from the 2014 Commonwealth Fund reporting for 2011–2012, http://www.commonwealthfund .org/publications/fund-reports/2014/apr/2014-state-scorecard.

10. Mississippi State Department of Health, "1999 Report on Hospitals," http://msdh .ms.gov/msdhsite/_static/resources/122.pdf; Rural Health Information Hub, "Critical Access Hospitals," https://www.ruralhealthinfo.org/topics/critical-access-hospitals.

11. Unless otherwise noted, all quotations from Michael Adcock are from an interview with the authors, February 8, 2017.

12. Richard L. Summers, Kristi Henderson, Kristen C. Isom, and Robert L. Galli, "The Tenth Anniversary of TelEmergency," *Journal of the Mississippi State Medical Association* 54, no. 12 (2013): 340–341.

13. Kristi Henderson, quoted by Louise Plaster in "Can Mississippi Emerge as the South's Next Health Tech Hub?" in *Telemedicine* 2 (Fall 2015): 29.

14. Email from Ryan Kelly, February 1, 2017.

15. Ellen Zane, interview with the authors, August 9, 2016.

16. Data USA, "Ruleville, MS," https://datausa.io/profile/geo/ruleville-ms/ #income.

17. Gabriel Perna, "Mississippi's Diabetes Problem with Telehealth and Care Management," *Healthcare Informatics*, November 14, 2014.

18. American Diabetes Association, "The Cost of Diabetes," http://www.diabetes .org/advocacy/news-events/cost-of-diabetes.html.

19. Testimony of Kristi Henderson before the US Senate Committee on Commerce, Science, and Transportation, April 21, 2015.

20. Neil Versel, "Mississippi Telehealth, Remote Monitoring Pays Dividends for Diabetics," *MedCityNews*, September 13, 2016.

21. Summers et al., "The Tenth Anniversary of TelEmergency."

Chapter 6

1. Eric Larsen, "Lessons from the C-Suite: Anthony Tersigni, President and CEO of Ascension," The Advisory Board, December 10, 2014, https://www.advisory. com/research/health-care-advisory-board/blogs/at-the-helm/2014/12/qa-ascension-health.

2. Institute of Medicine Committee on Quality of Health Care in America, *Crossing the Quality Chasm: A New Health System for the 21st Century* (Washington, DC: National Academies Press, 2001).

3. Nina Martin, "The Growth of Catholic Hospitals, By the Numbers," *ProPublica*, December 18, 2013.

4. Unless otherwise noted, all quotations from John Doyle are from an interview with the authors, December 20, 2016.

5. Unless otherwise noted, all quotations from David Pryor are from an interview with the authors, December 2016.

6. Douglas McCarthy and Elizabeth Staton, "Case Study: A Transformational Change Process to Improve Patient Safety at Ascension Health," *Quality Matters: Innovations in Health Care Quality Improvement*, Commonwealth Fund, January 2006.

7. David B. Pryor et al., "The Clinical Transformation of Ascension Health: Eliminating All Preventable Injuries and Deaths," *Joint Commission Journal on Quality and Patient Safety* 32, no. 6 (2006): 299–308.

8. Wanda Gibbons et al., "Eliminating Facility-Acquired Pressure Ulcers at Ascension Health," *Joint Commission Journal on Quality and Patient Safety* 32, no. 9 (2006).

9. Unless otherwise noted, all quotations from Rhonda Anderson are from an interview with the authors, February 13, 2017.

10. Ryan W. Buell, "Compass Group: The Ascension Health Decision," Case 615-026 (Boston: Harvard Business School, 2014, revised 2016).

11. Loretta Chao, "Hospitals Take High-Tech Approach to Supply Chain," *Wall Street Journal*, October 21, 2015.

12. Kaiser Family Foundation, https://www.kff.org/health-reform/press-release/nearly-half-of-the-uninsured-or-15-7-million-people-are-eligible-for-medicaid-or-subsidized-affordable-care-act-coverage-analysis-finds/.

13. Dave Barkholz, "High-Deductible Health Plans Prompt Some Hospitals to Cut Low-Income Patients a Break," *Modern Healthcare*, December 10, 2016.

14. Paul Barr, "Ascension Health's Approach to Standardizing Its Operations," *Hospitals & Health Networks Daily*, March 18, 2015.

15. Anthony R. Tersigni, "It's Time to Come Together to Improve Our Healthcare System," *The Hill*, April 24, 2017.

16. Johnny Smith of Ascension, interview with the authors, July 2017.

17. See "PVF's Vision: High Efficiency and Keen Focus on the Patient," *Horizon: The Pacific Vision Foundation Newsletter*, Spring 2015, http://www.pacificvisionfoundation.org/wp-content/uploads/2016/01/PVF-Newsletter-single.page-Spring.2015.pdf; and Robert Crum, "An Innovative Ophthalmological and Financial Model for People at All Economic Levels," Robert Wood Johnson Foundation report, April 6, 2015. The report noted: "For the millions of Americans who are uninsured, indigent, or underinsured, medical care is delivered through a system that is both separate from, and unequal to, the care delivered to the rest of Americans."

18. Bruce Spivey, interview with authors, February 13, 2017.

Chapter 7

1. Email from Rushika Fernandopulle, September 16, 2016.

2. Unless otherwise noted, all quotes from Rushika Fernandopulle come from an interview with the authors, August 17, 2016.

3. Unless otherwise noted, all quotes from Liam Donohue come from an interview with the authors, August 18, 2016.

4. Unless otherwise noted, all quotes from Eric Wadsworth come from an interview with the authors, July 29, 2016.

5. In fact Eric Wadsworth, cofounder of Dartmouth's Master of Health Care Delivery Science program, has found that at Iora's center in his area, overall visits to specialists have gone down while visits to certain types of specialists have gone up.

Chapter 8

1. Ellen Zane, interview with authors, August 9, 2016.

2. Gary Kaplan, interview with the authors, August 3, 2016.

3. Richard M. J. Bohmer, "Virginia Mason Medical Center (Abridged)," Case 610-055 (Boston: Harvard Business School, 2010).

4. Michael E. Porter and Robert S. Kaplan, "How to Pay for Health Care," *Harvard Business Review*, July–August 2016; Brent C. James and Gregory P. Poulsen, "The Case for Capitation," *Harvard Business Review*, July–August 2016.

5. Zeke Emanuel et al., "State Options to Control Health Care Costs and Improve Quality," Center for American Progress, April 11, 2016, https://www.american progress.org/issues/healthcare/reports/2016/04/11/134859/state-options-to-control-health-care-costs-and-improve-quality/.

6. Gary Kaplan, interview with authors, August 3, 2016.

7. D. Cook et al., "From 'Solution Shop' Model to 'Focused Factory' in Hospital Surgery: Increasing Care Value and Predictability," *Health Affairs* 33, no. 5 (2014): 746.

8. Diane Daych, interview with authors, August 10, 2016.

9. Christy Ford Chapin, "How Did Health Care Get to Be Such a Mess?" *New York Times*, June 19, 2017.

10. Patricia A. McDonald, Robert S. Mecklenburg, and Lindsay A. Martin, "The Employer-Led Health Care Revolution," *Harvard Business Review*, July–August 2015, 38.

11. Mark Brohan, "Investors Pump $4 Billion into Digital Healthcare Startups So Far This Year," Internet Health Management, July 7, 2016.

12. Robert Pearl, "U.S. Health Care Needs a Wakeup Call from India," *USA Today*, January 29, 2017.

Appendix A

1. A. Haripriya et al., "Complication Rates of Phacoemulsification and Manual Small-Incision Cataract Surgery at Aravind Eye Hospital," *Journal of Cataract & Refractive Surgery* 38, no. 8 (2012): 1360.

2. D. F. Chang, "Tackling the Greatest Challenge in Cataract Surgery," *British Journal of Ophthalmology* 89, no. 9 (2005): 1073.

3. See the following articles on these points: R. D. Ravindran et al., "Incidence of Post-Cataract Endophthalmitis at Aravind Eye Hospital: Outcomes of More Than 42,000 Consecutive Cases Using Standardized Sterilization and Prophylaxis Protocols," *Journal of Cataract & Refractive Surgery* 35, no. 4 (2009): 629; A. Haripriya, D. F. Chang, and R. D. Ravindran, "Endophthalmitis Reduction with Intracameral Moxifloxacin Prophylaxis: Analysis of 600,000 Surgeries," *Ophthalmology* 124, no. 6 (2017): 768.

4. Stephen S. Rauh et al., "The Savings Illusion—Why Clinical Quality Improvement Fails to Deliver Bottom-Line Results," *New England Journal of Medicine*, December 29, 2011; John E. Wennberg, *Tracking Medicine: A Researcher's Quest to Understand Health Care* (New York: Oxford University Press, 2010).

5. See Vijay Govindarajan and Ravi Ramamurti, "Delivering World-Class Health Care, Affordably," *Harvard Business Review*, November 2013, 117.

Index

Acknowledgments

Although we've known each other for more than four decades, our intellectual journeys followed separate trajectories for many years. One of us (VG) was studying strategy and innovation in large US multinationals, and the other (Ravi) was doing the same with firms in emerging markets. Our paths intersected when Western multinationals became increasingly interested in emerging markets, and firms in emerging markets became increasingly interested in the rest of the world, including the United States and Europe. And so, in 2010, we began to collaborate around the topic of "reverse innovation." We first explored reverse innovation in analytical terms, and then we zeroed in on its relevance in a very important industry—health care. We published our initial ideas in 2013 in the *Harvard Business Review* article, "Delivering World-Class Health Care, Affordably."

This book is the culmination of six years of research on how the United States and other industrialized countries can benefit from innovations in health-care delivery in poor countries like India. Needless to say, those lessons are also relevant to other poor countries, where billions have no access to health care. Our research took us to more than two dozen hospitals, and we interviewed over 125 health-care executives in India and the United States.

For the first phase of our research, we are deeply indebted to the leaders of innovative Indian hospitals who threw open their doors to us. Among them are Dr. Aravind Srinivasan, Dr. R. D. Ravindran, and R. D. Thulasiraj of Aravind Eye Care System; Dr. N. Krishna Reddy and Dr. B. Soma Raju of Care Hospitals; Dr. K. S. Nayak of

Deccan Hospital; Dr. B. S. Ajaikumar and Dr. Naveen Nagar of HCG Oncology; Anant Kumar and V. Srinivas of LifeSpring Hospitals; Dr. Gullapalli N. Rao of LV Prasad Eye Institute; and Dr. Devi Shetty, Dr. A. Raghuvanshi, and Viren Shetty of Narayana Health. The logistics of our field visits and research were expertly organized by Mahesh Sriram.

For the second phase of our research, in the United States, we are grateful to Dr. Anthony Tersigni, John Doyle, and Rhonda Anderson of Ascension; Dr. Rushika Fernandopulle of Iora Health; Dr. Kristi Henderson, formerly of University of Mississippi Medical Center (now with Ascension); Dr. Bruce Spivey of Pacific Vision Foundation; Liam Donohue and Payal Divakaran of .406 Ventures; Diane Daych of Apple Tree Partners; Ellen Zane of Tufts Medical Center; Dr. Gary Kaplan of Virginia Mason Medical Center; Dr. Kevin Curtis of Dartmouth-Hitchcock; Dr. Richard Friedlander of Netcare (South Africa); and Anssi Mikola of HNG (Finland).

Several colleagues gave us constructive feedback, some of them multiple times, and shaped the book in profound ways. Among them are Lisa Adams, Dr. Don Berwick, Sujana Chalsani, Dr. David Chang, Dr. Elliott Fisher, Dr. Richard Fried, Robert Hansen, Punam Keller, Karen Koh, Tim Lahey, Russ Moran, Alan Mullaly, Merritt Patridge, David Puvirajasingam, Suzie Rubin, Steve Spear, Albert Wocke, Gary Young, and Mike Zubkoff. We owe a special debt of gratitude to Eric Wadsworth of the Tuck School and Dartmouth Medical School, who educated us on the US health-care system and fundamentally shaped our research design and strategy. We cannot thank Eric enough for his deep insights and generosity.

A project of this scale and scope requires resources. VG would like to thank Tuck School's deans—Paul Danos (former dean) and Matt Slaughter (current dean)—for their generous financial support. Ravi would like to acknowledge the support of Northeastern University's Center for Emerging Markets and its benefactors, particularly Dave Nardone and Venkat Srinivasan.

We were lucky to have an outstanding editorial team to help us with the book. The fabulous duo of Art Jahnke and Nancy Zerbey helped recast our research in an engaging, storytelling style. And at Harvard Business Review Press, we were fortunate to have as our editor the one-and-only Melinda Merino, who helped sharpen our arguments and make the book a whole lot punchier. Jon Zobenica was a meticulous copy editor, and Jennifer Waring oversaw production.

We would like to dedicate this book to our wives, our children, and their families, whose love and support have sustained us through this and every other project we've undertaken. We would also like to dedicate the book to three people who left us prematurely in the recent past. Here are a few words about each of them.

VG was extremely close to his brother Rangan who, after earning his undergraduate degree in engineering, went on to get his MBA from the prestigious IIM-Ahmedabad. Rangan knew more accounting than VG did, even though VG was trained as a CPA. That is what motivated VG to pursue an MBA. Later in life, deriving inspiration from VG, Rangan completed his doctorate in strategy, then published his doctoral thesis as a book, which he dedicated to VG. It seemed as though the brothers had come full circle. When he was diagnosed with cancer, Rangan was determined to write a book on the engineering principles of cost-effective industrial construction, based on his experiences as CEO of one of India's largest construction companies. VG and his wife, Kirthi, spent time with Rangan just before he passed away. What amazed them was how passionate Rangan was about his book project. He dictated chapter outlines to his executive assistant. He was in a race against cancer to finish it. He saw the book as his legacy. VG wishes he knew enough engineering to complete Rangan's unfinished manuscript.

Bala, Ravi's brother, was one of six siblings, all boys, born to middle-class parents. As the number five and number six siblings, Bala and Ravi were especially close and grew up together for their first seventeen years. When he was two years old, Bala developed a high fever that led to convulsions, which resulted in a lifelong physical disability. This disability limited Bala's activities—but never his spirit or his determination to lead a full life. He completed college, volunteered in a village for two years, got married, had a lovely family, and pursued a career as an HR executive. Whatever fate dealt him, Bala faced with courage and good humor. He always focused on the other person, not himself, and on the good news, never the bad. His courage, positive outlook, and big heart were an inspiration to all who knew him.

Drew was the older brother of Ravi and Meena's daughter-in-law, Paige. Drew trained as a pediatric cardiologist and married May Ling, also a cardiologist. With two-year old Claire they attended Paige and Bharat's wedding—as groomsman and bridesmaid—even though May Ling was due to deliver their second daughter, Norah, any day. A few years later, their third daughter Caroline arrived. Drew loved baseball and hanging out with his family. Then, out of the blue, he was diagnosed with advanced cancer. Drew and his loving family lived as normal a life as possible, even as he underwent treatment. Drew is sorely missed by his family and friends.

As we conclude this book on health-care innovations, we would like to dedicate it to the fond memory of Rangan, Bala, and Drew.

Vijay Govindarajan (VG), Hanover, NH

Ravi Ramamurti, Lexington, MA

About the Authors

VIJAY GOVINDARAJAN (VG) is widely regarded as one of the world's leading experts on strategy and innovation. He is the Coxe Distinguished Professor of Management at Dartmouth's Tuck School of Business and a former Marvin Bower Fellow at Harvard Business School. He was the first Professor in Residence and Chief Innovation Consultant at General Electric. With GE's CEO Jeff Immelt, he wrote the *Harvard Business Review* article "How GE Is Disrupting Itself," which introduced the concept of "reverse innovation"—any innovation that is adopted first in the developing world. In November 2012 HBR named reverse innovation one of the "Great Moments in Management" in the last century. Govindarajan is the *New York Times* and *Wall Street Journal* bestselling author of *Reverse Innovation* and a two-time winner of the prestigious McKinsey Award for the best article published in HBR. In the latest Thinkers50 rankings, he is rated the #1 Indian Management Thinker.

Govindarajan has been identified as a leading management thinker by influential publications including *Bloomberg Businessweek*, *Forbes*, the *London Times*, and the *Economist*.

Prior to joining the faculty at Tuck, Govindarajan was on the faculties of Harvard Business School, INSEAD (Fontainebleau), and the Indian Institute of Management (Ahmedabad, India).

The recipient of numerous awards for excellence in research, Govindarajan was inducted into the Hall of Fame of the *Academy of Management Journal* and ranked by *Management International Review* as one of the Top 20 North American Superstars for research in strategy.

Govindarajan has worked with CEOs and top management teams in numerous *Fortune* 500 firms to discuss, challenge, and advance their thinking about strategy. His clients include: Boeing, Coca-Cola, Colgate, Deere, FedEx, GE, Hewlett-Packard, IBM, JPMorgan Chase, Johnson & Johnson, New York Times, Procter & Gamble, Sony, and Walmart. He has been a keynote speaker in the BusinessWeek CEO Forum, HSM World Business Forum, TEDx, and the World Economic Forum at Davos.

Govindarajan holds both a doctorate and an MBA (with distinction) from Harvard Business School. Prior to this, he received his chartered accountancy degree in India, where he was awarded the President's Gold Medal by the Institute of Chartered Accountants of India for obtaining the first rank nationwide.

RAVI RAMAMURTI is an expert on strategy and innovation in emerging markets. He is the University Distinguished Professor of International Business & Strategy at Northeastern University's D'Amore-McKim School of Business. He founded and heads the university's Center for Emerging Markets. For more than thirty-five years he has studied the strategies of firms in and from emerging markets.

After earning his BSc degree (in physics) from St. Stephen's College, Delhi University, India, Ramamurti obtained his MBA from the Indian Institute of Management Ahmedabad, where he received a Gold Medal for graduating at the top of his class. He holds a doctorate from Harvard Business School, where he was awarded a Dissertation Fellowship grant.

In recognition of his "outstanding contributions to the scholarly development of the field of international business," Ramamurti was elected a Fellow of the Academy of International Business in 2008. He was elected by members of the Academy of Management to serve on the board of its International Management Division (2003–2008).

Ramamurti has been a visiting professor at Harvard Business School, at the University of Pennsylvania's Wharton School, and at MIT Sloan

School of Management. He has also been a visiting professor at Tufts University's Fletcher School, CEIBS Shanghai, and IMD Switzerland. He has been recognized globally for his thinking and teaching on strategy and innovation in emerging markets.

Along with doing research and consulting for firms and governments in more than twenty emerging markets, Ramamurti been an adviser to the United Nations, USAID, and the Fulbright Program. He was also principal adviser to the World Bank's board on privatization and to The Economist Group for its online courses on emerging markets.

Ramamurti's pioneering work on the strategies of multinationals from emerging markets, and how Western multinationals should respond to these new rivals, has led to the publication of six books in this area, including three with Cambridge University Press.

He has also published articles in leading academic journals, including the *Academy of Management Review, Global Strategy Journal, Journal of International Business Studies*, and *Management Science*, and in practitioner journals such as *California Management Review* and *Harvard Business Review*. His 2011 *Global Strategy Journal* article "Reverse Innovation, Emerging Markets, and Global Strategy," coauthored with Vijay Govindarajan, won the 2012 EBS Universität prize for Best Article on Innovation Management, and in 2017 it won the inaugural prize for the Best Article published in GSJ.

Ramamurti is a frequent keynote speaker in academic and practitioner meetings and is quoted regularly in the business press. His consulting clients have included several public and private firms in the United States and around the world.